D0081231

The Quest for Peace

James Turner Johnson

The Quest for Peace

Three Moral Traditions in Western Cultural History

PRINCETON UNIVERSITY PRESS

Published by Princeton University Press, 41 William Street, Princeton, New Jersey 08540
In the United Kingdom: Princeton University Press, Guildford, Surrey

Library of Congress Cataloging in Publication Data will be found on the last printed page of this book

ISBN 0-691-07742-8 (cloth)

Publication of this book has been aided by a grant from the Whitney Darrow Fund of Princeton University Press

This book has been composed in Linotron Sabon and Gill Sans

Clothbound editions of Princeton University Press books are printed on acid-free paper, and binding materials are chosen for strength and durability. Paperbacks, although satisfactory for personal collections, are not usually suitable for library rebinding

Printed in the United States of America by Princeton University Press, Princeton, New Jersey

CONTENTS

theological seminary. My thanks to all the staff members of these various repositories of wisdom who aided me at various times.

A person's ideas, I think, are always better conceived when honed against the perspectives of others. Thus I am especially glad to have had a number of kinds of interaction, structured and casual, with knowledgeable people (some of whom agreed, and some of whom disagreed, with me) during the period when I was working on this study. The casual contacts will have to be left anonymous, since there have simply been too many worthwhile ones to list them all here. The structured ones have been very numerous, too. I am grateful for a whole group of invitations to lecture on Western moral tradition on war at various colleges, universities, and professional meetings from 1983 to 1985, largely in connection with the particularly hot debate over United States defense policy that was being carried on during that period. These occasions brought me, as an interpreter of just war tradition, into close contact with persons who thought of themselves as pacifists of one or another sort, as well as with people who used just war modes of reasoning (or something akin to them) to reach pacifist conclusions. Among all these occasions I must mention several as particularly valuable for honing my thoughts: at Georgetown University in March 1983 and March 1984; at Duquesne University in March 1983; at Princeton University in May 1983; at the United States Military Academy in June 1983; at the University of Colorado in November 1984; at Wesleyan University in February 1985; and at the United States Army War College in April and September 1985. In addition I gave two "lounge seminars" on portions of this book in the Princeton University Department of Religion in 1984 and 1985, as well as a colloquium on another portion sponsored by my own department at Rutgers in 1985. Finally, I have benefited over the years from discussions in the Interest Group on War, Peace, Revolution, and Violence of the Society of Christian Ethics.

No mention, however, of any of the above should be taken to imply that anybody but myself is responsible for the interpretations of Western moral traditions concerning the quest for peace that I advance in this book.

As always, I am grateful to my wife, Pamela, and our children, Christopher and Ashley, for their forbearance and tolerance as well as their support and quiet pride in a husband and father who never strays far from reading other people's books and essays and writing more of his own.

Finally, my thanks to Sandy Thatcher, Editor-in-Chief of Princeton University Press, who has shepherded two previous books of mine into publication, for his encouragement while I was engaged in writing this one.

INTRODUCTION

The quest for peace has become one of contemporary Western culture's major moral concerns. That concern, for many persons, is focused by the existence of nuclear weapons and the fear—for some even the expectation—that if these weapons were to be used in war, all life on earth would be destroyed. This is, for example, the message of Jonathan Schell's widely circulated book, *The Fate of the Earth*,[1] as it is of much other recent literature; the theologian Gordon Kaufmann, for example, finds in nuclear weapons the possibility of the ultimate rebellion of mankind against God, for now, Kaufmann argues, man has the power to undo God's creation itself.[2] Likewise the 1983 pastoral letter on war and peace of the American Catholic bishops puts its call for peace in the context of the urgency to avoid nuclear war,[3] and this same motivation is visible at the roots of a great multiplexity of contemporary antiwar, antiarmament sentiment and its political expression.

The quest for peace, however, is not a new creature of the nuclear age. It has a tradition; rather, the quest for peace has developed through several distinguishable moral traditions, each of which can be identified in the present historical context. In this volume, I identify three such moral traditions of the quest for peace and examine them in various stages as they have developed in history. The three are the just war tradition of setting limits to war, the sectarian pacifism of withdrawal from the world and its ills, and the political tradition of thought that finds the cure for discord among nations in the es-

[1] Jonathan Schell, *The Fate of the Earth* (New York: Avon Books, 1982).

[2] Gordon D. Kaufmann, *Theology for a Nuclear Age* (Philadelphia: The Westminster Press, 1985).

[3] National Conference of Catholic Bishops, *The Challenge of Peace: God's Promise and Our Response* (Washington, D.C.: United States Catholic Conference, 1983); especially compare sections 68-121 with sections 122-38.

tablishment of a new, more universal, and rightly constituted political order.

Some contemporary pacifists will object to including the first of these three, just war tradition, in a listing of moral efforts to achieve peace, for this stream of moral theory and practice after all justifies war. Yet it does not affirm *all* war: it sets limits to the use of force even as it legitimizes some such use, and it insists that war is justified only when it is for the purpose of bringing about peace. The just war idea constitutes in fact one of the major and most long-standing approaches to peace in Western culture. Were we to avoid it or rule it out of order here, we would miss a great deal in how people in this culture have sought to think about peace and how to achieve it—not only because of what this tradition in the quest for peace deals with in itself, but also because of the relation of the other two traditions to this one.

In fact, in this volume I will discuss just war thought principally as a way of throwing the other two traditions in the quest for peace into clearer focus. In other books[4] I have already treated just war tradition directly and in considerable detail. Here I will assume that previous work, referring to it as necessary and supplementing it where needful, but not concentrating so closely on the just war concept as on the other two approaches; for these need to have done for them what I have earlier done for just war tradition. This book, then, is mainly about the latter two streams of moral thought; yet it fits, like a new piece in a larger puzzle, together with my earlier work on just war tradition to form a more complete picture of how Western culture has sought to deal morally with the values brought to the fore by war and peace, violence and the avoidance of violence, the goals of human community, and the best ways to achieve and protect those goals.

Let us, then, look more closely at those other two traditions in the quest for peace, which form the chief focus of this book.

[4] James Turner Johnson, *Ideology, Reason, and the Limitation of War* (Princeton: Princeton University Press, 1975) and *Just War Tradition and the Restraint of War* (Princeton: Princeton University Press, 1981).

Both of them are, in their respective ways, highly idealistic, in that they proceed from a conviction that peace, in the limited sense of the absence of war and violence, is a possibility for at least some elements of human life in history, and that along with this elimination of violence will also be present the fullest flowering of other human values. Such idealistic conviction and expectation, common to these two traditions, sets them off sharply from just war tradition, which proceeds from a deeply rooted assumption that the world of human history will always be one in which violence is present, in which values are threatened by the forces of injustice and evil, and in which such peace as is achieved is always, by nature, limited and temporary and can never be expected to become universal and eternal.

Apart from a common idealism about peace, though, these two remaining traditions differ profoundly. One of them seeks to solve the problem of war and violence not for the world as a whole, but only for particular communities living lives withdrawn from some or all participation in the world wherein these disturbances are manifested. This approach to peace is most strikingly and consistently displayed in the pacifism of Christian sectarian movements; here I follow such sectarian pacifism from the medieval Waldensians through the Swiss Brethren, a sixteenth-century Anabaptist sect, to the contemporary "peace churches," the lineal descendants of this earlier radical Christian sectarianism.

The third tradition, instead of seeking to withdraw from the evil world to a place where the ideal life can be lived and the ideal form of community created, looks instead to the transformation of the world itself into a new form of community in which violence and war will, being out of place, wither away and in which the ideal life will thus become possible for all. Some such transformation of the world is generally what is meant when the word "utopian" is used, and thus in the analysis below I reserve the term "utopian" for this tradition, calling the other one "sectarian." In their common idealism about the possibility of peace in history, though, both are in a fundamental sense utopian by contrast to just war tradition.

The third tradition in the quest for peace coalesces most visibly in the thought of Renaissance humanism, most specifically in the writings of Erasmus. Broadly speaking, it envisions the solution of the problem of war to be in the creation of a more inclusive society, a "superstate," in which (because there will no longer be petty states to squabble among themselves) there will be no wars. This is the core concept right along from Erasmus's medieval forebears through his own writings to the "perpetual peace" theorists of the Enlightenment era to nineteenth- and twentieth-century internationalism.

The main line of this tradition is unabashedly internationalist, depicting the very existence of particular states as the root of war and holding out the creation of a universal political community as the most fundamental element in achieving the utopia in which peace will reign. Concerning this view, what I am calling the "superstate" is greater in two senses: it is both larger and above all currently existing sovereignties. But what if each of these sovereignties could itself become self-sufficient, so that it would have no reason to seek what other states might possess, and what if each one were at the same time to be so manifestly capable of self-defense, because of its internal sufficiency, that no greedy neighbors could realistically contemplate attacking it? Finally, what if an individual state's own virtue were so clear for all to see that its neighbors, and their neighbors, and so on, would restructure themselves accordingly? This concept is Rousseau's and before him that of the fourteenth-century theorist Marsilius of Padua; it is a vision of a utopian "superstate" in a different sense. Individual polities remain, though not necessarily the same ones as before, and each of them is in itself a "superstate," able to provide all the goods of community for its citizens, including the total absence of strife. This is historically a variant on the utopian "superstate" theme, and thus I treat the internationalist and the localist streams of thought not as separate traditions, but as two aspects of the same tradition.

The kinship between these ways of thinking is thematic as well as historical: each growing internationalist "superstate" must, until the final universal polity is achieved, behave in the way the minor tradition conceives that ideal individual polities will behave. We shall see this below in connection with the "perpetual peace" concept, in which the elimination of intra-European wars is sought through various schemes for an internationalist federation of European sovereignties. Yet, at the same time, the elimination of wars with non-Europeans would be achieved by the new inner strength and unity of the Europeans, which would deter potential enemies from attacking. Despite the connection exemplified here, however, a tension remains between these two ways of thinking: the main line of the tradition is inevitably imperialist in its universalism, while the minor line is, in the best possible sense, nationalist in its localism. At their extremes the two are as oil and water, fundamentally immiscible. Together, though, the two aspects of this tradition in the quest for peace tend to correct and embellish each other.

The earliest proponents of both these kinds of thinking about the achievement of peace through the creation of a superior state are to be found in the Middle Ages. Specifically, here I will discuss Dante's *De Monarchia* as exemplifying the first stages in the main line of this tradition, with the *Defensor Pacis* of Marsilius of Padua exemplifying an approach akin to that later taken by Rousseau.

Indeed, so far as coherent, continuous traditions in the quest for peace are concerned, these simply do not begin to coalesce before the Middle Ages. Why, then, does this study open with a consideration of the attitudes of the early Christians?

I give two answers to this question. The first lies in the frequently made claim that Christianity, by its nature and in its early history, was pacifist, and that Christian acceptance of violence and war came about only with a loss of moral purity that coincided with the age of the Emperor Constantine. Normatively this historical interpretation is used to argue that if contemporary Christians would be faithful to the moral insights of true Christianity, they must return to the pacifism of the earliest Christians. The vitality of this claim in the existing literature, in popular belief, and in current debate requires that it be examined. If it holds up, then the Christian component of just war tradition dissolves; it would no longer be possible to regard it as Christian, even though it came from the Church. What may be less apparent, but is no less true, is that if this interpretation holds at face value, the humanistic utopian tradition of the quest for peace also vanishes as a possibility for Christians, because insofar as early Christianity rejected violence, war, and military service, it did so as a religious community withdrawn as far as possible from the larger world; that is, as a sect. Where that withdrawal disappears, the rejection of violence, war, and military service is altered; but where it persists, neither the just war nor the "superstate" approaches to peace may be admitted to have validity.

A great deal more remains to be said, but I will postpone that until the first chapter. For now, I add only that this interpretation, while seeking to find normative value in historical fact, actually reads currently held normative values back into its interpretation of history. The argument of those who advance this interpretation, to put it crudely, is something like this: we are Christians and pacifists; we identify with those early Christians of the first three centuries; therefore, they must have been pacifists like us. The problem is that, even apart from the logical fallacy here, the historical evidence simply does not sustain such a claim.

The second reason for beginning with the early Christian attitudes toward war and military service is that the debate from this period provided the terms for concepts that took shape in the Middle Ages and even in the modern period. It is not absolutely necessary to go back so far to make sense of what was reasoned and believed later, but doing so gives a fuller picture. Not only is this true for the thought of such major figures as Augustine, whose influence on medieval religion and politics was so pervasive. It is also, for example, somewhat enlightening to find Clement of Alexandria, a Christian scholar of the second century, arguing in ways that presage both later just war thought and the "superstate" approach to securing peace. Likewise, in the opposition to idolatry—and thus to much of life in the Roman state—of Clement's contemporary Tertullian of Carthage, we sense a flavor of later sectarianism that might otherwise be missed. Finally, to place the debate over what the early Christians believed regarding war and military service into the cultural context of the first four centuries allows us to demystify their beliefs and attitudes somewhat, to understand them as responses to a flesh-and-blood world, and to prepare for doing the same with the developments in moral attitudes from later periods. Moral beliefs do not emerge from a cultural and historical vacuum but are shaped in response to concrete historical contexts. What is absolute or sacred in the moral beliefs and attitudes of the medieval and modern periods cannot simply be that they are in conformity with what the early Christians believed, for these, too, had their moral convictions shaped by historical experience. Explicitly treating early Christian attitudes on war, peace, and military service thus clears the way for a more thorough and objective assessment of later positions that directly or implicitly refer back to these.

One might raise another question. Why not begin even earlier, with the Hebraic *shalom* of the Old Testament and the ideas of peace found in Greek and Roman antiquity? My answer is that this would involve us in a task with sharply diminishing returns. There are, to be sure, important ideas to be found in these earlier cultures, and other studies have focused on these. Johannes Pedersen, Gerhard von Rad, and Walter Eisenbeis have explored the meaning of the biblical word *shalom*;[5] other biblical scholars have examined the cultural implications of this concept of peace in the contexts of tribal life, national life in the kingdoms of Israel and Judah, and eschatological expectation as exemplified by the prophets Isaiah, Deutero-Isaiah, Jeremiah, and Ezekiel.[6] That such a literature

[5] Johannes Pedersen, *Israel, Its Life and Culture* (London: Oxford University Press, 1959), vols. I and II, particularly pp. 263-311; Gerhard von Rad, "Shalom," in G. Kittel, ed., *Theologisches Wörterbuch zum Neuen Testament*, 10 vols. (Stuttgart: W. Kohlhammer, 1932-1979), vol. II, p. 400ff.; Walter Eisenbeis, *Die Würzel Sh-L-M im Alten Testament* (Berlin: Walter de-Gruyter & Co., 1969).

[6] See, for example, the discussions in Roland de Vaux, *Ancient Israel, Its*

exists makes it all the less pressing that I carry the present study back into the Old Testament period. Similarly, Gerardo Zampaglione has examined the ideas of peace in classical antiquity, focusing separately on the Greeks and Romans before turning to the Old Testament and then to Christian doctrine.[7] Certain common themes run through the Hebrew *shalom*, the Greek *eirēnē*, and the Roman *pax*, notably the concept that "peace" is a state of completeness and well-being, not just—or perhaps not even mainly—the absence of war. Indeed war may, in all these concepts, be necessary to ensure the peace—that is, the wholeness and well-being—of the community in question.

For the purposes of understanding the development of Western moral tradition concerning the quest for peace, however, it is not necessary or even particularly helpful to go back into this earlier historical period. History has a way of filtering ideas and channeling their remainders into particular streams. For better or worse, the concepts of peace that obtained in antiquity were filtered and channeled by the same cultural developments that made Christian religion the central cohesive force of Western society in the Middle Ages. For the development of the moral traditions I treat in this book, these earlier ideas are important only in the forms in which they existed in the cultural memory of Western society after this society achieved cultural cohesiveness and self-consciousness; that is to say, from the era of medieval Christendom forward.

Broadly speaking, to trace the development of a moral idea through the history of a culture requires that one begin at the beginning of that idea. The problem, however, is to figure out where and when the moral idea in question actually had its genesis. Or rather, this is one side of the problem. For such an idea to be of more than antiquarian interest, it must have a contemporary referent, and this complicates the task of following it back in time and cultural context. If we carry our search for origins back too far, either we lose touch with the

---

Life and Institutions (New York: McGraw-Hill, 1961) and W. Robertson Smith, *The Religion of the Semites* (New York: Meridian Books, 1956).

[7] Gerardo Zampaglione, *The Idea of Peace in Antiquity* (Notre Dame and London: University of Notre Dame Press, 1973).

contemporary referent that makes the search morally significant, or else, trying desperately to keep in touch with today's moral concerns, we may fall into reading those concerns into a distant historical context where their presence is foreign and distorts the whole picture we are trying to bring into focus. This is, as noted earlier, what I think is wrong with the standard pacifist interpretation of the moral attitude toward war and peace in the early Christian Church. The danger is as great or greater as we move further back in time and cultural context. The greater the intensity of our contemporary moral and emotional attachment to the idea in question, the more acute these problems become; and this is especially so with the ideal of peace, which (together with the other moral ideas that form a kind of penumbra around it in contemporary Western society) carries a great freight of powerful moral commitment.

The task in the present study is to keep some contact with that moral commitment while at the same time not being blinded by it. We need to know whence our moral ideals and ways of thinking normatively have come; thus, we ought to pay attention to the history of ideas and the development of moral tradition. In this way we employ history as a means of learning more about ourselves, the full dimensions of what we believe, and who our fellows in moral community are from ages prior to our own. We may gain insight by learning how they thought about problems similar to the ones that confront us in our own time. But all we can do from the perspective of our present concerns and commitments is pose questions to this past; we may not rewrite it so as to make its answers those which we today find most congenial or convincing. This study is thus an effort to let the moral traditions treated speak for themselves.

The origins of this book are to be found in my previous historical work on just war tradition. There I began with the medieval coalescence of this tradition as a broad cultural consensus on the justification and limitation of war and violence, following the development of this consensual body of theory and practice into the modern period through international law, military praxis and codes of conduct, religious teaching, and the work of moral theorists. There remained, though, two large issues that I purposely avoided in these earlier studies: the question of the minority moral position that has paralleled just war tradition throughout history, but that rejected violence and war instead of seeking to incorporate them into a larger scheme of justice, and the question of how far the moral concepts, attitudes, and practices regarding war that obtained in the medieval and modern periods continued or contradicted those of the premedieval age. The present study began, then, as an effort to go back into that earlier period to resolve the question of continuity and as an effort to explore the development of the moral tradition of pacifism as it related to the just war idea. This book, though, is not just about pacifism; at least not about pacifism in the sense mentioned, that of total rejection of violence and war. Sectarianism rejects the ways of society first of all, and violence and war only as included in that larger rejection. Violence and war are thus not the central evil here; they are but expressions of it. Violence itself is depicted as evil in the humanistic utopian tradition, as we shall see clearly below in Erasmus; yet this is in tension with that aspect of this tradition which always accepts war against those who would disrupt the peace. This is no absolute pacifism after all. In fact, absolute pacifism of the sort I originally set out to study works its way in and out of both sectarianism and utopianism, though neither of these is fully or characteristically best understood as opposed to violence and war as such. My initial idea, then, was to focus on such opposition and its sharp contrast with just war tradition; once into the study, however, I found a truer picture could be had only by focusing on a more positive goal, the ends of peace. Yet, this required that I reassess the pacifism of opposition to violence and war in relation to those ends, and the resulting new focus on the development of moral tradition concerning the quest for peace required further that just war thinking be incorporated into the overall examination of this development. The result is the present study, which I regard as supplementing and, in a way, completing the work I have done earlier on Western moral doctrine on war.

The Quest for Peace

CHAPTER I

CHRISTIAN ATTITUDES TOWARD WAR AND MILITARY SERVICE IN THE FIRST FOUR CENTURIES

A. Were the Early Christians Pacifists?

1. *A Standard Contemporary Interpretation*

What was the attitude of the early Christians toward war and military service? A widely accepted contemporary account goes something like this: Jesus was a pacifist who accepted neither the use of violent means to advance his message nor the resort to violence in self-defense. The early Church, following this example, was also pacifist in both these senses. Pacifism remained an essential characteristic of Christianity until the time of Constantine early in the fourth century; but Constantine and his successors effected a revolutionary change in the relation of the Christian Church and the Roman Empire, bringing the Church and its leaders into such close proximity to the state that the Church lost its earlier purity and became accommodated to the needs of the secular empire. In Christian thinking about war and military service the effects of this revolutionary change appeared first in Ambrose of Milan and then, more systematically, in Augustine of Hippo, generally regarded as the father of Christian just war doctrine. With Augustine, then, the effects of the Constantinian compromise between Christianity and empire triumphed over the attitudes that were normative among Christians for the first three centuries; in the case of attitudes toward war and military service, the normative pacifism of pre-Constantinian Christianity was displaced by just war theory, which justified participation in war by Christians in service of the state.

Such is this interpretation of early-Christian moral attitudes toward peace, war, and military service. It varies in detail, of course, depending on the narrative intent of the author giving it; yet the general shape of this account is widely presupposed in contemporary Christian writings on war. It is an interpretation rooted in pacifism; indeed, its concept of a Constantinian "fall" of the Church is an idea that, historically, was associated chiefly with the critique leveled by radical Christian sectarians against the Church of Rome. Yet it is striking that in contemporary discussions of morality and war this account of the Church's first four centuries has spread far beyond its pacifist beginnings. A broad spectrum of Protestants and Catholics alike has been influenced, for example, by the thesis of Roland Bainton in *Christian Attitudes toward War and Peace*, one of the most widely read statements of this interpretation. Bainton writes as follows in a chapter titled "The Pacifism of the Early Church":

> The three Christian positions with regard to war . . . matured in chronological sequence, moving from pacifism to the just war to the crusade. The age of persecution down to the time [of] Constantine was the age of pacifism to the degree that during this period no Christian author to our knowledge approved of Christian participation in battle.[1]

Similarly, the second draft of the 1983 pastoral letter of the American Catholic bishops put the matter this way:

> [F]rom the writings of leading theologians of this period [the first four centuries], it is clear that there was a certain level of opposition to military service based upon particular gospel passages. . . . Indeed, when contemporary Christians who are committed to pacifism or non-violence read the writings of early theologians such as Tertullian and Origen, they often focus upon the passages

[1] Roland H. Bainton, *Christian Attitudes toward War and Peace* (New York and Nashville: Abingdon Press, 1960), p. 66.

which specifically criticize military service on the grounds that it involved killing.[2]

Much more unequivocal, as should be expected, are the statements of authors writing from a peace-church perspective. Guy Franklin Hershberger's *War, Peace, and Nonresistance* is a case in point. Speaking of evidence from the early church that soldiers had been baptized, this Mennonite historian comments, "the records do not tell us whether these men continued as soldiers after their baptism or not. The most reasonable presumption, however, would be that they did not."[3] A few lines later, he adds, "The writings of this period [the early Church] are strongly nonresistant in their general tenor, . . . so that it is quite unlikely that anyone remained both a soldier and a Christian for any length of time during this period."[4] Hershberger proceeds to give examples of such writings, then turns to the "astonishing and shocking" change he observes in Christian attitudes on war in the time of Constantine and afterward: "[T]he church gave up its nonresistant position and became the religion of the imperial state. . . . No doubt the most important factor in bringing about the change . . . was the gradual growth of moral laxness during this period. . . ."[5] Hershberger speaks of "heathen hordes" flocking to the Church who could not meet its earlier high moral standards;[6]

[2] National Conference of Catholic Bishops, "The Challenge of Peace: God's Promise and Our Response" (second draft), *Origins*, vol. 12, no. 20 (October 28, 1982), p. 311; cf. the final version of the pastoral, National Conference of Catholic Bishops, *The Challenge of Peace*, paragraphs 111-15. A sharply contrasting position is that of John Helgeland in "Christians and the Roman Army, A.D. 173-337," *Church History*, vol. 43, no. 2 (June 1974), pp. 149-63, 200. Helgeland insists that such opposition to military service as existed among the early Christians was based in opposition to idolatry rather than in an abhorrence of killing.

[3] Guy Franklin Hershberger, *War, Peace, and Nonresistance* (Scottdale, Pa., and Kitchener, Ont.: Herald Press, 1969), p. 69. Cf. Helgeland, "Christians and the Roman Army"; cf., also, Luke 3:14 and Acts 10, where nothing is said about such baptized soldiers leaving military service.

[4] Ibid.

[5] Ibid., pp. 70-71.

[6] Ibid., p. 72.

Augustine's just war doctrine was for him only "a plausible theory" that attempted to "reinterpret the nonresistant teachings of Christ and the Scriptures in a compromising way so as to make them fit the lower moral standards which the church had adopted."[7]

Another contemporary pacifist author, Jean-Michel Hornus, characterizing the development of Christian attitudes to war in the early centuries as a "progressive 'slide,' "[8] makes Constantine himself an example of gross immorality and insincere Christianity, citing his "murder" of his wife and son, his "protection" of pagan religion, and his postponement of baptism.[9] The changes made by the Church at the time of Constantine were thus, for Hornus, tainted with guilt by association, and nothing good can be found in them.

The significance of this account of the early Christian attitudes toward war is not, though, in its interpretation by peace-church authors; rather, its significance is to be found in the wider acceptance given to this account in contemporary religious debate by persons and institutions not belonging to this explicitly pacifist tradition. The influence of Bainton, himself a Quaker "associate," has far transcended peace-church boundaries: that a sizable contingent of contemporary Catholics can accept a version of this interpretation of early Christian moral attitudes, as illustrated above, bears witness to its spread across denominational boundaries into branches of Christian religion not traditionally pacifist. In another example, the Protestant theologian Walter Muelder simply takes for granted "the pacifism of the early church" as part of "the legacy of the churches to the ecumenical movement on the issues of war and peace."[10] Ironically, this interpretation of early Christian history has become common fare even among non-

[7] Ibid.

[8] Jean-Michel Hornus, *It Is Not Lawful for Me to Fight*, revised ed. (Scottdale, Pa., and Kitchener, Ont.: Herald Press, 1980), p. 213.

[9] Ibid., chapter 6.

[10] Walter G. Muelder, "Pacifism and the World Council of Churches," chapter 9 (pp. 153-168) in Thomas A. Shannon, ed., *War or Peace: The Search for New Answers* (Maryknoll, N.Y.: Orbis Books, 1980), p. 153.

pacifists, who (while regarding just war theory as the proper expression of Christian involvement with the world) accept the historical interpretation that this adjustment to secular involvement is a product of the age of Constantine and think of the pre-Constantinian period as a time of pacifism rooted in Christian separatism.[11]

The most complete and thorough expression of this interpretation of early Christian attitudes toward war and military service is that of the English pacifist C. John Cadoux in *The Early Christian Attitude to War*, published in reaction to the First World War.[12] This is a comprehensive and thorough examination of all the evidence that exists for the pacifism of the early Christians, marked simultaneously by the expressed intention to weigh this evidence fairly on its own terms and by a certain superciliousness on Cadoux's part toward anyone who did not agree with him.[13] For reason both of its comprehensiveness and its perspective, this work is often appealed to by contemporary authors wishing to argue the normative pacifism of the early Christians.[14] Cadoux depicted this pacifism as

[11] Cf. William V. O'Brien, *The Conduct of Just and Limited War* (New York: Praeger, 1981), p. 4.

[12] C. John Cadoux, *The Early Christian Attitude to War* (New York: The Seabury Press, 1982, originally published at London: Headley Bros., 1919). One of Cadoux's purposes was to revise the interpretation that had earlier been given to the early Christian attitude to war by the German historian of Church doctrine Adolf von Harnack in his *Militia Christi* (first published in German in 1905). Harnack depicted the early church as somewhat mixed in its attitude to war and military service and did not find in just war tradition the radical break with earlier attitudes that Cadoux did after him. Both these books from an earlier era have been entered into recent argument about proper Christian attitudes toward war and the military, Cadoux's by a 1982 reprint and Harnack's in 1981 by the publication of an English translation with introduction and annotations. The scope of the scholarly argument between Harnack and Cadoux is analyzed in the introduction to the new English edition of *Militia Christi*. See Harnack, *Militia Christi: The Christian Religion and the Military in the First Three Centuries*, translated and introduced by David McInnes Gracie (Philadelphia: Fortress Press, 1981).

[13] See Cadoux, *The Early Christian Attitude*, pp. 213, 248, 261, and elsewhere.

[14] Cf. Hershberger, *War, Peace, and Nonresistance*, p. 65.

not only normative but universal in the early Church, treating evidence of Christian involvement in war or military service as exceptional, temporary, and the mark of attitudes less than perfectly Christian (owing, for example, to new converts or to a moral decline on the part of the Church as a whole). As in the account outlined above, he found a rapid subversion and disappearance of this "true" Christian position on war and the military to have taken place in the age of Constantine:

> It is generally thought that, with the accession of Constantinus to power, the Church as a whole definitely gave up her anti-militarist leanings, abandoned all her scruples, finally adopted the imperial point of view, and treated the ethical problem [of war] as a closed question. Allowing for a little exaggeration, this is broadly speaking true.[15]

A few lines later he notes approvingly the deploring by some historians of "the immense compromise to which the Church was committed by her alliance with Constantinus."[16] Christian acceptance of war and of participation in military service was "the result, not of any attempt to solve the ethical problem on its own merits, but of a more or less fortuitous combination of circumstances."[17]

Appearing clearly in Cadoux is an ethical judgment about the nature of true Christianity that also runs throughout contemporary statements of the standard pacifist account. We glimpse this judgment above in his reference to solving the ethical problem "on its own merits"; for a true Christian to do so, Cadoux was convinced, could not lead to just war tradition. In short, his position was this: *true* Christianity rejects violence and war, following the example of Jesus; the early Christians themselves lived out this example and rejected all involvement with war and any military service for themselves; when Christians later accepted such involvement, however conditionally, it was a betrayal of the earlier ethical purity; this betrayal is

[15] Cadoux, *The Early Christian Attitude*, p. 256.

[16] Ibid., p. 257.

[17] Ibid., p. 261.

identified with "compromises" the Church made beginning with the reign of Constantine. Cadoux's historical interpretation is thus linked to a prior moral decision about what true Christianity can allow. This ethical judgment appears in three guises: in statements affirming his own pacifism and suggesting that nonpacifist interpreters of the early Christian attitude to war have been biased;[18] in the superciliousness with which Cadoux, especially toward the end of his book, dismisses those of differing opinions;[19] and in the overall structuring of his argument on "the early Christian disapproval of war." The greater part of this argument is carried on under these topics: "The Condemnation of War in the Abstract," "The Essential Peacefulness of Christianity," "The Christian Treatment of Enemies and Wrongdoers," "The Christian Experience of Evil in the Character of Soldiers," and "The Christian Refusal to Participate in War."[20] These topics—as well as the content of the arguments subsumed under them—reveal a judgment of Christianity as "essentially peaceful" and of war and military service as "evil" and to be condemned. With such a base it is impossible to see in any form of Christian acceptance of war anything but a fall from the truth. And, as already noted, that is precisely what Cadoux and contemporary statements of the standard pacifist account declare to have taken place.

The problem is that this account of early Christian history is both dead wrong and misleading in its depiction of the historical evidence. Two issues of interpretation confront us here: first, whether the ethical judgment is a fair reflection of early Christian attitudes on war and military service or not; and, second, whether the historical development to be observed in the first four centuries is in fact what the pacifist account represents it to be. The first requires a closer look at the evidence from the period and its interpretation in this account, aided by recent studies of the early Christians in their social context and of the general social history of the Roman Empire in this pe-

[18] Ibid., e.g. pp. 14-15.
[19] Ibid., e.g. pp. 183, 193, 213, 232, 249-50, 261.
[20] Ibid., pp. vi-vii.

riod. The second also requires such a closer look; yet it necessitates as well an inquiry into the extent of pluralism among the early Christians and an estimation of the effect of such pluralism in developing attitudes toward war and military service. This chapter undertakes such a re-examination, beginning with the major evidentiary sources as interpreted by Cadoux and others who render early Christian attitudes toward war and military service in terms of the standard account.

2. *Major Planks in the Platform of the Standard Account*

Cadoux himself recognized the problem of misinterpretation introduced because of moral commitments, but he did not apply this recognition to himself; instead, repeatedly in the introduction to his book, he criticizes earlier authors as misrepresenting the attitudes of the early Christians precisely because these authors were *not* pacifists.[21] Toward the eminent historian Adolf von Harnack he was kinder than to most; yet Cadoux represents his own intention to be "to present the material more proportionately and comprehensibly—and even, on a few points—more accurately"[22] than Harnack had done in his *Militia Christi.* The possibility that his own perspective might introduce an opposite bias apparently did not occur to him. Cadoux was, though, at least conscious that other interpretations of early Christian attitudes on war existed and that they had to be taken into account; contemporary purveyors of the pacifist account are much more matter-of-fact in simply assuming that no other interpretation is worth taking seriously.[23] For this reason their styles differ: Cadoux is more interested in arguing the case for his interpretation, while later,

[21] See particularly Cadoux's dismissal of Bethune-Baker as "allowing his prepossessions in favour of a particular theory to mislead him" (ibid., p. 9) and of Bigelmair because his "leanings as a Roman Catholic here and there unduly influence his judgment" (ibid., p. 10).

[22] Ibid., pp. 13-14.

[23] Cf. Hershberger, *War, Peace, and Nonresistance*, p. 64ff.; Muelder, "Pacifism," p. 153; Jean Lasserre, *War and the Gospel* (Scottdale, Pa., and Kitchener, Ont.: Herald Press, 1962), pp. 53-59.

derivative authors tend toward mere exposition of this position or toward moral argument made on its basis. Nonetheless, all employ essentially the same evidence, and we need now to ask what this evidence is.[24]

I will focus on three kinds of arguments and the evidence employed to support each. The first identifies the rejection of war with a rejection of bloodshed and violence as such; the second builds on the disapproval of war and military service expressed in the writings of certain important early Christian theologians taken to be representative of a universal rejection of war among the early Christians; and the third has to do with early Christian service in the Roman army. Let us examine these in turn.

B. The Rejection of Violence and Bloodshed

The argument that early Christianity rejected all violence is typically made by reference to the teachings of Jesus. Cadoux, for example, argues that the commandment "Thou shalt not kill" has a more general force than "Do no murder"; it forbids killing as such.[25] Here he expressly connects this commandment to killing in war; later in the argument, he broadens it to include even judicial use of violence for punishment. Jesus, he declares, was determined "to take no part in the use of physical violence in the judicial punishment of wrongdoers."[26] Cadoux

[24] In this discussion I will not attempt a point-by-point analysis of all the evidentiary sources cited by Cadoux and the interpretations given them. Cadoux sought to do this with Harnack, and the result was a book four times the size of Harnack's. With these two seminal studies available in current editions, there is no need here to retrace the steps of each of the authors one by one; a comparison can easily be carried out by anyone interested in their debate. My intention here is considerably more modest in scope, if perhaps more fundamental in terms of perspective. Among the sources regularly cited as evidence for the standard pacifist interpretation are some that themselves raise questions about the accuracy of this account of early Christian views on war and that argue for a revision of this interpretation. In my analysis I will discuss only these significant sources.

[25] Cadoux, *The Early Christian Attitude*, p. 21.

[26] Ibid., p. 29.

also highlights Jesus' teaching of nonresistance in the Sermon on the Mount;[27] this is the central theme in Hershberger's argument about the message of Jesus on violence.[28] Discounting statements of Jesus that might be read to imply that he accepted participation in warfare by his followers, Cadoux sums up his own reading of the evidence in no uncertain terms—terms that would be accepted generally among authors favoring the standard pacifist account:

> Jesus both abjured for himself and forbade to his disciples all use of physical violence as a means of checking or deterring wrongdoers, not excluding even that use of violence which is characteristic of the public acts of society at large as distinct from the individual. On this showing, participation in warfare is ruled out as inconsistent with Christian principles of conduct.[29]

Now, the issue here is not so much *what* Jesus taught as the context in which he taught it and how it was understood by the early Christians. There is general agreement among New Testament scholars as to the strong eschatological element in early Christianity: Jesus was expected to return soon, and the old order would pass away to be replaced by a new one.[30] One recent work goes further, calling early Christianity a millenarian movement and stressing its apocalyptic expectations and separatist ethic.[31] Whether we go this far or not, recognizing the eschatological nature of early Christian religious faith requires that, to understand it correctly, we shift our attention away from the evil of violence as such in the continuing world toward the evil of this world itself and the expectation that it will soon pass away—perhaps in the midst of divinely instituted violence, as the Christian book of Revelation has it. Such an

[27] Ibid., p. 22.

[28] Hershberger, *War, Peace, and Nonresistance*, pp. 43-64.

[29] Cadoux, *The Early Christian Attitude*, p. 31.

[30] See, for example, Albert Schweitzer, *The Kingdom of God and Primitive Christianity* (New York: The Seabury Press, 1968), especially part III.

[31] John G. Gager, *Kingdom and Community: The Social World of Early Christianity* (Englewood Cliffs, N.J.: Prentice-Hall, 1975).

approach contrasts sharply with the interpretation given in the account discussed above, according to which the rejection of violence produces an ethic that, in its purity, defines the living witness of Christians in distinction to that of the rest of humanity ("the world"), which does not pass away but may be expected to live alongside the Christian community. The alternative view, which follows from the recognition of the eschatological faith of the early Church and its sectarian relationship with the larger world, is that it is life in the world that is to be rejected, since soon this world itself as it now exists will be no more; hence, in particular, Christians should not involve themselves with the state, whether in the taking up of arms, the administering of judicial punishment, or whatever. Cadoux, arguing for the former against the latter position, gives a glimpse into his inner priorities, arguing that "what many might consider this blind attachment to peace and this blind horror of war" offers in fact "a better solution" to the problems of penal justice and strife among nations "than had yet [before Jesus] been given to the world."[32] In short, Cadoux was a transformist; the early Christians were not.

To summarize the issue, even if we accept that Jesus himself and his followers in the early Church rejected involvement in war, judicial violence, and the like, there is still a considerable difference whether they did so because they regarded violence itself as always and inexorably evil or whether they did so because of a desire to separate themselves from the world so as to live the morally pure life of the "new age" that they expected soon to dawn. These two perspectives define two essentially different reasons for rejecting war and military service. If the former is chosen, then the standard contemporary pacifist account is correct in depicting the acceptance of military service and the rise of just war theory as signs of a loss of moral purity in the Church at around the time of Constantine. In this view, as Hershberger and other contemporary peace-church

[32] Cadoux, *The Early Christian Attitude*, p. 66; cf. Hershberger, *War, Peace, and Nonresistance*, pp. 57-58.

authors rightly argue, the true Christian life must be one of nonviolent nonresistance.

But what if the eschatological interpretation of Jesus' teaching and the early Christian position is accepted as correct? Then it becomes possible to explain why the Church could gradually move to a limited justification and acceptance of violence for judicial punishment and just wars and of Christian participation in meting out such violence. In this view, the growing realization that the last days were not immediately at hand implies an increasingly less radical separation from the world at large, or else it implies a revised understanding of what was meant by the expectation of a new form of life in a new age. Both these sorts of adjustment were in fact made, the majority of Christians taking the former tack and a minority, the hermits and later the monastics, taking the latter. This dual adjustment, which took place throughout the Christian movement over an extended period—at least from the end of the first century (perhaps earlier, in some views) through the fourth—is an argument that the eschatological interpretation of the earliest Christian ethic is the better one. It also suggests an alternative and better way to conceive what may have happened in the development of Christian attitudes toward war and military service.

One of the difficulties inherent in the standard pacifist account is how to explain the suddenness of the church's about-face toward the military that this school of thought represents as having taken place; this interpretation deals with the difficulty by focusing on the person of Constantine and the revolutionary changes he instituted in the relation of church to empire. The Church, it is argued, experienced its own internal moral revolution in response to this new state of affairs. The new ethic on war enunciated by post-Constantinian fathers such as Ambrose and Augustine reflects this total turnaround and is thus inconsistent with the ethic on war of the pre-Constantinian Church.

The idea of such a sudden revolutionary change is, nonetheless, hard to swallow. It means, among other things, that the Church itself, the conviction with which its members held to its ethical teachings, and the personal strength of its leaders must be denigrated. Only if the bishops of Constantine's time are depicted as not understanding what was at stake or as acting out of naked self-interest can one make sense of their collaboration in Constantine's reforms and their encouragement of his actions bringing church and state closer together. Only if the mass of Christians of this period are represented as already somewhat distanced from an earlier ethic of moral purity can it be understood why they accepted the actions of their leaders without raising a general complaint. There were, to be sure, elements of resistance among both the leadership and the laity of the Church, but it is simply a fact of history that this resistance was localized and not general. Closer study of these elements of resistance suggests that they were rooted not simply in a desire to be more faithful to primitive Christian teachings, but rather in conflicts between the Romanized cities and a hinterland populated by persons of local indigenous ethnic groups.[33]

In any case, recognizing that in general both the mass of Christians and their leadership were prepared to accept what developed under Constantine and his successors—and not only to accept it passively, but to work at advancing it—suggests that something was happening in their attitudes toward life in the world well before Constantine came upon the scene. But to grant this calls into question the very idea of a Constantinian "revolution," and it forces the question of change back earlier, when there is no convenient scapegoat like Constantine to blame for the alleged loss of moral purity in the Church's attitude to war and the military.

In fact, as we shall see below, there is clear documentary evidence of a sizable presence of Christians in the Roman army from the year 174, and from this may be inferred an earlier acceptance of the possibility of military service for Christians,

[33] The most outstanding examples were in Asia Minor and North Africa: the Montanists and Donatists. Cf. Diana Bowder, *The Age of Constantine and Julian* (New York: Harper & Row, 1978), pp. 67-70; Peter Brown, *Religion and Society in the Age of St. Augustine* (London: Faber & Faber, 1972), p. 242ff.

dating perhaps to the beginning of the second century, which was precisely the time when the crisis in the expectation of a new age was experienced. This is not to suggest that in the year 100 Christians suddenly began deciding in significant numbers that they should join the army; indeed, the pagan critic of Christianity Celsus, according to the Christian theologian Origen, asserted around 180 that Christians refused service in the army. This, of course, directly contradicts other evidence, and the contradiction suggests that if Celsus was writing in good faith, he simply reflected Christian teaching as he knew it in his own locality. The contradictory evidence, as well as reason, suggests that Christians in different areas came to different conclusions about how to adjust to the world in the aftermath of their disappointed original hope for an early coming of the new age, just as different sectors of Christianity came to different positions on certain matters of doctrinal substance.[34]

These are matters to be explored more fully below, but together they outline an interpretation of the early Christian position on war and military service rather different from that found in the standard account. This alternative picture is one that highlights the initial eschatological separatism of the earliest stages of the Christian movement, in which not violence as such but close involvement in the affairs of the world was to be shunned, followed by a gradual adjustment to such involvement in the wake of the realization that the new age was not immediately at hand—an adjustment that took place in different ways and at different rates among Christians in various parts of the empire, and one that did not compromise earlier moral purity but instead sought ways to direct it into life

[34] The regional differences are most obviously manifested through the heresies: Gnosticism was principally found in Egypt; Montanism originated in Phrygia in Asia Minor and spread to North Africa; Donatism was North African; Arianism was a movement confined to segments of the Eastern (Greek-speaking) Church and to those Germanic tribes converted to Christianity by Arians. Beyond these, there were real differences between the Latin and Greek churches on such fundamental issues as the meaning of salvation (moral perfection or divinization of the soul) and forms of worship. In the face of such multiplexity it is difficult to make a credible claim that early Christians were universally pacifist in moral doctrine.

within the world at large. If we pursue this interpretation of the development of early Christian attitudes toward war and military service, it is not necessary to hypothesize a revolutionary change in these attitudes in the time of Constantine, along with the associated negative implications such a hypothesis requires regarding the laxity and moral complacency of the fourth-century Church. Rather we are led to think of a gradual consolidation of a positive moral acceptance of participation in affairs of the state, including military service and war, which paralleled a rejection of violence in other parts of the Church that also rejected Christian involvement in the wider society in ways well beyond those associated with the military. (Tertullian, who will be discussed below, is an excellent example of the latter sort of Christian in this period of development.) If the Church of the first century in fact rejected war and military service—and lacking direct evidence, this is impossible finally to determine either way—it was because of their eschatological hope that they would soon be living in a new age. Beginning with the second century, though, there is increasingly hard evidence. And, as we shall shortly see, this evidence presents a picture not of a single doctrine, but of plurality; not of universal rejection of war and military service, but of a mixture of acceptance and rejection of these phenomena in different sectors of the Christian world.

C. The Rejection of War by Prominent Authors

Roland Bainton has observed a correlation between the hard evidence of Christians in military service and Christian writings deploring such service. Only after about 180, he notes, does there appear "a number of more or less explicit condemnations of military service," and thereafter the two kinds of evidence—of Christians serving as soldiers and of denunciations of such service by other Christians—parallel each other.[35] These parallel phenomena present a problem: Who were these people on both sides of the issue? How representa-

[35] Bainton, *Christian Attitudes*, p. 72.

tive were they of broader attitudes within the Church? The standard pacifist interpretation has no hesitancy in ascribing the greater representativeness to the antiwar figures; it is this ascription that we must now test.

The various statements of the pacifist account all agree on who were the major figures opposing Christian participation in war and military service from the late second century (when evidence of explicit opposition first appears) through the early fourth century, when acceptance of such participation by Christians began to emerge as the normative position of the Church. These figures include Clement of Alexandria, writing about the year 200 (who can, however, be cited on both sides of the issue); his Latin-speaking North African contemporary Tertullian; Origen, whose major work *Against Celsus*, in which he briefly treats the moral problem posed by war, appeared in 248; and Lactantius, whose relevant works come from the period 305-314. Supporting evidence is found in the Canons of Hippolytus, whose exact date is uncertain but the first edition of which appeared about 235, in some of the writings of Cyprian of Carthage from about the same period, and in the narratives of certain Christians martyred because they refused military service; these last come from the latter half of the third century.[36] Two of the authors mentioned, Clement and Origen, came from Alexandria; Tertullian, like Cyprian, was a Carthaginian; Hippolytus was a Roman; Lactantius lived and wrote first in Nicomedia, in western Asia Minor, and later in Gaul. The two Alexandrians wrote in Greek, while the rest used Latin.

Authors like Cadoux and others who argue for the generality of pacifist attitudes in the early Church find in the geographic, linguistic, and temporal distribution of these authors evidence of how widespread was the position on war and military service that they all, though in various ways and to various degrees, somehow shared. But unless one comes to this

[36] See Cadoux, *The Early Christian Attitude*, part II, for discussion of these and other figures who opposed war for Christians; for a convenient chronology, see pp. xii-xvii.

evidence with the previous assumption of broad and general Christian opposition to war and military service, it would be difficult to argue this way, for this evidence is, like the Platte River in Colorado, "a mile wide but only a foot deep." The period represented here is fully two hundred years; though all educated persons in this era knew both Greek and Latin, the linguistic division between the authors cited was not unimportant; they reflected widely differing cultural and personal experiences; and, finally, they had different relationships to the developing Christian doctrinal orthodoxy of their respective times and places. Here are six authors, widely separated by all these measures: it is more reasonable to view them as individuals rather than as representatives of a broad consensus, especially since their writings coincide precisely with the growth period of evidence showing acceptance by *other* Christians of participation in war and military service. The large picture, then, would be one of pluralism on this moral point, not of a pacifist "purity" that was gradually being whittled away as imperfect Christians more and more compromised their beliefs to participate as citizens or subjects of the empire. The advantage to examining these antiwar figures as individuals is that we may thereby learn something more about the nature of that pluralism as Christian religion developed during this two-hundred-year period.[37]

I will not, however, treat all these authors but only three of them, Clement, Tertullian, and Origen. The reason is one of economy: by examining them it is possible to show the variegated nature of attitudes toward war and military service even among Christian authors generally cited as exemplifying a primitive Christian pacifism. My purpose is to sketch only the main outlines of the plural positions that actually obtained, so as to show that the resolution of the matter of Christian participation in war reached in the fourth and fifth centuries did

[37] This discussion will be brief, since the substantive positions of these early Church fathers have been much analyzed; I will concentrate on the problems in the standard pacifist interpretation of the meaning of these positions. See, also, Helgeland, "Christians and the Roman Army," for an alternative to the standard pacifist account of these fathers' arguments.

not spring up overnight in the period of Constantine. Examination of Clement, Tertullian, and Origen is enough to satisfy this purpose.

1. *Clement of Alexandria*

Clement, one of the earliest authors in this group, is also one of the most ambiguous in his attitude toward war and military service, and in this ambiguity is revealed something of the reason why Christians, as the debate developed, could take different sides on these issues. In general terms Clement was quite certain that to be Christian is to be "educated, not in war, but in peace," saying in one place, "We do not train women like Amazons to be manly in war, since we wish even the men to be peaceable."[38] Perhaps on a more fundamental level, he elsewhere suggests that mankind itself is "in reality a pacific instrument,"[39] an observation that fits well with Clement's general conception of Christianity as a form of higher *gnōsis* or knowledge that, while yet possessed by only a few, was in principle accessible to all humankind. In Clement's perception, not even all Christians had attained the fullness of knowledge; the Church included "learners" as well as "gnostics."

Thus the picture that emerges from Clement's writings is of a spectrum of stages of development in which the lower stages of the Christian life might be closer, in at least some regards, to the pagan world than to the world of the fully enlightened Christian Gnostic. In such a concept the practical position to be taken on war and military service could not be a simple, unambiguous one of opposition, despite the ideal of peace. Indeed, Clement in several places employs language that suggests he accepted military service as one possible occupation alongside others (he mentions farmers, sailors, and merchants) in

[38] Clement of Alexandria, *Paedagogus* I.xii.98; *Stromata* IV.viii.61. Citations of Clement in English are from the translations of his works found in Alexander Roberts and James Donaldson, eds., *The Ante-Nicene Fathers* (Buffalo, N.Y.: The Christian Literature Publishing Co., 1885), vol. III.

[39] Clement of Alexandria, *Paedagogus* II.iv.42; cf. Cadoux, *The Early Christian Attitude*, p. 64.

which a Christian might develop toward full *gnōsis*.[40] But while it is readily conceivable that, on the attainment of such full enlightenment, a Christian could continue in the occupation of farming, what Clement says about the essential peacefulness of Christianity may be read, as it is by Cadoux and other pacifist writers, to suggest that a soldier could not likely so continue.

In Clement, then, are revealed harbingers of the debate yet to come; this is one of the most interesting aspects of his treatment of military service for Christians. He deplored war and represented Christianity as, in its fullest form, essentially pacific; yet he lived well after the crisis of expecting the new aeon had passed, and he depicted the fullness of Christian knowledge as something to be reached developmentally in this world. He could thus accept military service as one possible occupation in which Christian growth could occur without subtracting from the blessed vision of peace that he saw in Christian teaching. As a result, his attitude toward military service for Christians was a foreshadowing of the distinction that later emerged, in both East and West, allowing military service for Christian laity but forbidding it to monks and clergy.

Similarly, Clement's was a concept in which Christians and pagans might serve together in maintaining the goods afforded by the stability and lawfulness of the empire and a peace that even if relative was real. This vision was reinforced by his knowledge that Christians were, in fact, in his own time serving in the army, by the cosmopolitanism of life in Alexandria, and by the fact that his age was one in which persecution of Christians was reduced to infrequent and local instances. Clement's experience was of a pluralistic empire in which Christianity was accorded its place alongside the many other religions and quasi-religions of the day; in many ways, it was a quite modern concept. The superiority of Christianity, Clem-

[40] Clement of Alexandria, *Protrepicus* X.100; on this passage cf. Helgeland, "Christians and the Roman Army," p. 154, and Cadoux, *The Early Christian Attitude*, pp. 232-33.

ent believed, would gradually become evident in this social environment; he did not expect any sudden apocalyptic overthrow of the world he knew to bring in the kingdom of Christ. In his view Christian responsibility toward the world was not to reject the state and withdraw into sectarian separation, but rather to carry on the search for enlightenment while at the same time pursuing one of the multitude of occupations necessary to sustain the world.

The compromise of which the standard account speaks was thus already present in Clement, more than a century before Constantine; yet it is clear that for Clement what was at stake was not the watering down of a pure form of Christianity, but its exact opposite. The movement he conceived was not a downward deterioration, but an upward metamorphosis—an ever more generalized and widespread growth throughout society toward such purity as was represented in the lives of the Christian Gnostics. The acceptance of military service for Christians who were not yet fully enlightened does not appear in his thought as a loss of the ideal; rather, it is presented as a form of support for the goods of the imperial order in which Christian growth—as necessary for soldiers as for farmers, sailors, and merchants—could take place.

2. *Tertullian*

For Clement's contemporary, the Carthaginian theologian Tertullian, quite the opposite was the case. In Tertullian's view, to become involved with the world meant dire peril to the faith and moral behavior of any Christian, and the ideal form of Christian life was one lived in rejection of such involvement. In his treatise *On Idolatry*,[41] written about the year 200, Tertullian not only laid out this position frankly, but gave examples of occupations Christians should avoid as implicitly idolatrous. A Christian should not be a silver- or goldsmith or a woodcarver, because much of the livelihood of people in

[41] Roberts and Donaldson, eds., *The Ante-Nicene Fathers*, vol. III, pp. 61-78.

those occupations came from making idols for pagan clients; a Christian might be neither a student nor a teacher, since what was studied and taught were the classics of Greek and Roman literature, full of stories about pagan gods; a Christian might not belong to the Roman civil service, since (to use a modern term) the "oath of office" was a form of pagan sacrifice; and for the same reason, no serious Christian could be a soldier in the Roman army.

The same theme appears in Tertullian's other work that explicitly treats of military service, *On the Soldier's Crown*,[42] written a decade later. Here the subject is not the general duty of Christians to keep pure from taint by the world; it is a specific instance in which a Christian soldier refused, citing his Christian faith as reason, to wear the laurel "crown" required as part of his "dress uniform" on public occasions. To Tertullian the "soldier's crown" was implicitly idolatrous because of its association with the official paganism of Rome, and apparently the soldier in question judged the matter likewise. This incident tells us two important things, apart from cementing the fact that Tertullian's main concern in opposing military service for Christians was idolatry: we learn implicitly that Christians were serving in the army stationed in North Africa at that time and that the normal duties of soldiering appear not to have raised a problem of sufficient magnitude to excite either the conscience of the soldier who later refused to wear the laurel "crown" or the pen of Tertullian. These two pieces of information are consistent with the overall picture we also glimpse through Clement, one in which Christian service in the army was an established fact, though not without opposition by some members of the clergy and some soul-searching on the part of individual soldiers.

Tertullian was a Montanist, adhering to a morally strict sectarian movement within Christianity that was especially strong in North Africa right up to the time of Constantine. Christian orthodoxy was still in the process of formation in Tertullian's time (and for some time afterward), and it is only

[42] Ibid., pp. 93-104.

in retrospect that Montanism can be labeled heterodox. In its heyday it was a contender for orthodoxy itself, and the vision of Christian life it projected was a sharp alternative to that found in non-Montanist circles in the Church. Tertullian wrote as much against other Christians (not of his persuasion) as against pagans; he was an apologist for a concept of Christianity that he fervently believed was right and against one he just as fervently believed was fundamentally wrong.[43]

Tertullian, and Montanism generally, promoted a Christianity that held itself apart from the ways of the rest of the world and stressed personal moral purity within that separated Christian community; in these respects it resembles the Christianity of the first century, which was also separatist and morally stringent. Yet it would be a mistake to find here the only legitimate line of descent from the Church of the first century: *both* Montanism and the developing orthodoxy came out of that first-century beginning, and the links between the beliefs of the early Church and those of the non-Montanists were also strong. The sectarianism of the early Church was one defined both by the small size and geographical scattering of the Christian communities and by their eschatological expectations. The separatism of the Montanist movement was rooted in neither of these, but in a kind of spirituality that also found expression—within the same North African culture—in Manichaean dualism. This was a spirituality of rejection of the world as a moral statement, and the statement thus made, while given Christian form, was not uniquely Christian. Tertullian's rejection of military service, along with other "idolatrous" occupations, was thus not a statement of "pure" Christianity as opposed to the acceptance of these occupations by other, "impure" Christians. It was rather one side in a struggle for dominance between two concepts of Christianity, each with its own agenda and each able to claim roots in the beliefs,

[43] It is not relevant that Tertullian formally became a Montanist only after the publication of *On Idolatry*; his sentiments in that work are clearly congruent with Montanism.

practices, and traditions established by the first-century Church.

3. *Origen*

Sometime about 180 the pagan writer Celsus criticized Christianity in his *True Discourses*, and in 248 the Alexandrian theologian Origen gave a formal response to this criticism, in *Against Celsus*. What the pagan writer had actually written has been lost; all we know of it is what Origen reports. On the subject of war this is little enough. Origen's response, though, forms one of the pillars of the standard account. Cadoux terms Origen "the prince of early Christian thinkers"[44] and, about Origen's attitude toward the subject of war and military service, comments: "Practically the whole of the eight chapters that come last but one in Origenes' reply are taken up in justifying the Christian attitude of aloofness from all forms of violence in service of the state."[45] (This is stretching the point a bit, as we shall see in a moment.) Hershberger, who calls Origen "one of the outstanding early church fathers,"[46] quotes him as saying, "For we no longer take 'sword against nation,' nor do we learn 'any more to make war,' having become sons of peace for the sake of Jesus. . . ." And, Hershberger adds, "In another place Origen specifically states that Christians do not serve as soldiers or magistrates for the emperor."[47]

Is it right to make Origen so central to the position that third-century Christianity was opposed to war and military service? The first element in an answer to this question must be an examination of what Origen actually did say about this topic. *Against Celsus*, while an important apologetic work, is but one in Origen's total body of writings, and his fame rests more on his achievement as a theologian and biblical commentator in the other works than on his performance as apolo-

[44] Cadoux, *The Early Christian Attitude*, p. 129.

[45] Ibid., p. 131.

[46] Hershberger, *War, Peace, and Nonresistance*, p. 67.

[47] Ibid.

gist.[48] War and military service for Christians were not a major scholarly concern for Origen. He wrote on these topics only in *Against Celsus*, and what he wrote there is, contrary to Cadoux's implication, but a very small portion—something less than two percent—of the whole work. What Origen actually said in these few pages repeats the general theme, already found in Clement and in earlier writings, that Christianity is essentially peaceful; also like Clement, Origen made his peace with the fact of war, though he made it in a way different from his predecessor's. As already observed for the case of Clement, this general concept of Christianity runs across the whole spectrum of Christian attitudes toward war and military service, both in the first Christian centuries and since. By itself, though, this concept yields no certain evidence about where to place any given early Christian author on that spectrum. As we shall see below, just war thinking and not only pacifism is compatible with such a general opposition to war. We must look for other evidence than this if we are to label a given early churchman a pacifist.

As to Origen's own version of this general concept of Christianity as teaching peace, we need to consider the context in which the above-cited sentence quoted by Hershberger falls. It comes in a section of *Against Celsus* wherein Origen is responding to Celsus on the matter of obedience to law, and particularly to Celsus' opinion that "the various quarters of the earth were from the beginning allotted to different superintending spirits, and were distributed among governing powers, and in this manner the administration of the world is carried on."[49] Origen's response is that the "superintending spirit" followed by Christians is Jesus, and that his law is one that aims at the reformation of all those laws of the different "governing powers." The law of Christians is a "spiritual law"; it is "exalted above the hills," and its excellence is able to be recognized and admitted by "men who make a profession of su-

[48] See, for example, Jean Daniélou, *Origen* (New York: Sheed & Ward, 1955), parts I and II.

[49] Origen, *Against Celsus* V.xxvi. English citations are from the edition in Roberts and Donaldson, eds., *The Ante-Nicene Fathers*, vol. IV, pp. 395-669.

perior attainments in wisdom and truth." Then, a few lines later, follows the sentence quoted by Hershberger, which in immediate context is employed by Origen to exemplify how Christianity has gone beyond the law of the Jews.[50] It is what one discovers when the inquirer climbs "up to the mountain of the Lord." The sentence on the peacefulness taught by Christianity thus, in context, aims at demonstrating how high is the goal taught by Christianity. The excellence of this way of living is one that can be granted by persons "of superior attainments in wisdom and truth," regardless of whether they are Christian or not.

Here Origen writes from his role as proselytizer and interpreter of Christian teaching to potential pagan converts; this role, after all, provided his livelihood, and it was a natural one for him. But we must ask whether the position he expresses here is essentially different from that already observed in Clement: a conception of Christian perfection as the highest possibility for human life, one that even pagans can recognize, and one that is to be sought through a developmental process in which not only individuals, but even "governing powers," may gradually be drawn up toward "the mountain of the Lord." Celsus had implied that Christians were disobedient to the laws; Origen's reply is to set up Christian teaching as the highest of all laws, one toward which others already established might be expected to gravitate. Far from being revolutionaries or criminals, Christians already have their eyes fixed on this higher law, and others may be expected to do so, too, when confronted with it.

The above passage is thus not really about *war*, or opposition to war, at all; it is about the peacefulness that Christianity teaches and that represents *the goal of all law*. Where Origen does treat the question of war and military service directly, it is in a totally different context three books later, in response to Celsus' charge that Christians ought to "honor the king" and "to help the king with all our might, to labor with him in the maintenance of justice, . . . to fight for him, or lead an army

[50] Ibid., V.xxxiii.

along with him."[51] Origen's reply is to argue that Christians already do honor and support the ruler, but by their prayers, not by military service; and these prayers are a more efficacious service to the empire: "[N]one fight better for the king than we do. We do not indeed fight under him, although he require it; but we fight on his behalf, forming a special army—an army of piety—by offering our prayers to God."[52] (Of course we know that for some time now Christians had in fact performed military service; indeed, there were almost certainly Christian soldiers when Celsus was writing his attack on Christianity. Thus, neither Celsus nor Origen reflected this reality.) Celsus had wondered what would happen if everyone behaved like the Christians; Origen's response is that if all Romans were to become Christians, God would fight for them against their enemies.[53] And Christians go beyond merely following the lead of others: "if Celsus would have us lead armies in defence of our country, let him know that we do this too," polemicized Origen;[54] but the armies so led were armies "of piety" as mentioned above.

It is clear from these concluding chapters of *Against Celsus* that Origen did in fact oppose military service for Christians; yet *how* he did so is more the stuff of just war, or even holy war advocacy than of pacifism. Origen envisions God as acting in response to Christian prayers in the service of "a righteous cause, and for the king who reigns righteously, [so] that whatever is opposed to those who act righteously may be destroyed!"[55] This kind of concept is a common feature of holy war doctrine right through history.[56] Origen's position is thus not so much a rejection of violence as a relocation of it—from Christians, who must keep "their hands pure," to God, who is not bound by the requisites of such purity.

[51] Ibid., VIII.lxviii, VIII.lxxiii.

[52] Ibid., VIII.lxxiii.

[53] Ibid., VIII.lxix.

[54] Ibid., VIII.lxxiv.

[55] Ibid., VIII.lxxiii.

[56] Cf. Bainton, *Christian Attitudes*, pp. 111-16, 136-51; cf. Johnson, *Ideology*, chapter II and epilogue.

This was nonetheless a serious attempt to grapple with the tension between the inherited high teaching of peace on a general level and the empirical experience of continued life in a world that is not peaceful, where force must sometimes be used in the service of good ends. Origen was factually wrong in saying that Christians did not serve in the Roman army; they had done so by his time for more than a century, and Julius Africanus, a contemporary with whom Origen corresponded, was even a Roman general. Origen's hyperbole in this regard had a rhetorical purpose not dissimilar to Tertullian's claim that no genuine Christian could serve in the army. His apologetic against the pagan Celsus was, with respect to the matter of military service, also an argument against Christians of his own time who substantially agreed with Celsus' point and who sought to resolve the matter by serving the values represented by the empire with their bodies, not simply with their prayers. Like Tertullian, Origen defined his concept of Christianity as above and apart from such bodily service, in the interests of Christian purity. There is much in Origen's overall framework of thought on this matter that recalls Clement; yet, for Origen, the practical distinction between the "learner" and the Christian "gnostic" had disappeared, with the result that "keeping their hands pure" of violence became the only way of following the "spiritual law" of the "superintending spirit," Jesus.

Origen was like Clement and Tertullian, yet different from both. If in Clement can be glimpsed the outlines of the later just war teaching, and if in Tertullian can be found a position suggestive of later Christian sectarianism, in Origen both these elements can be found as well as a third one: a holy war concept in which God fights alongside pagan Roman armies to uphold the righteousness for which Rome stands. Thus, rather than the clear-cut pacifism imputed to Origen by the standard pacifist account of early Christian moral attitudes, we in fact find in him but another particular strand in the pluralistic fabric of developing Christian thought on war during the early centuries of the Church.

D. Early Christian Service in the Roman Army

1. *The Sociological Character of the Early Church*

One of the most perplexing problems in understanding the attitude of the early Christians toward war and military service is the lack of much direct evidence from the period, along with the ambiguity of the scanty evidence that does exist. What does this absence imply? It is possible to speak, as Cadoux does, of "the essential peacefulness of Christianity," citing such evidence as Paul's calling for "the reconciliation of Jew and Gentile" in Ephesians and Jesus' "Happy are the peacemakers" from the Sermon on the Mount.[57] But earlier, while arguing for the Christian condemnation of war "in the abstract," he concedes, "The conditions under which the books of the New Testament were written were not such as to give occasion for Christian utterances on the wrongfulness of war." The absence of direct evidence from the first century does not deter this writer, who proceeds to cite as evidence for the condemnation of war from the New Testament period forward the positions of Tatian and Clement of Alexandria, both of whom lived in the next century, and still later sources.[58] Such sources as these, though—individual, scattered in place and time, and from no earlier than the middle of the second century—tell us nothing reliable about the earlier period.

It is because of this that an argument based on the sociological character of early Christianity has also been employed by expositors of the standard pacifist interpretation. For example, Bainton, writing about the period before 170, comments:

> The subject of military service obviously was not at that time controverted. The reason may have been either that participation was assumed or that abstention was taken for granted. The latter is more probable.[59]

[57] Cadoux, *The Early Christian Attitude*, pp. 58-59.

[58] Ibid., pp. 49-57.

[59] Bainton, *Christian Attitudes*, p. 68.

Bainton then goes on to give a classic expression of the argument for early Christian pacifism from the urban sociological character of early Christianity:

> The expansion of Christianity had taken place chiefly among civilians in the urban centers. Few as yet were converted while in the army. Converts not already in the ranks had many reasons against volunteering, and they were not subject to conscription. As slaves or freedmen many were ineligible.[60]

Hershberger puts the matter similarly: "It should . . . be remembered that the earliest Christians, for the most part, were slaves and Jews and women, few if any of whom were eligible for political office or to serve as soldiers. . . ."[61]

There is a considerable difference between arguing that the earliest Christians were opposed to war and military service because they identified these phenomena as evil and arguing that, in Bainton's words, "abstention was taken for granted" among them. Logically one can move from the first to the second, but not the other way, especially if the sociological make-up of the earliest Christians is held to be such that many or most Christians were ineligible for military service and hence did not have to think about it. That is to say, tying the rejection of war and military service to the sociological character of early Christianity may create more problems for the standard account than it solves. Let us explore this further.

It is generally accepted that early Christianity was almost exclusively an urban phenomenon once it expanded out of Palestine. The best direct evidence of this from the early Church itself is the letters of Paul, directed to Christians in urban centers located along the principal trade routes of the eastern Mediterranean world, and the scholarly attention given this phenomenon has correspondingly centered on the Pauline evi-

[60] Ibid.

[61] Hershberger, *War, Peace, and Nonresistance*, p. 64.

dence.[62] From Paul there also appears a picture of the sociological character of the Christians in this period. Traditional interpretation has rendered this as a Christianity made up, in Hershberger's phrase, "for the most part [of] slaves and Jews and women."

Two factors make this concept of early Christianity significant for the argument that the early Church was opposed to war and military service. First, recruitment for the army drew almost entirely on the rural population, where soldierly characteristics were more likely to be found than in urban areas; and second, many of these early Christians belonged to social groups whose members were not in any case liable for service in the legions. Furthermore, the cities where early Christianity flourished were far removed in this period from the presence of war, which was a phenomenon limited to the frontiers of the Roman Empire. The only city- and town-dwellers who were likely to enter the army as common soldiers were volunteers, and there was no pressure to volunteer. Slaves and freedmen were in this period explicitly excluded from military service, and insofar as Christians belonged to these categories, they could not join the army even if they wished to do so. Finally, there was little reason for interaction between serving soldiers and peaceful townspeople in normal times: they inhabited two essentially different worlds.

But it is to be observed that this reveals nothing for certain about the *attitudes* these early Christians may have had toward the army as such; toward military service as a possible option for them, other Christians, or other individuals close to them personally; or toward war. All it says for sure is that the sociological character of the early Church meant that military service for Christians was not a pressing issue. If it is argued—on the basis of the general peacefulness of Christianity and evidence of explicit Christian pacifism projected backward from

[62] See, for example, Gerd Theissen, *The Social Setting of Early Christianity: Essays on Corinth* (Philadelphia: Fortress Press, 1982); Wayne A. Meeks, *The First Urban Christians: The Social World of the Apostle Paul* (New Haven and London: Yale University Press, 1983); and Gager, *Kingdom and Community*, chapter 4.

the second century—that the Church of the first century was actively opposed to war and military service for its members, one might reply that this was a common urban attitude, not limited to Christians but a feature of a concept of life shaped by town living, commerce, and the habits of living in orderly, well-policed communities. In short, the urban character of early Christianity provides a *background* for investigation of Christian attitudes toward war and military service during the first hundred or hundred and fifty years of the Church; but the *details* about the attitudes to be painted upon that background must be provided from somewhere else.

2. The Roman Army and the Roman World

Before we can address the specific matter of Christians in the army of Rome, we need first to inquire what this army was like. From where did it draw its soldiers? What portion of the able-bodied men of the empire were under arms in the period with which we are concerned? Where were the various units of the army stationed? What were the functions of the army? And finally, what impact did the army have upon life in the interior of the empire? We have already anticipated some of these questions; now let us confront them directly.

In the Roman Republic the army had originally been constituted by a levy of the able-bodied male citizens, just as had been the practice of the Greek city-states. Civilian social ranks were reflected in military rank, with the result that the officers (tribunes, legates) were drawn from the equestrian and senatorial classes and the common soldiers from the ordinary citizens, or plebs. The rank of centurion, nominally that of the commander of a unit of one hundred men (that is, a unit about the size of a company in a modern army), was an in-between position; centurions were promoted from among the body of common soldiers for reason of merit and length of service, but the responsibility they held in the army was essentially that of an officer. The military historian Hans Delbrück calls the rank of centurion a combination of the modern ranks of first sergeant (the highest noncommissioned rank) and company commander (normally a captain in modern armies).[63] Continuing this analogy, Roman tribunes were the equivalent of modern battalion and regimental commanders (lieutenant colonels and colonels) and legates were the equivalent of generals. The rank of camp prefect was held by the senior centurion. Below the centurion were lesser ranks which changed designation from time to time, corresponding to the modern ranks of corporal and sergeant.

This fundamental structure of the army remained the same right through into the imperial period, with one extremely significant change. The republic had got its common soldiers by a levy on the plebs, leaving aside slaves and freedmen and citizens of conquered territories. As time advanced, though, this method of raising an army no longer sufficed. Roman successes in battle had made Rome the master not only of Italy but of North Africa, Gaul, Spain, and an increasing part of the eastern Mediterranean world; in addition, there was a lengthy border to protect against raids by the various tribes of Germans. Instead of the army being raised for limited periods as it had been during the early period of the Republic, then disbanded when the specific emergency was over, a standing army gradually became necessary for occupation and police purposes and for border protection. Military service under such conditions could not continue to be imposed solely on the citizens of the city of Rome, who were fundamentally civilians with families, property, and businesses to attend.[64]

Already in the republican period, a first step taken to ease this burden and provide for military needs was to broaden the base of potential soldiers by extending citizenship to new areas incorporated under Roman government. A later step, essentially a variant on this one, was to grant citizenship to men (usually barbarians) who joined the Roman army. This was

[63] See further Hans Delbrück, *History of the Art of War within the Framework of Political History*, vol. I: *Antiquity*, vol. II: *The Germans*, and vol. III: *The Middle Ages* (Westport, Conn., and London: Greenwood Press, 1975-1982), vol. I, pp. 429-36.

[64] On this and the following discussion, see further ibid., vol. I, pp. 283-96 and 412-36, vol, II, pp. 161-200.

the pattern by which Rome raised and maintained its legions in the latter period of the Republic. (Caesar's legions in Gaul were typical, having a minority of soldiers who were Roman by birth.) The same pattern continued into the Empire. Still the rule against enlistment of slaves obtained, ruling out a considerable part of the total male population, though that against taking on freedmen as soldiers was eased beginning in the second century, thus allowing the army to become a vehicle of upward mobility for some of these. (This may also have had an effect on Christian enlistments in the army, since a considerable number of Christians in this period were freedmen.) Gradually the relaxing of pressure on the civilian population of Rome proper, and then of all Italy, was carried to the extreme that, beginning with the Emperor Septimus Severus, Roman citizens resident in Italy were exempted from military service. At the same time, the armies in frontier areas were increasingly staffed by local persons, though the officer corps remained restricted to the Roman nobility. Eventually this too changed, as local notables were brought into the nobility and individuals were promoted through the ranks to centurion, then to tribune. (Crossing this social boundary was unheard of in the Republic and early Empire; it became more common as barbarian peoples, who had a less rigid social structure, became more numerous in the army under the emperors of the third and fourth centuries.) Finally, in 260, in a complete reversal of republican practice, members of the senatorial class were excluded from military service, thus making way in the highest ranks for professional soldiers who had been promoted because of their ability.[65]

Aside from the exceptions noted, there was a legal obligation of military service for all Roman citizens through this entire period, though it was almost never enforced by conscription. The manpower needs of the Roman army were met during the imperial period almost entirely by volunteers.[66] Lo-

[65] Peter Brown, *The World of Late Antiquity* (Cambridge: Harvard University Press, 1978), p. 24.

[66] Harnack, *Militia Christi*, p. 67, n. 1, citing Theodor Mommsen; cf. Delbrück, note 63 above.

cal conscription was occasionally utilized, but in general it was easier—and caused less domestic unrest—to enlist barbarians and persons from the rural fringes of the empire (like the future emperors Diocletian, Galerius, and Constantine) as volunteers than to conscript Roman citizens from the towns of the interior. Furthermore, the former made better soldiers.

By the beginning of the Christian period, then, the internal character of the Roman army was quite different from that of the early Republic. This later army was one of individuals who made soldiering their profession; it was, in the strict and nonpejorative sense of the term, a mercenary army. There was a fixed term of enlistment of twenty years for common soldiers, followed by a pension. Soldiers serving in the legions were forbidden to marry, but this legal prohibition was not uniformly enforced, and in any case it did not keep legionaries from entering common-law relationships and having children. After the term of service, such relationships might be legalized. The prohibition of marriage, moreover, did not extend to officers or to members of the frontier forces, or *limitanei* (about which more below).

Roman society was generally one in which there was little mobility across occupational lines: sons were brought up learning their fathers' occupations, and daughters their mothers' tasks. Applied to the army, this meant that soldiers' sons were likely to become soldiers themselves. Among officers the principle even became, in the third century, a compulsion: one son of each officer father was required to enlist or provide a substitute.[67] This continuity from father to son is significant for understanding the development of a Christian presence in the army. It is, for example, the route through which Constantine rose to power. But, on the ordinary level, it means that where we find hard evidence of numbers of Christians performing military service, this can be taken as prima facie evidence that there had also been Christians in the same legion in

[67] Cf. the case of Maximilian in 295: see Cadoux, *The Early Christian Attitude*, pp. 149-51; Harnack, *Militia Christi*, pp. 97-98; Helgeland, "Christians and the Roman Army," p. 158.

the previous generation, and perhaps even in the generation before that—though in each earlier generation the total numbers would be expected to diminish.

The percentage of men under arms in the first Christian centuries was not large, compared to the total population of the Empire. (This was a considerable reversal from the period of Augustus, when demographic pressures had required measures to broaden the base for recruitment.)[68] With cavalry and auxiliaries a Roman legion numbered about 10,000 men.[69] The total number of legions varied considerably over time, from forty under Caesar, then up sharply to seventy-five or more during the Civil Wars, back down to eighteen in the time of Augustus and up again to thirty-three in that of Septimus Severus.[70] The total number of men under arms stayed at roughly this last figure until the reforms of Diocletian, when the organization of the army was reshaped, new types of units were added, and its strength was roughly doubled to about 600,000 men.[71]

This was the nature of the army in the time of Constantine. Concerning the impact of the army on society in general, the army's distribution was in some ways more important than its total size. Roughly half of the total men under arms during the first three Christian centuries were not in the main army itself but were *limitanei*, auxiliary forces whose function it was to guard the *limes*, or border, between Roman territory and the Germanic tribes. The *limitanei* were themselves Germans, and they were paid by being given land on which to live along the *limes*; title to this property remained with the emperor, but the condition of use was simply that a male member of the family bear arms in the *limitanei*.[72] Thus the property in question normally passed from father to son, as did the profession of arms. This organization was provided for totally outside the regular

[68] Delbrück, *History*, vol. II, pp. 194-95.

[69] Ibid., p. 164.

[70] Ibid., p. 162.

[71] Brown, *Late Antiquity*, pp. 24-25.

[72] See further Delbrück, *History*, vol. II, pp. 218-19, 258, 295-96, 317-36, 341, 347.

organization and provision for the legions, who were paid in money raised by taxation. The population of the Empire's interior thus had to support only about half the total number of men under arms, or about 150,000 soldiers. (This is considerably less than the size of a modern division.) The history suggests that this was considered a bargain, or at least no heavy burden, by the populace in general. There are no records showing serious public resistance against giving financial support to the army during the four hundred years prior to Diocletian's reforms in about the year 300, when the rapidity and magnitude of the change and the efficiency of new methods of tax collection brought forth a negative reaction from ordinary people and the conservative aristocracy alike.[73]

Members of the *limitanei*, as already mentioned, were stationed along the frontier to prevent barbarian incursions. Units of the regular army—that is, the legions—generally were stationed in the area where they were raised, though they were subject to being sent elsewhere for particular duties. In peacetime the duties of these soldiers were essentially those of policemen and public guards. It was in these functions that soldiers and civilians were most likely to have contact. But, at any time in any particular locality, only a small portion of the total force of a given legion needed to be thus engaged; so except in times of crisis, such contact was unlikely to involve more than a small number of soldiers in a much larger civilian population. Larger communities, where governmental functions were centered and where a large population base made it easy to support large troop units, saw more soldiers; smaller communities and rural areas were likely to have no regular contact with soldiers.

The changing shape of the army during the latter part of the third century and the early part of the fourth provides the immediate background upon which to view the official Christian acceptance of military service during and after the reign of Constantine. Above, I have suggested that opening the army to freedmen may have positively affected Christian enlistment.

[73] Brown, *Late Antiquity*, p. 25.

More fundamentally important was the transformation of Roman society and of the army itself so that governmental leadership of the empire on all levels came increasingly not to be restricted to those of aristocratic birth, but was opened up to persons of merit and achievement who had more modest origins. This change was well under way all through the third century; it became more pronounced in the latter quarter of that century; and, with Diocletian and his successors, appointment to official posts because of merit and not aristocratic background became a guiding principle. Thus the changes that had begun in the army became extended to the government of the Empire, and personal advancement through achievement in military service could lead to high civilian status and power, as well. Peter Brown describes this effect:

> The army was an artesian well of talent. By the end of the third century, its officers and administrators had ousted the traditional aristocracy from control of the empire. The great reforming emperor of the age, Diocletian, was the son of a freedman from Dalmatia; his nominee, Galerius (305-11), had herded cattle in the Carpathians; another of his colleagues, Constantius Chlorus (305-06), was an obscure country-gentleman from near Naissus (Nis). . . . They, and their successors, chose servants of similar background. The son of a pork butcher, of a small-town notary, of a cloakroom attendant in the public baths, became the praetorian prefects on whom the prosperity and stability of the eastern parts of the empire depended under Constantine and Constantius II. The reign of Constantine, especially the period from 324 to 337, saw the final establishment of a new "aristocracy of service" at the top of Roman society.[74]

There is in all of this a considerable circumstantial case to explain why Christians might have come to identify more closely with the Roman state and its government, and with the army and possible service in it. That they *did* so is settled; this is to

[74] Ibid., pp. 26-27.

suggest at least part of the reason *why* they did. Traditionally, historians of Christianity have focused upon changes in the membership of the Church. As Christianity became less and less a religion limited to the lower classes (the poor, slaves, and former slaves), and moved into the middle and upper classes, so the argument goes, the Church came to mirror the naturally higher level of involvement in public life characteristic of the latter sort of persons. This argument contains a part of the truth, but only part, and it must be recast to take account of recent social-historical work on the early Church.

First of all, as John Gager has noted, in Roman society one's *class* (senator, equestrian, pleb, freedman, slave) did not dictate *status*: a person of quite low social class might have a very high status, including both personal influence and wealth.[75] But since political power was exercised by those of high class, there existed an implicit tension between persons of high status and the hereditary aristocracy; and so long as the aristocracy retained governing power, this tended to produce alienation from the state on the part of those who had risen in status because of merit and hard work.

Second, as Gerd Theissen and Wayne Meeks have shown, the Pauline churches at least included some members of high social status, including wealth. These were not, in fact, despite what earlier interpretations have tended to suggest, churches made up of the dregs of society, but rather of the upwardly mobile; and membership in the Christian community was for such persons a vehicle of upward mobility.[76] So long as there was no conflict with their theological views, such persons were likely to seek to rise socially by such ways as became available to them. This meant, first of all, involvement in trade; in the second and third centuries, it also meant entry into the army.

The social transformation that brought Christianity into a relation of acceptance and support of the state was thus not simply a result of changes within the Church itself; it was also

[75] Gager, *Kingdom and Community*, pp. 97-106.

[76] Cf. Meeks, *The First Urban Christians*, chapters 2 and 3; Theissen, *Social Setting*.

a result of changes in the larger society. Nor was it the expression of a growing moral laxity, as has often been asserted, though it clearly *was* a reflection of a changing attitude toward self and world on the part of Christians. Where Christian military service is concerned, insofar as there was no explicit negative attitude toward this (and, as argued above, the early Church manifested a plurality of attitudes toward war and military service), the avenue of social advancement offered by the army represented a kind of vacuum into which Christians were drawn by reason of their social aspirations.

It is important to realize that for Christians thus attracted into military and civilian government service (as for Christians attracted, let us say, to a life of trade, where there was also some opportunity for mobility), these ways of life represented positive goods; this entry into vocations closely connected with the state is simply misunderstood when identified, as it is in the standard pacifist account, as a "compromise." Clement of Alexandria, if not Tertullian, understood this, and Clement's developmental model of individual Christian growth offers useful insight into the possible motivations of persons who were determined both to seek Christian knowledge and to live responsibly in the world. Clement was not yet Augustine, and the *Paedagogus* was not yet *The City of God*; but there is clearly an affinity between Clement's views on how individuals could become transformed and Augustine's on the gradual transformation of the city of earth. The emergence of just war doctrine, in which a general suspicion of war and a preference for peace are coupled to a justification of military service as a means to preserve and protect certain values, is thus not an entirely post-Constantinian development, but one that is rooted in the reasons for which Christians entered the Roman army as early as the second century.

3. Christian Military Service from the Second Century through the Time of Constantine

Some evidence exists, from the New Testament itself and from other sources of the first and early second centuries, concerning soldiers who were converted while serving.[77] In the pacifist account of the attitude toward military service in the early Church, the assumption is clearly that there were very few such converts and that the soldiers affected left the military profession after their conversion.[78] This is, however, an assumption only, deriving from a perspective in which the general disapproval of war and preference for peace in Christianity is read to imply total abstinence from military service on the part of "genuine" Christians. But of course Christian just war thinking also begins from the same general base of preference for peace and opposition to war; from this general Christian attitude, it is impossible to tell anything about the practical normative decisions of Christians in this period or at any other time in history.

It is possible to agree with some confidence with the standard account that the first-century Christians avoided military service; yet the reason, as I have argued above, lies not in their general feeling of abhorrence toward war, but in their holding themselves aloof from the kingdom of Caesar in expectation of the imminent coming of the kingdom of Christ. In this period there is likely to have been strong pressure, felt from both outside and inside, for converted soldiers to leave military life if possible and to join the gathered communities living in eschatological expectation. But leaving military service was not easy. The fixed term of enlistment was twenty years for soldiers up to the rank of centurion, with severe physical disability the only regular reason for discharge. Even soldiers who were only marginally fit for duty were kept in the army to perform such services as they could, so that it would not be necessary to pay them a pension and get no good from them.[79]

For these reasons, it is missing the reality of Roman military life to suggest easily that soldiers converted to Christianity then left the army; in reality, they could do so only at the end of their enlistment period or leave as deserters—and deserters could not expect to remain undetected if they lived in the close

[77] For discussion see Harnack, *Militia Christi*, pp. 65-71, and Cadoux, *The Early Christian Attitude*, pp. 228-29; cf. Cadoux, pp. 96-98.

[78] See, for example, Cadoux, *The Early Christian Attitude*, p. 228.

[79] See further Delbrück, *History*, vol. II, pp. 161-200.

confines of the urban Christian communities of the first century. It is more likely that many Christian converts stayed in the army, maintaining what fellowship they could with the local Christian community where they were stationed. In this way a small nucleus of Christian soldiers might form in particular legions over time, especially as the eschatological hope of an immediate end to the age waned. This would inevitably have had the effect breaking down hostility on the part of civilian Christians toward the life of the soldier as such. It also helps us to understand the well-evidenced fact that, beginning in the second century, there were in fact not inconsiderable numbers of Christians in the army.

Bainton summarizes the evidence with characteristic pithiness. Commenting on Celsus' apparent assumption that there were no Christians in military service, he writes:

> But [Celsus] was mistaken. In the very decade in which he wrote, we have our first testimony of Christians in the army, in the so-called Thundering Legion under Marcus Aurelius in the year 173. From that day forward the evidence of Christians in the ranks increases. Tertullian in his *Apology*, written in A.D. 197, refuted the charge of misanthropy leveled against the Christians by pointing to their presence in the palace, the senate, the forum, and the *army*. His stern rebuke in the *De Corona* (A.D. 211) to voluntary enlistment is a witness to the practice which he condemned. During the persecution of Decius in A.D. 250, we have a reference in Cyprian to two soldier martyrs. The number of Christians in the army must have increased during the latter part of the third century, because . . . Galerius sought to weed Christians out of his forces. . . . How numerous were the Christians in the army at the commencement of the fourth century we have no means of knowing. . . . Cadoux has conjectured that they must have been relatively few because no sovereign would readily deprive himself of a tenth or even a twentieth of his military power.[80]

[80] Bainton, *Christian Attitudes*, pp. 68-69.

This last reference to the judgment of Cadoux requires some comment. We recall that Diocletian had increased the total size of the army to approximately 600,000. Subtracting the *limitanei*, which remained at about the same strength as earlier, this leaves 450,000 in the legions, the auxiliaries who fought in support of the legions, and the new units (*comitatenses*), who were heavy cavalry made up chiefly of Romanized barbarian tribesmen whose custom it had been from time immemorial to fight on horseback. Thinking only in the raw percentages picked out of thin air by Cadoux, this means somewhere between 22,000 and 45,000 Christians in the army at the beginning of the fourth century—a not at all inconsiderable figure, and certainly not "relatively few." But such raw percentages are misleading. Galerius might have sought shortly to rid his portion of the army of Christians, but his command was in the East; Constantius, in the West, protected the Christians under his command, and we know that the army he passed on to his son Constantine had significant numbers of Christians in it. Indeed, what else can be made of the evidence of the Milvian Bridge incident in 312, when Constantine is supposed to have received a vision and, in any case, took his troops into battle under the Chi Rho symbol (made up of the first two letters in the Greek "Christos") except that there were sufficient Christians in his forces for this symbolic standard to have a special meaning?

All this is, of course, an extrapolation from between the lines of hard historical evidence. That hard evidence is this. Beginning in 173 (or 174) with the case of the *Legio Fulminata*[81] (the "Thundering Legion"; actually, the term *fulminata* means "thunderstruck"), we know there were significant numbers of Christians in the army, and that the numbers of these Christian soldiers continued to grow, despite occasional efforts to purge Christians from the army, through the second and third centuries and into the age of Constantine. We may estimate the number of Christian soldiers at the beginning of the fourth

[81] See further Cadoux, *The Early Christian Attitude*, pp. 229-32; Helgeland, "Christians and the Roman Army," p. 157.

century in the tens of thousands. They were, however, unevenly distributed. If the *Legio Fulminata* was largely or even significantly Christian, as the evidence suggests, this says nothing definite about the other legions (and it says nothing at all about the *limitanei*, who largely remained pagan). Similarly, even if a local or regional commander succeeded in totally purging Christian soldiers from his command at one or another time during this period from the 170s to the early 300s, there were other commanders who, like Constantius, ignored imperial edicts to purge Christians and actively protected Christian soldiers in their legions.

We have, then, a picture of gradual growth in Christian acceptance of military service, perhaps not large in total percentages but significant in absolute numbers, and more significant in both respects in some elements of the army than in others. This growth parallels the development in some Christian circles (such as Montanism) and among some Christian theologians of an opposition to military service. *Both* are part of the total picture of the Church's developing attitude toward war and military service during the first four centuries. Without recognizing the increasing acceptance of military service (and of participation in public life and service of the state generally), it is impossible to make sense of the developments that took place in the fourth century, when Christians, though still a minority, gained ascendancy in the halls of government and in the army. But without understanding that these developments always seemed to those in opposition to represent a selling out of "true" Christianity, it is not possible to make sense of the evidence usually cited by persons who use the word "compromise" to describe the changes under Constantine (as a Victorian might speak of a lady's having "compromised" her virtue). To speak of these changes as "compromising" Christianity is implicitly to take sides in the debate of the second, third, and fourth centuries over which of the developing strands of doctrine and practice represented the "true" Christianity: it is not an exercise in finding objective truth, but one of partisanship.

Something more remains to be said about when Christian

acceptance of military service actually began. I have already suggested that for soldiers who converted to Christianity during the first century, the only real choice was between martyrdom or remaining in the army and attempting to practice the faith there. I have also suggested that more are likely to have done the latter than is admitted in the standard pacifist account, and that this likelihood increases with the waning of eschatological hope toward the end of the first century. It now needs to be added, also as suggested earlier (though in another context) that the hereditary pattern of occupations in Roman life also points to this being the time when a significant Christian acceptance of military life began to be felt. If in the *Legio Fulminata* of the 170s there was a legion that was entirely, mostly, or even only significantly Christian (the evidence is unclear), then in the previous generation it is almost certain that there were Christians, though presumably in smaller numbers, in that legion, and likewise for the generation of the grandfathers of the soldiers of the 170s. With the grandfathers' generation we are in the first decade of the second century, the period coincident with the waning of imminent eschatological expectation in the Church at large and the parallel transformation of the Church away from its sectarian, eschatological separatist form. Though it is necessary to set the date by inference, rather than by direct evidence from the early 100s that there were then Christian soldiers in the Roman army, and while some evidence suggests an even earlier date, it is nonetheless possible to say conservatively and with some certainty that here—and not in the age of Constantine two centuries later—is where the decisive change began to take place.

That change, moreover, was not a "fall" of the Church away from apostolic purity. *Both* the subsequent pacifism and the acceptance of military service that led eventually to just war theory were movements away from the position of the first-century Christians, who avoided the issue because it was not pressed upon them and because they thought the world of Caesar would soon pass away. The real revolution in Christian thought came when the effort began to be made to wait for a much longer period within the world, wherever one might be situated, before salvation might come; and then, in a modification rising out of this attitude, to attempt to shape the world while waiting; as an implication of the experience of gradual transformation that was going on in one's own soul. Constantine, Ambrose of Milan, and after him Augustine and Christian just war doctrine were among the results.

E. The Anatomy of the Constantinian Synthesis

1. *Pluralism and Change*

Not the least of the difficulties with the standard account of Christian attitudes toward war and military service in the first four centuries is that this account ignores the implications of the pluralism and change that were endemic to this period, both inside and outside the Church. Within the Christian faith, the doctrinal pluralism, for example, was so great as to beg the question whether it means anything at all to speak of "the Church" during this period. A short list of the controversies familiar to any historian of early Christianity would include the dispute over whether Christianity was to remain substantially a Jewish sect or not, the struggle for dominance among the major Christian communities, and the debates over Gnosticism, Marcionism, Sabellianism, Monophysitism, Montanism, and Arianism—to name only the most salient controverted issues. There were differences between East and West, most notably centering around the ambiguities imposed by the two different scriptural languages, Latin and Greek, and around the Eastern concept of salvation as divinization as opposed to the Western one of salvation as moral transformation. Bishops sometimes thwarted each other on purpose, for private or political reasons, as when Origen was ordained by Palestinian bishops despite the fact that his own bishop in Alexandria had refused to ordain him because he had castrated himself.

Out of all this controversy Christian religion developed and grew, but in almost every controversy it would have been impossible at the time to say which direction the main line of development would—or should—take. The Arian bishops and priests certainly thought their understanding of the relation of Christ to God the Father was the right one, just as their Trinitarian opponents were convinced of the rightness of their own position; large numbers of Christians supported each view. So it was in the struggle over Montanism in which Tertullian was involved; likewise in that over Christian faith as *gnōsis* in which Clement of Alexandria took a prominent position that orthodoxy later backed away from. Early Christianity was far from monolithic, whether in doctrine, social make-up, language, cultural context, political preference, or virtually any other measure one might apply; nor was it monolithic in historical cross-section at any time during this period, or longitudinally monolithic throughout this period. At any one time there was pluralism, and over time there was change. This context provides yet one more reason why we should expect to find a plurality of attitudes toward war and military service during the first four centuries, and not a universal pacifism that was subverted and compromised in the time of Constantine.

Outside the Church there were also pluralism and change, and these affected all the institutions of Roman society in this period. This society was, in many ways, quite fragile. Peter Brown, speaking specifically of the Empire of about the year 200, describes it as held together by a "delicate . . . sleight of hand."[82] He notes the great cultural and political distances that separated the cities grouped around the Mediterranean shore, and connected by a relatively easy sea passage, from the rude and primitive inland towns united only by roads built to facilitate the movement of administrators and troops. Roman life, Brown comments, "had always tended to coagulate" in the coastal cities, "in little oases, like drops of water on a drying surface." Indeed, "the aristocrat would pass from reassuringly similar forum to forum, speaking a uniform language, observing rites and codes of behaviour shared by all educated men; but his road stretched through the territories of

[82] Brown, *Late Antiquity*, p. 14.

tribesmen that were as alien to him as any German or Persian."[83]

Yet in the third century all this began to change decisively, and the thin veneer of Graeco-Roman culture began to give way to influences from the hinterland. The first Christian centuries were the age of religious syncretism: Roman paganism had to make its peace with the cult of the Great Mother, prominent among the aristocracy; with that of Mithras, which spread widely in the army; with that of Thrice-Greatest Hermes, the old Egyptian deity Thoth in Gnostic garb; and others besides the new Christian movement. That coexistence with these other religions was possible made early Christian separatism stand out all the more obviously, creating pressure for Christian coexistence, as well. These same centuries were also the age of rival philosophical schools, some almost religions in themselves, which proselytized far and wide among persons of culture and education; for Christians to penetrate the same circles, it was necessary that there be a respectable Christian "philosophy" as well. From this period comes the link with Neo-Platonism—itself a movement that arose at this time—which later characterized Christian thinking from Augustine to Boethius to Bernard of Clairvaux and beyond.

The latter half of the third century, though, was a time of the strongest incentives for change. This was the period when the new Sassanian dynasty took over Persia, shattered Roman armies sent against them, and overran Syria, Silicia and Cappadocia. Not only did this create a political threat so serious that Roman soldiers had to be withdrawn from the West to shore up the defenses in the East; the vigor of the Sassanian society exposed the Roman world, especially in the East, to new cultural influences from the Mesopotamian region. We have already seen, in discussing the Roman army, how Roman society revived and reformed itself administratively and militarily to meet the new political and military challenges of this period. Now it is necessary to re-emphasize that such reform itself injected new social and cultural elements into the life of the em-

[83] Ibid., pp. 12-13.

pire, engendering new pluralism and further pressures for change. Out of this context, the Christianization of the empire under Constantine in the next century should be seen as an effort to re-establish some kind of unity and commonalty across all the diversity that existed.

2. *The Emergence of Just War Thinking*

A. THE CONTEXT

It is possible, without crossing one's fingers too firmly or implanting one's tongue too strongly in the cheek, to regard Clement of Alexandria as the first Christian just war thinker. Clement did not employ the term "just war," but clearly he regarded military service as justified to protect the goods represented by the Empire, even if not justified in any ultimate respect. Clement had no idea of a *jus in bello*, or restraints on the right use of force, but there can be discerned in his thought a very general *jus ad bellum*, or how and when the resort to military force might be justified. As given in classic form during the late Middle Ages, the *jus ad bellum* requirements were right authority, just cause, right intent, a reasonable hope of success, the end of peace, that the use of force be expected to do more good than harm, and that force be the last resort. In Augustine, often regarded as the father of Christian just war thinking, the first four of these were unambiguously present; but while the rest can be read from a later perspective as implicit in his writings, he did not treat them explicitly. In Clement can be found two of the three *jus ad bellum* ideas enunciated by Augustine: just cause (protection of the goods represented by the empire) and right authority (possessed by the emperor). Ambrose, Augustine's predecessor and mentor, whose *Of the Duties of the Clergy* is often cited as a first step toward the just war theory of Augustine, also cited only these two requirements that were to become classic (though he augmented his *jus ad bellum* with elements drawn directly from Roman law, as did Augustine after him).

The point is not that we should look for a fully worked out

just war theory in Clement, for we will not find one even in Augustine. Such a concept coalesced only after the work of such medieval canonists as Gratian and his successors, theologians such as Thomas Aquinas and Peter of Paris, and the theorists of the secular *jus gentium*, and after the development of a self-conscious code of chivalric behavior among the knightly class.[84] Even Augustine's thought, which several hundred years later played a central role in the definition of the medieval just war idea, lay fallow in the centuries immediately following the fall of Rome and the transformation of the western part of the Roman Empire into independent Germanic kingdoms (subjects about which I shall say more in the next chapter). The point of noting that Clement argued similarly to Ambrose and Augustine is to suggest that the implications of Christian thought that led to the formulation of the just war idea could be recognized long before either of these later writers, and could be recognized in the East as well as in the West.

The moral issue before all these writers, as before all Christians then and always, was a simple one: May a Christian ever take part in violence; and, particularly, may he perform military service? Christian doctrine was generally opposed to violence, but opposition to military service, where it occurred, was founded not only on this general presumption against bloodshed, but also (and more importantly) on an attitude that only in separation from the affairs of the secular world could Christianity be true to itself. Christian pacifism in its characteristic form has blended these themes together, and it did so from the very first. The achievement of just war theory was, by contrast, to combine this general attitude of opposition to violence and bloodshed with a limited justification of the use of violence by Christians. This limited justification required that the use of force be to protect a value that could not otherwise be protected, and it justified military service as an instrument for such protection of value. The presumption against violence nonetheless remained, so that the justification could never be-

[84] See further Johnson, *Just War Tradition*, chapter V, and *Ideology*, chapter I.

come absolute: permission was always accompanied by limitation. Just war theory thus emerged as a blend of these two themes.

The difference—and it is a crucial one—between Christian just war theory and Christian pacifism lies not in a different attitude toward war; both regard it with suspicion as something less than the ideal to be reached in the kingdom of Christ. Both are, in fact, forms of the quest for peace. Rather, the difference between them resides in which *second* principle is added to this common attitude of opposition to war and violence. For Christian pacifists this principle comes in the form of separation, as with Tertullian, Origen, and subsequent monasticism as well as with the medieval sectarians and those of the Radical Reformation centuries later. For Christian theorists of just war, as for later utopians, the second principle was that Christians might responsibly take part in securing the temporal goods represented by the state, goods which pointed toward those of the heavenly kingdom even if they did not yet coincide with them. The problem, though, was how to articulate this latter principle. Clement did it by suggesting that Christian learners still might be soldiers, but he left open the question of whether one who had achieved enlightenment (*gnōsis*) ought to remain in military life. This was in fact no real solution, both because it focused on the development of the individual and because it failed to address the fundamental question of whether such participation in securing the goods of the world might not in some cases be a positive duty, imposed by Christian ideals themselves, and not merely a permission granted to those who had not yet achieved Christian perfection. The step Clement took was an important one which, as earlier suggested, anticipated the practical compromise later reached in the Church. However, as a rationale taking seriously the idea of Christian moral responsibility in the world, it did not go far enough, and the significance of Ambrose and Augustine as the originators of just war thought is precisely that they did address the implications of this responsibility seriously and in full breadth.

The just war idea required a synthesis between Christian ideals and the moral relativity of the world of history—the "secular" world; literally, the world of "this age." For Christians who took the direction of pacifism, no such synthesis was desired or acceptable.[85] In the realm of theory, Augustine's depiction of the gradual and inexorable transformation of history by grace, in *The City of God*, achieved such a synthesis—explaining how individuals and societies alike might be understood in terms of the "already" and the "not yet" and laying on individuals living within this historical context the moral obligation to respond to grace whether or not doing so would serve their private secular ends. But this theoretical model is only part of the story behind the development of just war theory as a Christian synthesis with the world: there was also a practical level on which this synthesis was achieved. It is arguable which has been the more important. Surely both levels of development were necessary; yet, since there has been much written on the theoretical accomplishment of the view of history in *The City of God* and very little on the achievement of the practical synthesis, I will focus here on the latter. This approach is also the one that more closely accords with the social-historical, and not doctrinal, perspective on which I have been drawing.

It is proper to think of this synthesis on the practical level as a "Constantinian" synthesis, not only because as emperor Constantine himself initiated and furthered it, but because its later development presupposed that close formal relation between Christianity and empire which characterized the Constantinian age. But again, much has been written on the development of church-state relations in the time of Constantine, and this is not our concern here. If we are to focus on the emergence of the peculiar lines of synthesis found in just war theory, we must begin with Ambrose, who wrote about war in 386-387, fifty years after the death of Constantine.

B. AMBROSE OF MILAN

As already suggested, Ambrose of Milan was not "the first to formulate a Christian ethic of war," as one scholar puts it

[85] For a modern version of this view see Hershberger, *War, Peace, and Nonresistance*, chapter 9.

and others have argued.[86] But he was the first to attempt consciously to blend together implications drawn from Christian morality with requirements for the waging of war established in Roman practice. Such blending was to become a central and characteristic feature of just war tradition in its medieval and modern development,[87] as it was more immediately in the thought of Ambrose's protégé Augustine.

Louis Swift has summarized the elements in the synthesis achieved by Ambrose.[88] Ambrose was a bishop whose influence on secular policy was considerable, and he had occupied a high civil office in the service of the state before becoming bishop. He possessed a classical education as well as a knowledge of the Christian Scriptures and tradition. The synthesis between these two cultures that Ambrose defined with respect to war may in certain particulars be questioned, but the *structure* of that synthesis is what interests us. As a professional administrator, he came to such a task quite naturally.

Ambrose, like Augustine after him, knew his Cicero, and his views on the *jus belli*, the right or justification of war, began with Cicero's. Fundamentally, these followed Roman practice: justified wars should be defensive in nature, agreements should be honored, unfair advantage should not be taken, and mercy should be shown the defeated.[89] Yet Ambrose went beyond secular Roman law and practice in suggesting that war might be waged for the purpose of protecting Christian orthodoxy,[90]

[86] Louis J. Swift, "St. Ambrose on Violence and War," *Transactions and Proceedings of the American Philological Association*, vol. 101 (1970), p. 533. Cf. Bainton, *Christian Attitudes*, pp. 89-91.

[87] See further Johnson, *Ideology* and *Just War Tradition*.

[88] Swift, "St. Ambrose," pp. 533-35.

[89] Ambrose of Milan, *Of the Duties of the Clergy*; cf. Swift, "St. Ambrose," p. 534. Citations of Ambrose are from Philip Schaff and Henry Wace, eds., *A Select Library of Nicene and Post-Nicene Fathers*, second series (New York: The Christian Literature Co.; Oxford and London: Parker & Co., 1896), vol. X: *Of the Duties of the Clergy*, pp. 1-89; *On the Christian Faith*, pp. 199-314.

[90] Ambrose, *On the Christian Faith* 2.14.136-43; cf. Swift, "St. Ambrose," p. 534. Somewhat earlier (1.27.129) in the same vein, Ambrose had asserted that "the bravery which guards the fatherland in war from the barbarians or defends the weak at home or [one's] allies from robbers, is full of justice."

a position also taken by Augustine in urging the use of the army to coerce the Donatists of his own day to accept orthodoxy. Ambrose spoke positively of *fortitudinam bellicam*, the courage of the soldier, and praised the man who defended his country at personal risk;[91] here it is impossible to tell whether he was speaking as a Roman, a Christian, or both. A clear step beyond the secular—and beyond many earlier Christian writers, as well—was his argument that even in the private sphere it is a moral obligation of the Christian to use force, if necessary, to defend another. This is not a matter of such use of force being merely optional and justified, but justified because morally obligatory: in Ambrose's own language, "He who does not keep harm off a friend, if he can, is as much in fault as he who causes it."[92] Such a position is all the more striking because it does not descend from reasoning about the justness of self-defense; indeed, Ambrose explicitly rejects, on Christian terms, fighting back against an aggressor in defense of self, even when the attacker is doing evil.[93] Thus the Christian basis of his reasoning that the use of force is sometimes justified stands out in high relief: his argument was not simply a development of Roman self-defense law or of Stoic natural-law reasoning about duties to the self, but was derived from a Christian duty to show love to the neighbor.

In all this Ambrose anticipated Augustine's fuller thought on morality and war. In another important respect he expressed the growing consensus about the proper relation of the Church as an institution to the practice of war. Here he was quite explicit and quite firm: "The thought of warlike matters seems to be foreign to the duty of our office," Ambrose wrote to his priests, and "it is not our business to look to arms, but to the forces of peace."[94] When the basilica at Milan was threatened by imperial troops, Ambrose set his own example by resisting passively rather than seeking to defend the basilica with arms.

Bainton comments, "Ambrose furnished two of the ingre-

[91] Ambrose, *Of the Duties of the Clergy* 1.41.211.

[92] Ibid., 1.36.179.

[93] See further Swift, "St. Ambrose," p. 537.

[94] Ambrose, *Of the Duties of the Clergy* 1.35.175.

dients of the Christian theory of the just war: that the conduct of the war should be just and that monks and priests should abstain."[95] In fact, Ambrose contributed a good deal more than this. He achieved a practical synthesis of Christian and secular thought, which is expressed on two levels. First, he drew together Roman practice and Christian moral theory so as to define the moral obligations of Christian individuals both as soldiers and as persons in authority. Where military force is necessary to protect the goods represented by society, including the persons of neighbors in that society who are being unjustly menaced by others, the Christian is justified in using defensive force. Indeed, in some circumstances he is, for Ambrose, *obligated* to do so. This is a fundamental challenge to the view that the most moral course for Christians, in whatever circumstance, is to avoid violence. Second, Ambrose differentiated between the offices of clergy and laity with respect to the employment of force: while lay persons may themselves take up arms in just causes, clergy must resist evil not by bearing arms, but only by passive resistance. This concept, on both levels, remains at the heart of the just war tradition in its subsequent medieval form. Equally important, it both reflects earlier Christian attitudes, pacifist rejection of military service, and acceptance of such service, described above in this chapter, and puts them together into a synthesis. To label this synthesis a "compromise" would be to suggest—wrongly—a fall from grace in this version of Christian moral obligation regarding the use of force. Rather, it combines opposed Christian attitudes already established, and then blends the result—a limited acceptance of Christian participation in the use of force together with established secular Roman traditions on the legitimation of war. This was the synthesis achieved by Ambrose.

C. AUGUSTINE

Ambrose began to synthesize Roman and Christian thought on war into a single doctrine, but he did not complete the task

[95] Bainton, *Christian Attitudes*, pp. 90-91.

in a systematic way. Frederick Russell, while admitting that Ambrose's "diffuse analysis" was a "potent compound," goes on to degrade it with the comment, "Yet it remained an unstable amalgam of examples of Old Testament wars and Roman morality serving as a clumsy weapon against barbarians and heretics." Russell notes that Ambrose did not examine the question of right authority or provide "a systematic grounding of the just war on both Old and New Testament moral principles." For him Ambrose's thought remained too closely bound to assumptions about Roman imperial authority, and by contrast the greatness of Augustine's just war thought was that it was "independent of the connection with Rome."[96] Whether Ambrose's use of conceptions borrowed from Roman law and governmental practice was for good or ill is a matter of interpretation; contrary to Russell, I judge it to be a strength in the bishop of Milan's thought. It is simply not true, moreover, that Augustine's just war thought was "independent of the connection with Rome," as we shall see below. It would not be as important a contribution to the historical development of Western moral doctrine on war if it were independent of such connection.

Augustine, and not Ambrose, is in fact generally regarded as the father of Christian just war doctrine. Besides the judgment of historians such as Russell, theological ethicists such as Paul Ramsey can find in Augustine "the genesis of noncombatant immunity,"[97] while a proponent of the idea that the Christian Church was pacifist until the age of Constantine speaks only of Augustine in discussing the theological adjustment that produced the just war idea.[98] And, to be sure, Augustine's influence has run deep: in the Middle Ages the great canonist Gratian turned to Augustine thought when, in the *Decretum*, he sought to lay out the Church's teaching on what constituted right authority, just cause, and right intention in

[96] Frederick H. Russell, *The Just War in the Middle Ages* (Cambridge, London, New York, and Melbourne: Cambridge University Press, 1975), p. 15.

[97] Paul Ramsey, *War and the Christian Conscience* (Durham, N.C.: Duke University Press, 1961), pp. 34-39.

[98] Hershberger, *War, Peace, and Nonresistance*, p. 73.

war.[99] Subsequent canon law followed this lead, and in the next century the theologians did so as well: Aquinas's often-cited references to Augustine in his discussion of war do not go beyond those of Gratian.[100]

The influence Augustine had on late medieval and modern thought should not, however, obscure the fact that, in real terms, his teaching on just war did not become authoritative Church doctrine until the twelfth century and later; or the further fact that, if we think in terms of a unified, consensual, and continuing body of thought and practice, there is no just war tradition prior to its coalescence in the Middle Ages around concepts drawn from canon law, theology, secular law, chivalric morality, and the habits of relations among princes.[101] That is to say, for the seven centuries between Augustine's death and the publication of Gratian's *Decretum*, the Bishop of Hippo's thought on war did not have the authoritative character it would later take on. For practical purposes, moreover, there was in fact *no* just war doctrine in the Church from the time of Augustine until the Peace of God movement in the tenth and eleventh centuries (discussed in the following chapter) began to open up debate on the protection of noncombatants and the authority to wield the sword.

This is not to demean Augustine's critical thinking about morality and war, but only to suggest that its originality and significance ought not be blown out of proportion. Seen in the context of the late classical age, Augustine built on a Christian understanding of responsibility for the world that was already forming early in the second century, an acceptance of some Christian participation in just warfare that had already found expression in the thought of Clement of Alexandria two hundred years before him, and the beginnings of a synthesis between Roman legal concepts and Christian morality concerning war already begun by his mentor Ambrose, the bishop

[99] *Corpus Juris Canonici*, pars prior, *Decretum Magistri Gratiani*, secunda pars, causa XXIII, qq. I, II, IV.

[100] Thomas Aquinas, *Summa Theologica* II/II: q. XL.

[101] See further Johnson, *Ideology*, chapter I, and *Just War Tradition*, chapter V.

of Milan. Augustine's creativity lay not in his standing alone, apart from any predecessors, but in the fullness of the synthesis he finally achieved; and the significance of his thought on war resides in its ability to provide the fundamental terms around which a later synthesis, at once more complete and more durable, could be founded several hundred years after his death.

Where thought on war is concerned, then, the Constantinian synthesis is in fact the synthesis achieved by Augustine. A synthesis, moreover, requires a union between different things, and thus we need to question Russell's judgment that Augustine achieved a Christian just war theory "independent of the connection with Rome." His thought on war instead depended heavily on what had already been achieved by Ambrose in drawing together Christian ideas with Roman theory and practice, and beyond this it also incorporated elements in the Roman cultural consensus on war besides those utilized by Ambrose. It is equally illegitimate to suggest, as do the purveyors of the standard account, that Augustine's thought on war represents a capitulation to the ideals of secular society, as these were known to him through the Roman Empire. Rather, his just war theory was a genuine synthesis, bringing into a single unity elements from the Roman consensus and from Christian morality, and we must consider both of these if we are to understand the nature of his achievement.

Classical society, whether Greek or Roman, produced very little on the idea of restraints to be observed once a war was under way; and Augustine, while possessing a general idea that it is unjust to harm noncombatants,[102] likewise bequeathed no *jus in bello* to later generations. (Whether it is *implied* in his thought is another question, and I believe Ramsey is correct that one is; but Augustine himself did not draw out this implication in his comments on just war.) Classical Roman society did, however, achieve the beginnings of a *jus ad bellum*, a doctrine on when it is right to make war, and Augustine, like Ambrose before him, drew directly on this.

[102] Augustine, *The City of God* I.4, 7; in Whitney J. Oates, ed., *The Basic Writings of St. Augustine*, 2 vols. (New York: Random House, 1948), vol. II.

The very idea of a "just" war, a *bellum justum*, is a Roman concept. Long before Augustine's time, it had solidified around the requirement that the Fetial priests (the *fetiales*) rule on whether Roman arms should be employed in given circumstances and around the legal concept that just use of military force should be undertaken by the imperial authority and in response to at least one of three conditions: the need to repel injury, the need to retake something wrongly taken, and the need to punish wrongdoing already accomplished.The concepts of right authority and just cause, as well as the general idea of *bellum justum*, were thus part of the Roman side of the synthesis effected by Augustine.[103] A case might further be made that Augustine drew out of his classical heritage the prudential requirements that use of force not produce more evil than good and that it be a last resort, as well as the condition that just wars aim at the production of peace. This last in particular is a theme that runs throughout both Greek and Roman thought about when war is justified. We saw it earlier in Clement, and it also forms a part of the major Western philosophical traditions. Stated more fully, this is the idea that if the internal peace and tranquillity provided by a good state (like the Empire) is threatened by armed aggression from abroad, then there is a moral duty to fight back so as to protect that internal peace and the order and justice that lie behind it.

Yet Augustine clearly did not rest with the patterns inherited from classical thought and Roman practice. In place of the *fetiales* the Christian bishop now has a role in the determination of a just war, thought Augustine, and so did Ambrose before him. It is perhaps wrong to term the result a doctrine of holy war; for, whether it was Ambrose against the Arians in *De Fide Christiana* or Augustine against the Manichaeans and Donatists a generation later, the point was that wars fought on God's account are the *most just* of all wars. In these writings heretics and barbarians are condemned in the same breath:

[103] See Augustine's definition of "just war" in his commentary on Joshua, *Questiones in Heptateuchum* 6.10.

both troubled the peace of the Empire; both deserved armed coercion if necessary.[104]

Augustine also added an entirely new condition to the requirements for just war: it must be fought for a right intention. What characterizes such an intention? In his *Contra Faustum*, Augustine identifies the real evils in war; these are not death, which will come to all eventually anyway, but "the love of violence, revengeful cruelty, fierce and implacable enmity, wild resistance and the lust of power, and such like."[105] A right intention is the absence of these; more positively, it is an intention in accord with the other conditions of justice in resort to war. This new requirement of right intention, by contrast with the others mentioned, is a direct implication from Augustine's concept of Christian faith, both in its focus on the inward disposition and in its cataloguing of the sort of evil dispositions to be avoided.

In Augustine's theological concept of the history of individual salvation and of the development of the history of the world toward its final end, the city of God, inner motivation is a key feature. In Augustine's psychology, the gravitational force that draws anything toward a given end is its "love." Love, for Augustine, as for the Neo-Platonic philosophical framework in which he thought, is thus the attractive force that is manifested as the experience of being drawn toward something perceived as good. In fallen man the fundamental form of love is *cupiditas*, which draws man to seek his good in things of this world, while the saved man is motivated instead by a different love, *caritas*, which draws him through this life toward knowledge of the divine.[106] Similarly, the city of earth is founded upon *cupiditas*, while in the city of God *caritas* rules.[107] The problem of salvation, then, is the quality of human love, its right direction—whether toward the penultimate goods of this world or the ultimate good which is God. Hence,

[104] See Ambrose, *On the Christian Faith* 2.16.136-43, *Of the Duties of the Clergy* 1.40.195-98; Augustine, *Contra Faustum* XXII.74, 78.

[105] Augustine, *Contra Faustum* XXII.74.

[106] Augustine, *Enchiridion* CXVII-CXXI.

[107] Augustine, *The City of God* XIX.

death is not evil, because it may be the vehicle of union with God. But "implacable enmity," "the lust of power," "revengeful cruelty," and the like are all evil precisely in that they manifest a wrongful attachment to this world. One lusts after power or domination, for example, in the erroneous conviction that, by possessing it, one can possess all that is good and so find the greatest good for oneself.

But why, then, does not the desire to protect the goods of the Empire—or, for that matter, *any* "city of earth"—also qualify as a wrongful intention? Augustine answers this objection on several levels.

First, we may observe that it is clear throughout *The City of God* that Augustine regards Roman society as possessing a greater level of good than the societies of the barbarian peoples surrounding it. Moreover, Roman culture is precisely the vehicle through which God is gradually transforming history toward its perfection: Rome is the *civitas terrenae* that is gradually becoming the *civitas Dei*. To fight to protect this culture and its goods is thus a quite different matter than to seek to destroy it, as the barbarians were trying to do.

Second, Augustine's concept of some wars as authorized by God removes any possible objection that, at least in those wars, the ultimate good is not being served. Such wars are by definition wars of *caritas*, not of *cupiditas*.

Third, and related to this, Augustine distinguishes in the inner motivation of a soldier between killing the guilty because of a duty owed to God or the lawful public authorities and killing for any other reason.[108] Killing in a war determined to be just is thus morally justified, and it does not violate the commandment "Thou shalt not kill." Moreover, the soldier who kills in such a cause does not violate *caritas*, because like the executioner he may hate the enemy's sin without hating him as a person.[109]

Finally, if the motivation for a war is justice (revenging in-

[108] Ibid., I.xxi.

[109] Augustine, Epistle 153.3; cf. Louis J. Swift, "Augustine on War and Killing: Another View," *Harvard Theological Review*, vol. 66 (1973), p. 379.

jury, retaking something wrongly lost, repelling an unjust attack in progress) and peace, then the requirement of right intention is objectively met. Nonetheless, the peace Augustine has in mind is not identical with the temporal tranquillity of the earthly city; it includes this but goes further. What is added is also a significantly Christian element in Augustine's synthesis concerning just warfare, and it is important as well for the later development of the idea of peace in the Middle Ages. For both reasons, we need to explore this concept in Augustine somewhat more fully.

All men, writes Augustine, desire peace, even those who make war:

> For what else is victory than the conquest of those who resist us? and when this is done there is peace. It is therefore with the desire for peace that wars are waged, even by those who take pleasure in exercising their warlike nature in command and battle. And hence it is obvious that peace is the end sought for by war. For every man seeks peace by waging war, but no man seeks war by waging peace. For even they who intentionally interrupt the peace in which they are living have no hatred of peace, but only wish it changed into a peace that suits them better. They do not, therefore, wish to have no peace, but only one more to their mind.[110]

This is, of course, a purely temporal peace, and its limitations are suggested by Augustine's ironic language: "They do not . . . wish to have no peace, but only one more to their mind." Contrasted to it is "the happiness of the eternal peace, which constitutes the end or true perfection of the saints," which can be found only in the city of God: "[T]he end or supreme good of this city is either peace in eternal life, or eternal life in peace."[111]

The problem is to connect these two sorts of peace and show how they can be one. One answer is that nature itself tends to-

[110] Augustine, *The City of God* XIX.xii.
[111] Ibid., XIX.xi.

ward ultimate peace;[112] yet, in human nature disordered by sin, this tendency has been perverted, so that people desire the wrong things and contradict one another in seeking after them. "Not your peace, but mine" is an expression of this disorder in the plan of nature. In human societies, whether domestic or civil, it is necessary to establish means of correction to re-establish and preserve order in the face of disorder, and the social order thus established directly serves the cause of peace. The "well-ordered concord [*concordia*] of civic obedience and civic rule"[113] is the basis of civic peace, and it points toward the ultimate peace which is to be found in eternal life with God:

> The earthly city, which does not live by faith, seeks an earthly peace, and the end it proposes, in the well-ordered concord of civic obedience and rule, is the combination of men's wills to attain the things which are helpful to this life. The heavenly city, or rather the part of it which sojourns on earth and lives by faith, makes use of this peace only because it must, until this mortal condition which necessitates it shall pass away. . . . Even the heavenly city, therefore, while in the state of its pilgrimage, avails itself of the peace of earth, and . . . desires and maintains a common agreement among men regarding the acquisition of the necessaries of life, and makes this earthly peace bear upon the peace of heaven. . . .[114]

The immediate significance of this concept, in the context of Augustine's own time, was dual: it provided a theological justification of the goods of order, justice, and peace in civic society (the "city of earth"), and it related the peace of this society to the ultimate goal of man, the enjoyment of everlasting peace in God. The connection between these two kinds of peace provides an implicit critical corrective of the peace of the earthly city from the vision of the peace of the city of God.

[112] Ibid., XIX.xiv.
[113] Ibid., XIX.xvi.
[114] Ibid., XIX.xvii.

Thus, not all earthly cities are equal, either in principle or in practice: some have a more perfect order, a more perfect justice, a superior *concordia* (the quality of harmonious interaction among citizens), and some accordingly have a more perfect peace. The peace (and order, justice, and *concordia*) achieved by Rome was not the peace of God; yet, given the alternative social systems available, it most closely approximated that latter peace. "[I]t is in our interest that it enjoy [its] peace meanwhile in this life," wrote Augustine, for while the earthly and heavenly cities remain commingled, the saints profit from earthly peace. "And therefore the apostle also admonished the Church to pray for kings and those in authority, assigning as the reason, 'that we may live a quiet and tranquil life in all godliness and love.' "[115]

The just war synthesis achieved by Augustine was both Roman and Christian. It was not, Russell's suggestion notwithstanding, enunciated in such a way as to be set apart from the fortunes of imperial Rome. Not only was this theory strongly a product of Augustine's high estimate of the good of Roman society and of his deep personal attachment to Roman civilization; this idea of just war did not, as a matter of history, outlast the fall of the Empire, but was neglected until its recovery and extrapolation in the High Middle Ages. When Roman civilization broke apart and dissolved into quasi-barbarian kingdoms, Augustine's work on just war was remembered neither in the mind nor in military praxis. Indeed, as a synthetic achievement it depended on *both* its sources for its own life. When the just war idea was picked up again and developed, with significant reliance on elements of Augustine's thought, a new "empire" was forming, that of medieval Christendom. Ever since, the continued existence and development of this moral tradition on war has depended on the continuity and development of the broad culture that produced a new synthesis and that has renewed it, in one way or another, in subsequent eras.

Left to itself, without reason to enter into the life of the sur-

[115] Ibid., XIX.xxvi, quoting I Timothy 2:2.

rounding culture and take responsibility for it, the Christian movement might well have remained in its original sectarian aloofness; then, like the first-century Church, it would have been pacifist, rejecting war and military service as connecting Christians to the world from which they would be apart. Correspondingly, later Christian sectarian movements have typically (though not inevitably) been radical-pacifist; and, as we shall see in subsequent chapters, radical pacifism and Christian sectarianism have moved hand in hand, along with a rejection of the kind of synthesis achieved in Augustine thought.

Simultaneously, though, this synthesis has been repeatedly renewed, and the result has been the recurrence, in various guises, of the idea that to achieve ultimate peace, Christians must participate, by force if necessary, in securing the peace of this world. Just as they did in the first Christian centuries, these two contrary themes have continued to generate, throughout subsequent history, a tension as to what constitutes "true" Christianity and the most perfect peace.

CHAPTER II

PEACE, WAR, AND THE REJECTION OF VIOLENCE IN THE MIDDLE AGES

A. A New Cultural Context

1. *A Profound Change in Attitudes toward War*

In seeking to contrast human development in his own period to that prevailing in the state of "nature" Hugo Grotius, writing in the seventeenth century, commented that in "nature"—evidence for which he drew almost entirely from classical authors—only the practice of slavery mitigated the cruelty of war, while he and his contemporaries might also draw on Christian charity to inform the "modesty" necessary to restraint in war.[1] In fact, by the end of the Roman period in the West, a great deal had been done toward defining legal and moral limits to war, and to enslave vanquished enemies (rather than kill them) was already but one part in a larger cultural fabric of controls on war.

The just war doctrine of Augustine was perhaps the most advanced statement of this developing cultural concept of the place of war and the rules for prosecuting war; yet Augustine, as noted in the previous chapter, built on themes and lines of development that had already been defined in Roman society. The major terms of what much later would be called the *jus ad bellum* (defining justice in the resort to war) were established in Roman law and practice: these were the need for a just cause and a proper authority to authorize the taking up of arms. The goal of peace as understood by Augustine was conceived in an essentially similar way in his own time by Stoics and Neo-Pla-

[1] Hugo Grotius, *Of the Rights of War and Peace* (London: n.p., 1682), book III, chapter V, pp. 481-82.

tonists alike, as well as in a tradition reaching back to Aristotle and Plato:[2] it was an ordered peace with justice, not simply the absence of violence. Considerations of proportionality were nothing new to persons familiar with the need to balance aims and resources within the Roman state. Though Augustine performed a valuable service in knitting all these ideas together, the principal substantive contribution he made to this developing list of restraints on the resort to war was his concept of the need for right intention in a just war; this was a concept deeply touched by his understanding of the nature and effects of charity and cupidity in the human soul.

As for the *jus in bello*—restraints on the actual prosecution of war—the classical period bequeathed little, and Christian doctrine through Augustine added nothing directly to what was already there. Of course some of the *jus ad bellum* limitations bore implications for the conduct of war. In particular, the insistence on right authority meant that only soldiers could legitimately use the sword, and these were implicitly restrained from wanton violence by their superiors; considerations of proportionality meant holding back from the use of military resources and then not squandering them by using more than needed for a given goal; and the definition of right intention supplied by Augustine expressly ruled out "the cruelty of domination." As for restraints directed explicitly to the conduct of war, we are left with the practice of slavery as a substitute for killing vanquished enemies. This was little enough; yet it was something, given the alternative.

The distinguishing mark that runs through all this development, though, is that violence was conceived as a tool—a sometimes necessary tool, but one that should be subjected, when used, to control by overriding concerns having to do with the health and good order of society as a whole. Perhaps it is significant that the culture which produced this concept of the place of force in society was one in which the military arm was by design discrete; its functions were, in principle, determined by the need of the larger society to maintain its own internal peace with order and justice.

[2] See further Zampaglione, *The Idea of Peace*, chapters I and II.

In the Germanic tribal societies that the Romans knew first as barbarian antagonists, then as allies against other Germans, and finally as supplanters, the place of violence and of the military life was knit far more closely into the lives of ordinary individuals. Whereas in Roman society every member of a legion was supported by tens or hundreds of persons working at other tasks, among the Germanic peoples each adult male was a warrior who, during fighting season, was expected to present himself armed and ready under the command of his *hunno*, or clan leader. Thus there was no distinction between warrior and civilian, between military and civil leadership; in each case, the same individuals acted as one or the other according to circumstances. Traditionally, moreover, these societies had moved about as entire tribal groups; so unlike the legionaries, who were by design kept apart from women, children, and the concerns of familiy life, the Germanic warrior always knew that for him to fall in battle imperiled his personal and extended family group.

Correspondingly, to beat an enemy in battle tacitly made the fallen enemy's family and goods the possessions of the victor. In such circumstances as these, the restraints that were gradually unfolding in Roman law, morality, and custom were quite alien. The justice of fighting was determined in terms of immediate tribal concerns; the authority to fight was built into the combined system of heredity and valor by which tribal leaders were chosen and was, at least some of the time, ratified by vote of the warriors themselves; proportionality was calculated differently when the stakes were the loss of one's own family and possessions; and peace referred more to the absence of threats from outside society than, as in the Roman Empire, to a state of civil well-being. Finally, the Germanic societies were ones that glorified the way of the warrior, expected every male child to grow into a warrior, and looked down on peaceful farmers, merchants, and the like as inferiors. Each warrior, lacking interjection from superior authority, became his own judge as to when to take up arms and when to lay them down.[3]

In the new kingdoms established by the various Germanic

[3] See further Delbrück, *History*, vol. II, pp. 15-58, 387-406.

tribal groups on the ruins of the western Roman Empire, then, there was no fertile soil for the continued growth of the nascent just war idea. On the contrary, these kingdoms tended to glorify the role of the warrior and the violence by which personal valor and prowess could be proved. Whereas in the Roman system the imperial authority was established upon and supported by the civil society (the military arm in turn being created and utilized for the good of that society), the ruling authority in the new kingdoms was ultimately inseparable from the military loyalties that flowed up from beneath, and at least among the warrior class there was no systematic distinction between the civil and the military.

These starkly different societal structures represented and reflected quite fundamental differences of attitude toward war, peace, and the place of violence in society. The backdrop against which medieval antiviolence sentiment developed was thus a social system in which those who held a virtual monopoly on the means and use of force, the knightly class, also held the political power, and a value system in which this dominant class regarded personal military prowess as a mark of manhood. The potential for abuse of military power was thus great, and it tended to become greater or less abusive in proportion to whether the central political authority was relatively weak and spread out or strong and centralized.

2. *Approaches to the Rejection of Violence*

In medieval society, approaches to the rejection of violence ran along three general paths, and in these we can see beginning to coalesce the three major traditions in the quest for peace within Western culture. One of these paths led toward centralization of political authority; for where the individual knights and local barons were well policed by a stronger force from above, they were held back from using force to gain their personal ends. Though movement in this direction began earlier, among the various canon lawyers of the thirteenth century this led to an attempt to restrict the authority to use force legally to some centralized power—the pope, the Holy Roman emperor, regional kings, or some combination of these. This direction of thought fed strongly into the developing Church doctrine on just war. I have dealt with the canonists at some length elsewhere,[4] so I will not pursue this trend further here. A parallel development along the same general path, though, was the production of political arguments for the supremacy of the emperor over kings and pope, such as are found in the thought of Dante and Marsilius of Padua. Though their concepts are in some ways like the contemporaneous thinking of the canonists, especially the generation of canonists known collectively as the Decretalists, Dante and Marsilius argued on a very different basis. Though different from each other, they shared a common vision of the secular ruler's proper place, one that can best be understood as an extrapolation from an ideal representation of the Roman Empire. This concept strongly influenced the humanists of the Renaissance-Reformation period and can be identified, also, in the internationalist world-order pacifism of today. This approach to peace is one of the avenues to be examined in the present chapter.

Second, rejection of feudal violence could be accomplished by opting out of feudal society. The Church accomplished this in the monastic orders and, with less success, among the secular priesthood. The reasoning behind the former was, however, the more significant: those called to the religious life should abstain from the sword because Christ did so, and their calling implies possession of the grace necessary to live up to this perfection. Secular clergy had no such calling or extra measure of grace, and the canon law restraints on their taking up arms were by nature arbitrary, not always observed, and even less often enforced with any zeal. But perhaps a more interesting expression of this sort of rejection of violent society is to be found among those religious splinter groups—such as the Cathars; the *Unitas Fratrum*, or Bohemian Brethren; and the Waldensians—who chose a way of life much like that of

[4] Johnson, *Just War Tradition*, chapter V; cf. *Ideology*, chapter I, and Russell, *The Just War in the Middle Ages*, passim, which focuses almost entirely on the canonists.

the monks, but without official Church approval. In this chapter, such rejection of medieval violence will be examined through a look at the Waldensians and, to a lesser extent, the Cathars.[5]

Third, rejection of feudal violence could be accomplished by strengthening and channeling the values of the knightly class itself; this was the approach taken in the developing code of chivalry. That code came about side by side with a revived and somewhat more concrete concept of just war developed by ecclesiastical theorists: the former became the core of the *jus in bello* aspects of the newly elaborated just war idea, while the latter defined the *jus ad bellum*. I have elsewhere discussed this line of development in some detail,[6] and here I will treat it only as it bears directly on the quest for peace.

We are left with two main themes to be explored in this chapter: the vision of peace as expressed by political thinkers like Dante and Marsilius, who (though in significantly different ways) saw in the ideal of the Holy Roman Empire and the person of the emperor a plan for establishing a well-ordered society at peace with itself that might ultimately extend throughout Christendom; and the rejection of political violence undertaken by certain minority religious groups that, because of their own understanding of the Christian ideal and also because of the ecclesiastical disapproval and discipline leveled against them, chose the path of separation from society.

The former is "pacifism" only in retrospect, applying this term as it has come to be used in the twentieth century: neither Dante nor Marsilius thought of themselves as "pacifists," and both accepted violence as a necessary element in the establishment and preservation of peace. Nonetheless it is important to examine their concept of how to make the goal of peace a reality, for this kind of thought provides a bridge from the classical world to a certain kind of modern pacifism. In the background of the thought of these medieval political theorists lay the con-

[5] For discussion of the Bohemian Brethren see Peter Brock, *Pacifism in Europe to 1914* (Princeton: Princeton University Press, 1972), chapter 1; cf. pp. 509-511.

[6] Johnson, *Just War Tradition*, chapter V.

cept of peace accepted broadly by classical philosophy—indeed, by classical society in general—and ultimately made into a transcendent ideal in Augustine's heavenly city: this was the notion of a well-ordered, just society at peace internally, though it might have to utilize force of arms to maintain that state against disturbers of the peace both internal and, especially, external. In the classical context, this ideal was tied to the empirical reality of the Roman Empire; similarly, Dante and Marsilius tied their vision of a well-ordered society at peace with itself to an empirical political reality, the Holy Roman Empire. Their vision was already somewhat fanciful, though, as the empire on which they placed their hopes ruled only in parts of Italy and Germany and (even apart from the struggle with the papacy for political control there) coexisted alongside much more cohesive, less quarrelsome, and better governed states such as the kingdoms of France, England, and Naples. Later on, when this concept was taken up by the Renaissance humanists, the tie to empirical reality became still more strained, as symbolized by Thomas More's choice of name for his ideal kingdom—Utopia, or "Noplace."

If pacifism is understood as total rejection of violence, though, it is to the Waldensian movement, and slightly less to the Cathars, that we need look for a medieval expression of pacifism. The radical rejection of violence that characterized the first-century Christian Church, where this was one expression of a general rejection of "the world" and an imminent expectation of the end of that world, had flowed into two channels by the end of the classical period. One was monasticism; and the rejection of bearing arms characteristic of the monastic movement (if not always of every individual monk) was an expression of an overall way of life that also included vows of poverty, chastity, and humility and a withdrawal from secular society. The other channel included radical movements like Montanism which were the prototypes of later Christian sectarianism. The Waldensian movement, though it had important parallels with monasticism, was of this latter sort; and, well after its founding, the links that developed between it and the Radical Reformation testify to bonds of similarity there, as well. One interesting feature of Montanism, as we have seen in the first chapter, was that politically it was a reaction from rural, back-country areas against the type of Christianity found in the highly Romanized North African coastal cities. While Waldensianism was initially an urban movement, it soon retreated into the rural southern Alpine valleys which, closed off from easy communication with the outside world, rejected the domination of that world, and whose inhabitants, familiar with the relative simplicity of life in such an environment, rejected the style of Christianity represented by the official Church. The same rural-urban antagonism later appeared among the Swiss Brethren and other sectarians of the Radical Reformation, and it is a significant factor in understanding the form of pacifism expressed there.

Monasticism was, by nature, a world-rejecting and hence violence-rejecting phenomenon. But to follow the history of the development of Christian pacifism in the Middle Ages through monasticism would be mistaken. For in the mind of the Church and of the monks themselves, as well as that of ordinary, "secular" Christians, theirs was a form of life set apart from the world and able to be lived out only through the presence of a special divine grace manifested in the monastic "calling." Without such a vocation there was no possibility of living up to the standard of monastic abnegation, for the special grace that made this possible would not be present. In the phenomenon of medieval monasticism there was, to be sure, the pacifism of a radical rejection of the sword as a political tool; yet, because of the nature of monastic society as a representation on earth of the transcendent "city of God," where heavenly peace, order, and justice would obtain, this rejection could and did exist side by side with a secular society that accepted and sometimes (as in the case of the knights) even glorified the use of arms, and with a Church that likewise regarded the use of arms in such a society as a necessity that must sometimes be invoked to establish and maintain temporal order, justice, and peace. Monastic pacifism represented no challenge to the emergent just war tradition, which expressed this latter concept; indeed, almost without exception, the major theorists of the just war idea in the Middle Ages were themselves monks.

Only when the style of Christian life characteristic of the monks was held to be incumbent on all of Christian society was there a real challenge to the official consensus about the necessity of violence in temporal human government of the world. This was the claim of later radicals such as the Swiss Brethren of the sixteenth century, and it was the claim, as well, of the medieval Waldensians. By contrast to the monastic movement, Waldensianism was closer to the radical pacifism of the first-century Church, since the Waldensians made a claim on *all* Christians to reject violence. Yet for these medieval sectarians, as for such earlier groups as the Montanists, the situation was different: the majority of Christians in their own time held a quite different view of the matter. Thus, unlike the Christians of the first century, these later groups had to set themselves not only against the evils inherent in secular society, but also against a Church that, though representing the majority of Christians in their time, was represented as tainted with those very same evils. The same was true later of the sectarian pacifism of the Radical Reformation. For such groups as this, it was impossible to reach the kind of compromise achieved between the monastic rejection of the sword and the official Church acceptance of a limited political use of force in the interest of justice; for in these groups the presence of violence was itself the inherent negation of the values of a good society. Both these groups and the monks sought to bring the "city of God" to earth, but the radicals wanted to make this the way of life of the entire Church. Ironically, in whatever period of history, they have achieved only what was achieved in the monastic movement: enclaves of persons attempting to live by a stricter moral code than that of other persons who conceived themselves to be following a Christian life.

B. The Problem of Limiting Violence in a Violent Society

Violence was endemic to medieval society. In the fifth and sixth centuries, after the breakdown of Roman authority, Western Europe was divided geographically into regions controlled by more than two dozen distinct tribal groups, each of which was competing for space with its neighbors and, ultimately, with all the others.[7] These groups included indigenous peoples who, like the Celts, now pushed into the western areas (the Bretons, the Welsh, the Picts, the Irish); old enemies of Rome who had become allies, such as the Franks and the Alemanni; and later adversaries of the Empire, such as the Visigoths and the Vandals. Others were the Ostrogoths, the Rugians, the Thuringians, the Lombards, the Saxons, the Frisians, the Gepids, and the various Viking peoples. All these were in competition not only with each other, but with newcomers pushing in from the east, even as they had earlier done themselves. As each new group settled itself on the population already there, the latter were reduced to smaller and smaller landholdings as lands were distributed among the members of the new group. In a society lacking money, land—as an outright grant or as a leasehold contingent on continued good behavior—was the means of rewarding service given.

Thus we have the roots of the feudal system, with the peasants eventually reduced to serfhood and the warrior class controlling the land. But the land was distributed unevenly, even among these latter, and there was never enough to go around. Moreover, it was possible to lose land through malfeasance or, then as now, simply through not being able to make a living from it. In addition to individuals impoverished in these ways, there were young men, old enough to become warriors but not yet having inherited the family lands, as well as others, younger sons, who might never inherit. As a result of these social factors, there developed an entire subclass of men who possessed warrior (knightly) status by heredity but who had no lands and hence no personal means of livelihood. Wealthy lords employed some of these as personal retainers, paying them by furnishing their keep and their arms and holding out the promise of land at some later time. Others lived a catch-as-catch-can existence as mercenaries or brigands. In the latter

[7] This is graphically illustrated in Colin McEvedy, *The Penguin Atlas of Medieval History* (Harmondsworth, Middlesex: Penguin Books, 1961); see the maps on pp. 23 and 25.

category were also peasants and the sons of peasants who had lost their own lands. This pattern, established in the first generations after the collapse of Roman authority, extended and became commonplace in later centuries. The result was a continually bubbling stew of violent behavior at the social border between those who had land and those who did not, compounded by the tradition among the warrior class of using arms both to demonstrate manhood and to secure upward social mobility.[8]

The lines of distinction between *milites* (the term means "soldiers," but in the Middle Ages, at least into the eleventh century, it was used specifically for the personal retainers kept at the expense of a lord), mercenaries, and brigands were, moreover, somewhat blurred. Reading between the lines of the historical records, we can infer that the former were not above bullying behavior toward nonwarrior peasants, perhaps in much the same way that cowboys in the American West bullied and pillaged farmers when the latter were trying to establish themselves, or as Cossacks treated Jews in Eastern Europe during the pogroms. To the peasants who received such treatment, the *milites* of the local lord must have seemed little if any better than the bandits who lived in the security afforded by a nearby wilderness and who made periodic raids for provisions.

The *milites* were mercenaries in fact, though they were not paid in money, a scarce commodity; one way to keep them in check and also to occupy the armed bands of lawless pillagers was to make war and enlist all of them in one's army. For a given area this might be a double boon: if the forces marched away to invade a distant land, then the fighting would occur there, not in one's own home; and if the war were successful, some of the landless among the victors could be expected to remain there on new landholdings given in reward for service, or as newly employed retainers to the new landholders. But such wars were not always successful; and feudal wars, moreover,

[8] See further Delbrück, *History*, vol. II, books II and III; on the attitudes of persons at the interior of the empire see Brown, *Religion and Society*, pp. 53-54.

tended to be sometime things, with armies coming together in early summer and disbanding at the end of the fighting season in the fall. Then the troublesome bands of armed men returned home, used to taking whatever they wanted, and the pillaging would begin again.

This pattern is one that appeared again and again throughout the Middle Ages. The problem was worse in some periods than in others, and worse in some regions than in others. In general a strong central authority tended to suppress this sort of violence, which tended to increase when such authority was lacking. Likewise, areas close to centers of authoritative control tended to be more at peace, while those on the fringes of such control tended to be more prone to violence. Geography was a potent factor, since brigands flourished in areas where they could maintain a refuge in rugged terrain—mountains, forests, swamps. These areas also tended to be those most remote from the central government and often were contested territory between rival powers. Even in ignorance of political factors, one could almost identify the worst regions by studying a topographical map of Europe.

All this is important because it was the areas most prone to the sort of violence I have been describing that first experienced the impetus to restrain violence in the Middle Ages. That impetus was the Peace of God movement, whose initial target was precisely the bullying *milites* and those bands of armed men who lived on the edges of civilization, preying on settled areas. The Peace of God idea originally appeared late in the tenth century; about a generation later came the first appearance of a concept generally attached to it in historical interpretation, the Truce of God, and a century after that, in 1139, followed the ban on crossbows, bows and arrows, and siege weapons issued by the Second Lateran Council. This last was directed principally at mercenaries, who often were organized into fighting units around one or the other of these highly specialized and destructive weapons. In being thus directed, the Lateran ban can be regarded as finally closing the circle that the Peace of God first began to draw, circumscribing the violence of the three main groups of violent troublemakers in this period of medieval society—the *milites*, the brigands, and the mercenaries (who often became brigands when out of work).[9]

There are three caveats to be observed in interpreting these early antiviolence efforts and their interrelation. First, while there clearly are connections among them, they were exceedingly spread out in history (over a century and a half from the first appearance of the Peace of God idea to the Second Lateran Council), and it would be an erroneous compression of history to collapse them into a common movement. While collectively they hang together in certain ways, the differences among them are also important. It is more accurate, and for our purposes more useful, to think of them separately in terms of the immediate priorities each sought to address and the individual processes of development undergone by each. Second, while in some sense all three (but especially the Peace of God and the Truce of God) may be understood as expressions of a medieval "peace movement," this term ought not to be freighted with twentieth-century meaning. While some implications of these efforts may be read as expressing a kind of pacifism within the Church (which was the source of all three), the larger effects were on the development of just war thought. Third, and related to both the previous points, these efforts sought to restrain certain kinds of violence, but they ratified certain other kinds; in particular, the Peace of God movement had a perverse effect in encouraging holy war.

Now, what exactly were these three efforts to restrain violence? The beginnings of the Peace of God can be identified at the time of the Council of Le Puy in 975. Here, to follow the narrative of the French historian Philippe Contamine,[10] "Bishop Guy of Anjou assembled . . . the peasants and *milites* of his diocese 'in order to hear from them what their advice was for the maintenance of peace.' " On this same occasion he addressed them with the words, "Because we know that without peace nobody will see the Lord, we warn [all] men in the

[9] See further Johnson, *Just War Tradition*, pp. 124-31.

[10] Philippe Contamine, *War in the Middle Ages* (Oxford: Basil Blackwell, 1984), p. 271.

name of the Lord that they should be sons of peace." But the bishop went further, imposing on the *milites* an oath "to respect the Church's possessions and those of the peasants"—provisions that were ultimately to become the core of the idea of noncombatant immunity in late-medieval just war tradition. At the same time, this was not strictly a case of triumphant idealism; for, as Contamine also notes, there was resistance on the part of some of the *milites*, and this was put down by the force of arms by two powerful relatives of the bishop, the Counts of Brioude and Gevaudan. Contamine concludes: "That is to say, the peace movement was not directed against all the powerful (who had an interest in seeing that the goods of their dependants were protected) but simply against pillagers and troublemakers."

The subsequent development of the Peace of God idea, beginning with the Council of Charroux in 989, gradually diminished the protection extended to peasants and their property while making more explicit the immunity of ecclesiastical persons and property.[11] The high-water mark of this trend is the statement on noncombatant immunity in Gratian's *Decretum*, compiled in the middle of the twelfth century, wherein the protected classes of persons were explicitly listed, and defined by their relation to the Church as an institution: clergy (including bishops), monks, and pilgrims.[12] In the next landmark statement of canon law on this subject, that in the thirteenth-century *De Treuga et Pace* [Of Truces and Peace], peasants, their goods, and their lands had returned to the category of those

[11] For one expression of the effect of this idea on the knightly class, see the oath taken by Robert the Pious in the early eleventh century, quoted in Bainton, *Christian Attitudes*, p. 110: "I will not hurt the Church in any way. . . . I will not steal an ox, cow, pig, sheep, goat, ass, or a mare with colt. . . . I will not burn houses or destroy them unless there is a knight inside. I will not root up vines. I will not attack noble ladies traveling without husbands nor their maids, nor widows nor nuns unless it is their fault." What is still allowed by this is as interesting as what is forbidden. That this was an oath imposing *restraint* suggests a great deal about the earlier behavior of members of the warrior class.

[12] *Corpus Juris Canonici, Decretum Magistri Gratiani*, causa XXIII, q. VIII, canons IV, XIX.

who did not participate in war and thus should not have war made against them.[13] Gradually, other non-Churchly categories of persons were added to the list of noncombatants, until by the time of Honoré Bonet's *L'Arbre des battailes* [*The Tree of Battles*] in the fourteenth century the listing had come to include all sorts of secular persons who were noncombatants by virtue of their not being knights (a class-rooted distinction) or not being physically able to bear arms (a functional distinction). Peasants and clergy alike were defined in the former way, while such noncombatant groups as women, children, the aged, and the infirm belonged to the latter category. But Bonet's list (reflecting, I think, the societal consensus of his time) is, as I have argued elsewhere, the result of the growing impact of the chivalric code as a limitation on knightly violence; and by the fourteenth century it is quite clear that just war tradition, whatever its earlier history as a canonical and theological doctrine, was a statement of a broad cultural agreement on the justification and restraint of violence and war.[14]

In the shorter run, the effect of the Peace of God was not so much to protect peaceful noncombatants, wherever and in whatever social status they might be found, but to mark off who might legitimately resort to violence and for what ends. The Church by this doctrine attempted to remove its persons and property from being among the possible spoils of war, and all through this period canonical efforts (echoing Ambrose of Milan)[15] were made to rule out the personal use of arms by clergy and monks. But ecclesiastics still on occasion bore arms, and even when they did not, there were many instances of clergy and monks leading armed forces into battle or, as in the case of bishops who also functioned as the temporal lords of

[13] *Corpus Juris Canonici*, pars secunda, *Decretalium*, lib. I, tit. XXIV. See further Johnson, *Ideology*, pp. 43-46.

[14] See further Johnson, *Ideology*, pp. 64-80, and *Just War Tradition*, pp. 165-71.

[15] Ambrose, *Of the Duties of the Clergy* 1.35.175: "The thought of warlike matters seems to be foreign to the duty of our office. . . . [I]t is not our business to look to arms, but rather to the forces of peace."

their dioceses, sending out others under arms to do their bidding.[16] As a result, this side of the Peace of God movement carries with it a scent of self-interest on the part of the Church. The practical effect of the doctrine appears from this angle to be, "You (knights and nobles) may not fight against us (of the Church), but we may fight against you; our persons and property must be respected, but we do not extend that protection to other peaceful classes in society." Not only is such a position hardly pacific, it is self-centered in the extreme.

On the other hand, in the long run the idea of noncombatant immunity contained within the Peace of God developed into a much more universal concept with far-reaching implications. This is one of the two core ideas around which the *jus in bello* of just war tradition developed, and both modern humanitarian law of war and moral argument centering on the concept of discrimination are legacies of this slender tenth-century beginning. In the medieval context, the later development of noncombatant immunity as a consensual restraint on war was a result of the happy confluence between the Church's efforts to protect her own and moral ideas implicit in knighthood's code of chivalric conduct, as the latter developed into the basis of knightly self-awareness. Thus, in the fourteenth century Bonet could write, "[T]hat way of warfare [not observing the immunity of noncombatants] does not follow the ordinances of worthy chivalry or the ancient custom of noble warriors who upheld justice, the widow, the orphan and the poor."[17] Bonet could scarcely have had in mind the bullying *milites* and brigands from the time of Bishop Guy of Anjou; yet, even in the tenth century, such behavior as they practiced was opposed by others from the knightly class. For reasons I have discussed elsewhere, the goal of protection of noncombatants turned out to be implied by knightly self-interest, and this goal gradually became internalized and further developed in the chivalric

[16] See, for example, Contamine, *War in the Middle Ages*, pp. 434, 436-37, 442-43. The result was, as this author notes, to promote the idea of the crusade; see pp. 444-46.

[17] Honoré Bonet, *The Tree of Battles of Honoré Bonet* (Cambridge: Harvard University Press, 1949), p. 189.

code of the later Middle Ages.[18] The Church had some effect on this development; but knightly class-consciousness and the code of chivalry also influenced the Church's rather narrow and self-interested effort to protect her own. The result of the interaction between these two cultural forces was much more significant than either would have been by itself. In retrospect, this is the real importance of the Peace of God idea as an attempt to restrain violence.

In the shorter run, though, the effects were much more ambiguous: not only did the early effort to protect peasants as well as ecclesiastics degrade into protection for the latter only, but one of the effects of the Peace of God was to authorize and initiate violence, not just to restrain it. Again, though this could conceivably be termed a "peace" movement, it was anything but a *pacifist* movement; for in the name of the Peace of God the sword was employed to establish and maintain peace.

The first historical example of this outcome of the Peace of God movement has already been noted: the intervention of the Counts of Brioude and Gevaudan on the side of their relative, Bishop Guy of Anjou, to enforce the oath he exacted of the *milites* in his diocese. Such action by the authorities (the office and title of count, in this period, were borne by specific members of the knightly class who had been designated by the king to enforce royal authority in their regions; "count" was thus an office, not yet, as it later became, a noble rank in itself) suggests that they saw in the Church initiative an implicit reinforcement of the centralization of power that the kings (and their agents the counts) were trying to impose and that local barons and individual knights often opposed.

Another approach to the problem, however, surfaced some sixty years later: the organization, in 1038, of the first of the "leagues of peace" or "militias of peace," this time at the initiative of Aimon, archbishop of Bourges, who required "all the faithful aged 15 years or more to declare themselves enemies of disturbers of the peace and to promise to take up arms

[18] See further Johnson, *Just War Tradition*, pp. 131-50.

against them if required."[19] Whether organized with a long-term struggle in view or brought together for some *ad hoc* purpose, these peasant militias became a feature of life in troubled regions for the next century and a half. Typically they were convened at the initiative of a Church official and marched under Church banners, with the convener either commanding them himself or accompanying them to lend moral support while the command was taken by another. Their very existence, in a society in which for peasants to take up arms in their own defense was a challenge to the monopoly of arms claimed by the knightly class, testifies to the central authorities' lack of disciplinary power in remote areas. Because the central authorities were slow to act or lacked the power to act, these peasant militias were necessary, and in organizing them the local clergy were serving the cause of peace by deterring or punishing those who would engage in pillage.

Clergy did not always convoke these armed bands or march with them; in 1183, in Auvergne, a large group of Brabantines—out-of-work mercenaries—was brought to battle and destroyed by an "Alliance for Peace" made up of armed peasants under the leadership of a carpenter named Durand.[20] Yet, whether clergy headed such peasant militias or not, the "leagues of peace" provide witness to the problem of lawless violence posed by mercenary bands in this period.

Necessary for peace and order these leagues of peasants may have been; a force supplementing royal authority they may have been; yet, such militias must also have appeared very dangerous to that authority. The danger was not only that arming peasants challenged the knightly monopoly of power; kings and lower feudal lords could themselves happily arm non-knights when the occasion demanded. More serious was the implicit threat that a regional militia might set itself up as the governing body in the area it controlled, thus denying not only the coalescing feudal system but the authority of the king himself. The "Alliance for Peace" militiamen mentioned

[19] Contamine, *War in the Middle Ages*, p. 271.

[20] Delbrück, *History*, vol. III, p. 318.

above, after dealing with the Brabantines, turned against the local *seigneurs*, who then destroyed them. Equally serious was the implicit challenge to secular power on the part of the Church: even if canon law forbade clergy to bear arms, the example of the militias showed that the Church could wield secular power when conditions were right.

Responding to these last two sorts of challenge, the chief rulers of the tenth and eleventh centuries acted so as to place themselves alongside this movement, not against it. Louis VI was "obliged to ask for help from the bishops all over his kingdom to put an end to the oppression of bandits and rebels."[21] Louis VII, in 1155, followed with an act directed against breakers of the peace to "repress the ardour of spite and restrain the violence of brigands." Frederick Barbarossa proclaimed peace throughout Italy; other similar actions followed in train.[22]

To respond to the Church initiative in this way was shrewd policy, because it both headed off a church-state struggle (deferring it until the thirteenth century) and united the religious and secular powers in a common aim of removing the authority to use the sword from petty knights and lords and restricting that authority to the level of kings and emperors. That popes and bishops might also claim such authority was not yet a problem, for secular and religious authorities were still making common cause. That cause was, in effect, to establish order by restraining the violence of landless knights, petty lords, and brigands. For the Church, this was a means of protecting herself, her persons, and her property as well as the persons and property of peaceful peasants; for the kings and emperors, it was a means of consolidating their authority over the lesser feudal ranks. "The measures of Saint Louis and his successors against private warfare," writes Contamine, were "a logical continuation of the peace movement."[23] As we noted earlier, the Peace of God idea gave birth to the concept of noncombat-

[21] Contamine, *War in the Middle Ages*, p. 273.

[22] Ibid., p. 272.

[23] Ibid.

ant immunity as a restraint on war; now we must note, also, that it formed the context out of which, in the thirteenth century, canonists and political theorists shaped a renewed concept of right authority as part of the coalescing just war idea.[24]

Finally, the Peace of God movement also provided the historical context out of which the Crusades became possible. The effect of the Church's espousing temporal peace as a religious cause was to make it a pious duty to fight in order to establish such peace, and the Church herself did not hesitate to identify enemies of the peace for the pious to make war against. As we shall see below, the result was holy war.[25] Far from tending to suppress violence, this aspect of the Peace of God movement had the effect of fomenting it; far from restraining it, as in the case of the interjection of the new idea of noncombatant immunity, this aspect of the movement had the effect of legitimizing the unrestrained use of force for the cause of the faith.

We may responsibly spend much less time on the other two elements in the "peace movement" identified above, the Truce of God and the ban on certain weapons. The principal reason for this is that, as compared with the Peace of God, these efforts were derivative, and much of what has already been said about it applies also to these later attempts to limit violence. A second reason, though, is that neither the Truce of God nor the weapons ban produced the kind of broad effects and lasting results we have noted as coming from the Peace of God idea. Though these two later efforts endured for a time, neither became part of the emerging just war consensus on the limitation of violence formed in the later Middle Ages; nor did either have any perceptible effect on the radical pacifistic rejection of violence, whether in the Middle Ages or later. Thus they are simply not as important as the Peace of God, and it is enough to treat them in summary form.[26]

[24] See further Johnson, *Just War Tradition*, pp. 150-65.

[25] Cf. Contamine, *War in the Middle Ages*, pp. 278-80; Bainton, *Christian Attitudes*, pp. 109-116; Delbrück, vol. III, pp. 217-22.

[26] My detailed arguments for this judgment are given in *Just War Tradition*, pp. 124-31; cf. Bainton, *Christian Attitudes*, pp. 110-11.

While the Peace of God aimed at protecting certain kinds of persons and their property—broadly, those persons who did not themselves bear arms and engage in violence, and so ought not to have violence directed at them—the Truce of God aimed instead to eradicate the use of arms entirely during certain periods. In an early statement of the Truce of God idea, at the Council of Toulouges in 1027, the period of peace was to be each week from Saturday evening at the ninth hour until Monday morning at prime. This order, like the initial appearance of the Peace of God, had a very limited geographical scope, applying only within the diocese of Elne and the county of Roussillon.[27] In 1041 the bishops of Provence, writing on behalf of all the bishops of France, addressed a letter to the Italian bishops asking them to "receive" and maintain "peace and this truce of God which has been handed down to us from Heaven." In this letter the period of truce was defined as extending from vespers on Wednesday until sunrise on Monday, and it was to be observed "amongst all Christians, friend or foe."[28]

The regions in which the truce was to be applied gradually enlarged, as did the periods during which it was to be observed. Whole seasons of the ecclesiastical year were added: Christmas, Lent, the period from Rogations to Pentecost, the feasts and vigils of the Virgin, some saints' festivals.[29] Still, the Truce of God applied only among Christians, and this meant that violence could still be employed by Christians against non-Christians during truce periods. In practice this meant that violence could be directed against two main groups: infidels, as in the Crusades; and heretics, as in religious persecution.[30] The effect could be insidious. Since the Church enforced

[27] Contamine, *War in the Middle Ages*, p. 272.

[28] Ibid.

[29] See further ibid., p. 436; Richard Barber, *The Knight and Chivalry* (New York: Charles Scribner's Sons, 1970), p. 213 (who notes pessimistically, "[I]t is hard to find a single instance where a battle was postponed because of the day."); and Delbrück, *History*, vol. III, p. 249.

[30] See further Bainton, *Christian Attitudes*, pp. 111-16, and the discussion of the Waldensians and Cathars below.

the truce by imposing penance and excommunication, it in effect had the power to declare who was outside the faith and thus liable to be the subject of violence at any time of year, day in and day out. Where dissident religious groups like the Waldensians and the Cathars were concerned, it meant that they could be and were subjected to a continuous inquisition, carried out by the Church but with the aid of the armed power of the secular authorities. In the case of the Cathars, it even meant that they could have a bloody and relentless holy war directed against them.

In the Truce of God, then, as with the Peace of God, the effect was to enhance the right to use violence by the central authorities.[31] In the context of the time it was the Church's interest to have the powerful on her side; and, as already noted when discussing the Peace of God, they shared a common interest (though rooted in different reasons) in putting down private violence and eradicating dissident groups. That the Truce of God had this effect is certain; the nature of the effect—if any—on wars between the great nobles is harder to judge, but everything suggests that it must have been far more limited.

What might such a truce mean, after all, in an age when warfare largely consisted of sieges and not pitched battles? It surely was not interpreted to mean raising a siege for three days of the week and then reimposing it for the next four, as a strict interpretation of the truce might be thought to imply. Further, in realistic political terms, the Church was not able to discipline the powerful with heavy ecclesiastical punishments, for these were precisely the authorities on which the Church in other circumstances might have to depend for police action against miscreants. Finally, even where there were truces in wars between great powers during the era of the Truce of God, we should not overestimate the moral force of the Church in bringing to pass such cessations in fighting; then, as now, any commander might have had ample reasons of purely military nature to seek a truce and observe it once concluded. The enormous logistical and medical problems faced by medieval ar-

[31] Contamine, *War in the Middle Ages*, pp. 272-73.

mies alone made for "episodic" warfare. My own suspicion is that in wars among the great feudal powers the existence of the Truce of God offered a convenient excuse for periodic breathing-spaces, but such pauses would have happened whether or not the Church's truce existed. Contrarily, where these powers had no reasons of their own to ease military pressure on an opponent, the Church had little real ability to force them to do so. For such reasons as these, I suggest, the Truce of God did not endure as an effort to constrain violence. Its principal effect, in any case, was not to constrain violence but to consolidate it, and the peace that did follow from this aspect of the medieval "peace movement" was maintained by the swords of the high feudal authorities.[32]

The weapons ban imposed at the Second Lateran Council, and reaffirmed several times thereafter, represented a third avenue of attack on the kind of violence deemed wrongful or troublesome by the Church and the established powers. By this time—the Second Lateran Council convened in 1139—the centralization of power had increased considerably over that during the late tenth century when the Peace of God first appeared. The principal agents of private violence and possible challenges to authority were no longer unruly *milites* (a term now out of use for the knights and men at arms in a nobleman's household) or bands of local brigands. The former had been brought under firmer control, and the latter had largely been wiped out or forced further into the fringes. In the twelfth century, it was mercenaries who posed the greatest problems, and the weapons ban struck directly at them.

The mercenary problem took two forms. First, out-of-work mercenaries, as in earlier periods, often moved about as bands of pillagers, living off the countryside of whatever area they passed through. Second, mercenary bands sometimes seized castles or built their own fortifications, setting themselves up as the *de facto* rulers of the surrounding region, in defiance of

[32] See Bainton, *Christian Attitudes*, p. 116; Contamine, *War in the Middle Ages*, pp. 270-74; Russell, *The Just War in the Middle Ages*, pp. 183-86; Johnson, *Just War Tradition*, pp. 161-65.

the legitimate authorities.[33] In the first case they were no different from brigands; in the second they represented a revolutionary force. In either case, they needed to be held in check.

How did the ban on crossbows, bows and arrows, and siege weapons contribute to this end? The answer lies in the changed character of the mercenary phenomenon. In earlier periods, as for example in the time when the Peace of God first appeared, the typical mercenary was a landless individual who hired himself out for money or land, thus hoping to rise in the established social structure. Gradually this state of affairs changed. By the twelfth century the typical mercenary belonged to a well-organized band whose leader sold or bartered their services as a group and then himself paid his followers. This was the *condottieri* pattern, which reached its zenith in the fifteenth and sixteenth centuries, when Machiavelli derided it.[34] In the Middle Ages, what held these bands together (apart from the promise of gain) was expertise in one or another weapon that could be especially telling in the prevailing kind of warfare. Specifically, mercenary companies were formed around the possession and skilled use of bows and arrows and crossbows, neither of which were employed by knights but which could be devastating when used against knights, and siege machines, these being so expensive and difficult to transport and requiring so much skill to use properly that wealthy nobles preferred not to own their own but to hire mercenary companies specializing in their use.

From this it follows easily that the new-style mercenaries could be controlled by constraints placed on the use of their weapons. The knightly class in particular had good reason to favor such restraints, since there was no glory in falling in battle to an arrow shot by a commoner and since siege weapons represented the only significant threat to a nobleman seeking security from attack in his castle. Again, as in the case of the

[33] To combat such a band of mercenaries was the reason for the formation of the peasant army of the "Alliance for Peace"; see Delbrück, *History*, vol. III, p. 318.

[34] On medieval mercenaries see Delbrück, *History*, vol. III, pp. 313-21, 385-98, 505-522.

Peace of God and the Truce of God, here was an effort to limit violence that was really an effort to channel the control of violence into the hands of those authorities deemed legitimate. And it was ultimately because these very authorities found the banned weapons and the mercenary groups who employed them useful for purposes of their own that the Church's effort to limit violence by banning these weapons failed. For one thing, expertise in these weapons and men willing to fight for money were essential to the Crusades, to which the ban on these weapons was explicitly not extended. For another, subsequent history shows that princes were not at all hesitant to fill out their armies with such troops when they were serious about war. By the time of the Hundred Years' War (the fourteenth century) the ban had so faded from warfare, even among Christian princes, that even the briefest look at the tactics of the day shows that the presence of archers was taken for granted in an army (longbowmen for the English, crossbowmen for the French); these common soldiers were mercenaries.[35]

C. Sectarian Pacifism

The Peace of God, the Truce of God, and the ban on certain weapons characteristically employed by mercenaries were all efforts to approach the goal of peace by restraining violence. These efforts further had in common that they brought secular and religious authorities together both in establishing the limits to violence and in imposing the sanctions directed against disturbers of the peace—as these two sets of authorities collectively defined that peace. By following these efforts chronologically we have reached the middle of the twelfth century, and looking forward from this point we can observe several differentiable, though related, lines of medieval thought concerning violence and peace.

[35] See, for example, the discussion of the Battle of Agincourt in John Keegan, *The Face of Battle* (Harmondsworth, Middlesex: Penguin Books, 1983), and Charles W. Oman, *A History of the Art of War in the Middle Ages*, revised ed. (Ithaca, N.Y.: Cornell University Press, 1960).

The main line was the consolidation of just war tradition as a coherent and consensual body of thought and practice. As I have argued elsewhere, Gratian's *Decretum* (published around 1148) is the benchmark document for understanding the beginning of this consolidation;[36] yet, considerable development still remained in the thirteenth and fourteenth centuries before the just war idea would reach its classic form, and it was only during this development that it clearly came to represent a majority consensus within the culture that was medieval Christendom.[37] A fundamental theme in this development was carried forward out of the earlier "peace" efforts: that violence is an instrument; neither good nor evil in itself, but only so depending on who employed it, why, and how. In other words, this is the assumption that violence may be employed to restrain violence, the concept of the use of the sword in the service of peace. Viewed one way, this implied the justification of police action against miscreants and restraint in wars among European powers (if not yet in wars between Europeans and others). This has been the direction taken by just war doctrine proper since the late Middle Ages, and there has been an increasingly general claim that the restraints defined here ought to apply in all wars, whoever the belligerents.[38]

Viewed another way, however, the concept of the justified use of the sword to restrain violence and secure peace could imply that, under the conditions of an ideal state or a legitimate universal government, peace, order, and justice would all be established, and that at least the internal use of the sword within such a political community would be virtually or entirely abolished. This vision later fueled the utopian pacifism of the Renaissance humanists, as we shall see exemplified through Erasmus in the next chapter. In this chapter, though, we will examine it in its medieval form; for it is the motivating concept behind the idea of peace conceived by Dante and, in a

[36] See my discussion in *Ideology*, pp. 33-39.

[37] Cf. Russell, *The Just War in the Middle Ages*, pp. 292-308; Johnson, *Just War Tradition*, chapter V.

[38] See further Johnson, *Ideology*, chapters II-IV; *Just War Tradition*, chapters VI-X.

different if related way, by Marsilius of Padua, both of whom will be discussed in the concluding section of this chapter.

Viewed in yet a third way, the concept that the sword might be used to correct those who disturb the peace could become a justification for religious persecution at home and for crusades both at home and abroad. We have already seen how zeal for the Peace of God and the Truce of God led to Church involvement in armed action against violators; we have also seen that much of the force of these early "peace" efforts was toward restraining private violence while consolidating the right of the central authorities to employ violence against dissident groups. Breach of the Peace of God or the Truce of God was defined as a religious offense, since the Church had promulgated these efforts, and a rebel or dissident group that broke the terms of either thus became the enemy of both the Church and the secular authorities. It was a small step from this to the claim that the Church herself had the right to authorize violence against "enemies of the faith," whether infidels, heretics, or individuals or groups guilty of nothing worse than heterodoxy. We shall see how this development helped fuel a radical reaction against all use of violence, even that ostensibly in the name of peace.

A central issue in all these developments concerned the proper relation of the Church to the emerging state. Were the two coequal, the Church having precedence in the spiritual area, the state having precedence in the secular? Or did the Church possess a status superior to that of the state in all matters, even secular rule, by dint of the superiority of the spiritual over the material? Or did the state take precedence over the Church, not only in matters clearly having to do with secular rule, but in all ecclesiastical matters insofar as they related to the secular world? Because of the closely intertwined character of church and state all through the medieval period, these were not easy questions to answer; yet this did not prevent claims being made for each of the three positions.

Of greatest interest to the present discussion are the claims of the Church to have authority in matters both secular and spiritual. An epicenter of this position and of resistance to it was provided by the so-called Donation of Constantine, a document in charter form purporting to be from the Emperor Constantine and granting certain powers of temporal rule to Pope Sylvester and his successors in the Roman see. The document transferred to the popes "the city of Rome and all the provinces, districts, and cities of Italy or of the Western regions"—language that could be read as giving to the popes temporal sovereignty over the entire western half of the Roman Empire as it existed in Constantine's time.[39] In fact, the "Donation of Constantine" dates not from the fourth century, as it pretends, but from much later—probably from the latter part of the eighth century, when it was produced to bolster the claims of Pope Stephen II to temporal overlordship in certain regions of Italy. In any case, though, this document was generally accepted as genuine for several hundred years, until its spuriousness was demonstrated by Nicholas of Cusa in 1433 and again by Lorenzo Valla in 1440.[40]

The medieval use of this document was principally to support Church—and more specifically, papal—claims to supremacy over secular kings and emperors in the various church-state struggles that flared up at different times. So far as Church involvement in the use of force to suppress dissidence and private violence was concerned, there were ample reasons apart from this spurious charter for Churchly and secular authorities to cooperate toward this end. Nonetheless, radical-sectarian critics have regularly and consistently excoriated the "Constantinianism" of the Roman Church and laid this to the position based in the "Donation of Constantine." This was not a line of argument favored in the Middle Ages; rather, it is found principally in the present-day historical writings of radical-sectarian Christians, where it has become a commonplace theme. We need to attempt to understand the nature of this criticism and to explore what it means in the medieval context for relations among the Church, the secular au-

[39] Williston Walker, *A History of the Christian Church*, revised ed. (New York: Charles Scribner's Sons, 1959), pp. 186-87.

[40] Ibid., p. 187.

thorities, and heterodox religious groups such as the Waldensians and the Cathars.

"Constantinianism," as employed in this criticism, refers not simply to papal claims to secular authority (which was the issue in the Middle Ages), but more generally to all forms of Church involvement in the secular government of the world. Within this latter, broad sense critics attach the term more particularly to the authorization of force or the actual use of force by the Church in support of her own purposes in the world. Calling this "Constantinianism" identifies it with the compromise of Christian principles that radical sectarians, following the "standard account" discussed in the previous chapter, place in the era of the Emperor Constantine. Thus, for example, Hershberger speaks of "a state of ill health" that "has characterized considerable portions of the church more or less continuously from the time of Constantine to our own."[41]

The application of this argument to the medieval period is well exemplified by the contemporary Czech scholar of Waldensianism Amadeo Molnar. In a book on medieval Waldensianism revealingly titled *A Challenge to Constantinianism* Molnar singles out the "Donation of Constantine" as the root of the medieval idea of Church involvement in the affairs of the world:

> During the whole of the Middle Ages, the papacy did not hesitate to return to this text in order to guarantee a legal basis to its claims to temporal supremacy. This document, while a forgery, was nevertheless publicly thought to be true, but all the same it rested upon an important historical basis, that is the radical change of attitude of the western church towards society with the coming to power of Constantine.[42]

This "historical basis" is itself a myth, as I argued earlier; but, to paraphrase Molnar, perhaps what is important here is

[41] Hershberger, *War, Peace, and Nonresistance*, p. 72.

[42] Amadeo Molnar, *A Challenge to Constantinianism: The Waldensian Theology in the Middle Ages* (Geneva: WSCF, 1976), p. 47.

that, whatever its character as a true representation of history, it is "publicly thought to be true" by historians following the "standard account" and particularly occupies a place of honor in the historical self-understanding of contemporary heirs of radical sectarianism. But let us follow Molnar's argument a bit further:

> The Lombard poor and the Waldenses who followed their initiative were among the first to anchor their witnessing to Christ along the lines of an anticonstantinian choice. Constantinianism was, for them, not so much an historical fact as it was a theological and social situation.[43]

Later we find him describing persecution and the Waldensian attitude toward martyrdom in similar terms:

> The Constantinian church, having made recourse to force, was characterized by its attitude of persecuting power, whereas the Church of Jesus Christ is characterized in its temporal existence by an unlimited capacity for suffering, and when it is necessary, for martyrdom.[44]

Molnar reinforces this dichotomy a page later with a quotation from an early Waldensian, Durando d'Osca: "Let the church of God never inflict suffering, but always be ready to endure it."[45]

We are beginning to glimpse here the outlines of the radical pacifism of the Waldensian movement as it developed in the closing years of the twelfth century and the beginning of the thirteenth. Let us now back away from the question of "Constantinianism" for a bit and look at the emergence of Waldensianism more directly.

It appears clear that neither Peter Waldo (or Valdez) nor his immediate disciples wanted to reject the spiritual leadership of the Church of Rome or to challenge her temporal authority. Waldo, a rich Lyonese merchant, resolved in 1176 to seek the best way to God, and he was advised to follow that biblical

[43] Ibid., p. 50.

[44] Ibid., p. 64.

[45] Ibid., p. 65.

text central to monasticism, "If you would be perfect, go and sell all that you have and give it to the poor, and come, follow me" (Mark 10:21). This was standard medieval advice, and if followed in the expected way it would have led Waldo, after providing for his family, into the monastery. But, instead, he obtained for himself a translation of the New Testament and gradually gathered around himself a circle of disciples, composed both of women and men, who resolved to follow his example for living in apostolic poverty—in the world, however; not in the monastery. A similar development occurred at about the same time: the *Humiliati*, or "Poor of Milan" (the "Lombard poor" referred to by Molnar).

These movements possessed three characteristics that made them unwelcome to Church authorities. First, they were lay movements led by persons without formal education or ecclesiastical credentials who presumptuously interpreted the requirements of the gospel for themselves. Second, while quasi-monastic in nature, these movements included both men and women, and their communities were not in cloisters but gathered in the midst of the secular world. Last, they called on the whole of society to choose their way of life as the truly Christ-like way, thus implicitly challenging the established pattern of separation between monastic life, lived apart from the world according to the "counsels of perfection," and the life of other Christians, lived in the secular world according to the "precepts of morality." These lay movements, the followers of Waldo and the Lombard *Humiliati*, challenged the established institutions of the Roman Church; and that, we shall see, could not be tolerated.

The Waldensians at first attempted to remain within the existing ecclesiastical structure. In 1179 they applied to the Third Lateran Council for permission to preach. This was denied, not because they were heretical, but because they were ignorant laypersons. They proceeded to preach anyway, and in response to this direct disobedience Pope Lucius III excommunicated the Waldensians in 1184.[46]

[46] On these developments see further Walker, *Christian Church*, pp. 229-30.

At this point the history of the Waldensians as a radical-sectarian group may be said genuinely to begin. Excommunication did not discipline the Waldensians to bow to the authority of the Church; rather, it forced them underground. Inquisition and coercion by force followed excommunication as efforts to root out the Waldensians and turn them to orthodoxy; the result instead was to drive the movement out of the cities, where it had first taken hold, and into the rural valleys of the southwestern Alps or farther west into Languedoc, where the Cathar movement was already well established.[47] Further development of this movement would no longer be as a community openly expressing commitment to the ideals of the early Church, as interpreted by that community from the New Testament; now the Waldensians were themselves forced into a form of compromise with the world. Two classes of members developed, corresponding to the two tiers already in effect within Catharism. In the latter movement, a distinction was made between the "perfect" (or "pure," the meaning of the Latin term "Cathari") and the "believers." Among the Waldensians, the corresponding terms of distinction were the

[47] The Cathars (also known as Albigensians, after Albi, the largest town in the region where they were most concentrated) were a dualistic Christian sect that originated in the twelfth century in Languedoc. Though based in Christian teachings and regarding themselves as "good" Christians (by contrast with the official Church, which they regarded as corrupt), the Cathars held a Manichaean distinction between the spiritual world, ruled by God, and the carnal, physical, terrestrial world, which, ruled by Satan, was entirely evil. Its adherents fell into two groups, the *perfecti* ("perfect ones") and the *credentes* ("believers"). The former lived ascetic lives, abstaining from eating meat and from sexual contact. For the latter, however, such strictures were imposed only after receiving the rite of *consolamentum* shortly before death, after which they fasted until death. The Cathars were persecuted by both the Church and the state virtually throughout their existence as an identifiable religious group; and from 1209, when a crusade was directed against them, to 1244, when the last Cathar fortress fell, they were the objects of continual military pressure. Pockets of Cathar belief and practice persisted in the area south of Albi along the Spanish-French border well into the early fourteenth century, finally being subdued by an energetic local inquisition. See further Emmanuel L. Ladurie, *Montaillou: The Promised Land of Error* (New York: Random House, 1979), introduction et passim.

"masters" and the "friends." In both cases the former group, who lived out the full meaning of the doctrines they held, were a minority, and these were the ones for whom clandestinity was most necessary. The "believers" or "friends" formed a penumbra of support around the "pure" or "masters," maintaining overtly ordinary lives in the world but following the doctrines of the elite group insofar as possible and shielding them from the authorities. This proved a remarkably effective strategy, allowing the Waldensians to resist annihilation throughout the thirteenth and fourteenth centuries so that their movement could ultimately survive into the modern era. For the Cathars it meant that even after a crusade directed specifically at them, their heterodox beliefs could continue long after within the rural communities of southern France.

In short, the persecution directed against the Waldensians made them into a radical sectarian movement, drove them into clandestine existence, and brought them into contact with the Cathar movement, which was much more clearly heterodox in doctrine. For a time the history of these two groups ran parallel, but it is impossible to say anything with certainty about the degree of influence the one may have had on the other, or about the direction of such influence. Very little is known about either movement in the thirteenth century except through the records of their inquisitors. At the end of the twenty years of warfare (1209-1229) directed against the Cathars and their supporters by Pope Innocent III and the French monarch, there were no Cathars left who were able or willing to tell their own story in writing. Even though Waldensians in the region were caught in this same net of persecution, there was another center of this movement's followers farther east in the Alpine valleys; thus, Waldensianism maintained its integrity as a religious sect. For understanding the beliefs of the earliest Waldensians, however, this can be a source of hindrance as well as help because of a tendency to read back into the former the beliefs and teachings of later periods.

In the present book, my major concern is to understand the pacifism of the Waldensians as a sectarian group, and this is precisely an area where the evidence is often made to say too much. Interpreters generally agree that both the Waldensians and the Cathars rejected the taking of oaths[48] and the bearing of arms,[49] but there is disagreement as to the reasons each of the two persecuted groups did so and exactly when the twin refusals took hold in each group. For Gonnet and Molnar, for example—both sympathetic to Waldensianism—the Cathar refusal of oath and arms stemmed from their doctrine of dualism between good spirit and evil matter. For the pure, taking an oath or bearing arms degraded the spirit by involving the body in things of the world. By contrast, the Waldensians refused the oath as "unscriptural," and likewise "[t]heir nonviolence was not . . . an abstract and rigid principle" like that of the Cathars, but "a revolt against a Church of success and of conquests which had succeeded in wiping away the spirit of service and the passion of sacrifice."[50] Given the paucity of hard evidence about the beliefs of the two groups in the early thirteenth century, this smacks of special pleading. Both groups had significant doctrinal reasons for a stand against oath-taking and bearing arms, and both had exactly the same experience of being persecuted by the hand of the state under the authority of the Church. We simply cannot say what the Cathars may have actually believed about this, or that they were somehow more doctrinaire or "rigid" in their rejection of governmental authority and in their pacifism than the Waldensians.

What can be said is this: neither heresy made use of violent means; both had violent means employed against them. Later Waldensian opinion is unanimous that their strong nonviolence was a reaction against the use of violence by the Church in an effort to coerce orthodoxy.[51] This is certainly consistent

[48] Jean Gonnet and Amadeo Molnar, *Les Vaudois au moyen âge* (Turin: Editrice Claudiana, 1974), p. 169.

[49] See ibid., p. 179; Christine Thouzellier, *Catharisme et Valdéisme en Languedoc à la fin du XIIe et au début duXIII^e^ siècle* (Louvain: Editions Nauwelaerts; Paris: Beatrice-Nauwelaerts, 1969), p. 188; Contamine, *War in the Middle Ages*, p. 467; Molnar, *A Challenge*, pp. 64-68.

[50] Gonnet and Molnar, *Les Vaudois*, p. 182.

[51] See further ibid., pp. 182-83.

with the argument that Waldensianism (and Catharism as well?) was a reaction against the "Constantinianism" of the Roman Church. But later Waldensians, as well as their heirs among the pacifist sectarian groups of the Radical Reformation, certainly had no trouble finding scriptural warrant for the refusal to bear arms,[52] and so it is unreasonable to think of the pacifism of the Waldensians as one only or principally of reaction (though the experience of living in a heterodox religious community subject to violent persecution was undoubtedly a factor in cementing attitudes that, we have every reason to expect, were already present).

Understanding why this was likely requires that we reflect back on the parallels between the Waldensian movement and monasticism. What they did *not* share was monastic cloistering (the Waldensians first gathered within secular society and retreated to the fringes of that society only when forced to do so by persecution); rigid separation of the sexes (the original Waldensian community included both men and women, and later on members of both sexes achieved the status of "master"); their view of who should attempt to live by their ethic (for the monastic orders only those few could do so who had received a special vocation, while for the Waldensians, *all* Christians had received such a vocation by virtue of being Christians); and the Waldensians' view that their calling gave laypersons the right to preach to others.

What they did share, though, was an understanding that the Christlike life was one of poverty and avoidance of ties to "the world." With very few exceptions (even if those exceptions tended to be quite visible ones) monks held aloof from worldly office and the use of the sword that came with such office. If they did not take the feudal oaths of fealty that bound vassals to lords, regardless of the status into which they had been born, it was because by entering the monastic life they had removed themselves from the world of nature and had already begun to participate in the life of supernature. Their pacifism was based in the example of Christ; yet, doctrine also held, it

[52] Ibid., pp. 67-70, 181.

was possible to them only because they had received special grace along with their calling and because they lived a special life in enclaves apart from the secular world. So far as the secular world was concerned, the pacifism of the monks was to be honored as a matter of simple justice: they did not make war, and so they ought not to have war made against them.[53] This was noncombatant immunity defined by social function.

The Waldensians accepted the life of poverty, humility, and renunciation of secular authority, as did the monks. Yet the former did not cloister themselves, attempting instead to remain in the secular world, where they located their mission of preaching and witnessing. While monastics refused secular oaths, they were nonetheless bound in a feudalistic fealty to the authorities in their set-apart communities; when the Waldensians refused the oath, while still living in the midst of communities governed by secular authorities, it threatened the whole fabric of a social structure that depended fundamentally on the taking and keeping of oaths.[54] In the same way, for the monks to reject the sword while living apart in their enclaves of the heavenly city could serve as a continual reminder of the excellence of that ultimate end, for a world wherein violence seemed necessary to secure order, justice, and even temporal peace; yet for the Waldensians to reject the sword while living within such a world was a challenge to the goals secured by the presence of military force in the hands of rightly constituted authority.

Where Waldensian pacifism was concerned the problem was not simply, as Gonnet and Molnar have argued,[55] that the heirs of Waldo challenged a feudal structure in which armies were absolutely central (since the oath of fealty obliged one to serve as a soldier when requested by his feudal superior); rather, they must have seemed anarchistic, rejecting the goods secured by the presence of force along with that force itself.

[53] Such reasoning is implicit in the earliest canonical listings calling for clerical immunity; see, for example, *De Treuga et Pace*: *Corpus Juris Canonici, Decretalium*, lib. I, tit. XXXIV.

[54] Cf. Gonnet and Molnar, *Les Vaudois*, p. 180.

[55] Ibid., p. 180.

The flavor of this concern is given in the reports of the official investigators, as in the following exchange between the inquisitor Jacques Fournier and the Waldensian Raymond de Sainte-Foix in 1321. The record notes that the heretic admitted "that it is permissible for the secular authority to put to death or mutilate malefactors, for without such actions there would be neither peace nor security amongst men," that it is even "just and licit" to put heretics like the Manichaeans (that is, the Cathars) to death, that "those who kill or condemn malefactors or heretics to death may be saved," and that a just war is permitted to a Christian prince not only against pagans and infidels, but against other Christians in order to respond to insults or violent attacks, in cases of violations of faith and of disobedience.[56]

Clearly here the inquisitor was deeply concerned to establish the legitimacy of the use of force by the proper authorities where there was just cause; without this, the line of questioning suggests, there could be no society at all. The same line of questioning later would be applied to radical sectarian pacifist groups in the Reformation era, such as the Swiss Brethren.[57] In this case, the Waldensian Sainte-Foix ultimately is reported as rejecting participation for himself, even in such just violence as was named, because he was one of the "perfect." This is essentially, of course, the monastic answer as well; later, it was adopted by the sectarian pacifists of the Radical Reformation, as a way of attempting to assure the secular authorities that they were not anarchists otherwise intent on subverting right authority. But it was a difficult concept for the authorities to credit in the case of nonmonastic sectarian groups during both ages, since to their minds the acceptance of the goods of the society they governed necessarily implied a willingness to participate in its policing against domestic malefactors and its defense against external enemies.

I have earlier argued that the pacifism of the first-century

[56] Contamine, *War in the Middle Ages*, pp. 295-96.

[57] See James M. Stayer, *Anabaptists and the Sword* (Lawrence, Kans.: Coronado Press, 1972), chapter 6; John Howard Yoder, trans. and ed., *The Legacy of Michael Sattler* (Scottdale, Pa.: Herald Press, 1973), pp. 66-85.

Christian Church was one result of that community's rejection of the life of the world in order to live out its communal expectation of the imminent end of that world. It was not, on this understanding, violence itself that was evil, for God might employ violence; it was participation in an evil world that was already doomed but did not know it, and in the violence this world undertook for its own ends. Later, I argued, referring to such groups as the Montanists, the situation had importantly changed. The Montanists were also pacifists; they, too, followed a strict morality that kept them aloof from much that had to do with life in the secular world.[58] But their rejection of Roman society was in part political,[59] and their repudiation of military service stood in sharp distinction to the position of growing numbers of other Christians, who found such service to be one among the possible ways to take responsibility for the government of a world that, by this time, neither they nor the Montanists seriously believed would soon come to an end.

The Waldensians, like the Montanists, believed that they were recapturing the way of life of Christ and the Apostles (so, for that matter, did the monks). In rejecting the peace, order, and justice of the temporal world, they were seeking to serve a higher goal of community which they identified with the early Church and which they believed was already possible for any Christian to join in this life, without waiting for the afterlife. Structurally, they were challenging the social compromise that set the monastic enclaves of the city of God apart from (though set within) the cities of earth; this was what made them seem so dangerous to the existing social order. Their eschatology, like that of the monks, was a realized one: it was already possible, in their teaching, to live the life of the new age. Rather than waiting in gathered communities for the world to pass away (as the first-century Christians had done), the Waldensians sought to embody the already present end of that world as confirmed in their theology. Their pacifism, then, is directly comparable to that of medieval monasticism, which under-

[58] See above, Chapter I; cf. Tertullian, *On Idolatry*.

[59] See above, Chapter I.

stood itself in similar theological terms; yet it was radically different in holding that this rejection of violence (and the paired rejection of oath-taking) ought to extend to the whole of the Church. Since the boundaries of the Church were at that time coterminous with those of European secular civilization, this was a genuinely revolutionary idea, as both the religious and the secular authorities quickly recognized and as was reflected in the inquisition directed against the Waldensians.

It is against this background that we may return to the issue of whether the Church's "Constantinian" involvement with violence in the persecution of the Waldensians was an important factor in cementing the pacifism of the latter. Gonnet and Molnar put the argument succinctly: the Waldensians' nonviolence was "a revolt against a Church of success and of conquests which had succeeded in wiping away the spirit of service and the passion of sacrifice." [60] Or as Molnar puts it in another context, "[T]o endure suffering imposed by a false Christianity would be the sign of the true church: 'Let the church of God never inflict suffering, but always be ready to endure it.' "[61]

That violent means were employed in the suppression of dissident religious movements, and that the Church cooperated with secular authorities in the application of such means, is a characteristic of European history from the time of the Peace of God movement through the era of the Reformation and the Counter-Reformation. But the religious groups thus affected did not always respond nonviolently; in fact, most did not, as the history of the religious wars of the sixteenth and early seventeenth centuries shows. In the Middle Ages the crusade against the Cathars was resisted by noblemen who were Cathar sympathizers, and likewise groups of Waldensians sometimes resorted to violence against their persecutors.[62] In attempting to explain the latter, Gonnet and Molnar, both highly sympathetic apologists for Waldensianism, distinguish

[60] Gonnet and Molnar, *Les Vaudois*, p. 183.

[61] Molnar, *A Challenge*, p. 64, quoting the medieval Waldensian Durando d'Osca.

[62] See Gonnet and Molnar, *Les Vaudois*, pp. 183-86.

between the "Waldensian sympathizers" or "friends" and the "Waldensians *stricto sensu*, the 'masters,' the 'perfect' . . . , a distinction created by the imposed clandestinity of the movement."[63] This suggests exactly that kind of moral distinction which obtained between monks and others in the official Church; yet these authors want to insist that the Waldensians admitted no such distinction in the requirements of true faith. Earlier they state their thesis explicitly: "The testimonies are unanimous in affirming that the Waldensians without exception, French, Italians, or Germans, refused to take oaths [and] reproved all violence and all use of the sword in the service of justice, whether ecclesiastical or civil."[64] Nor did the later, radical heirs of this movement make any such distinction between the levels of obligation incumbent on different members of their movement.

In fact, though, these authors' discussion of the violent reaction that sometimes erupted against the Waldensians' persecutors sounds suspiciously like an effort to make excuses for it: the persecutors goaded the Waldensians into it; even the distinction between "masters" and "friends" was "imposed" by the need to live clandestinely to avoid persecution. *True* Waldensians were nonviolent. And so they were, or at least so they attempted to be, because of their understanding of the nature of the Christian life; yet, the instances of violence that did take place suggest that the experience of violent persecution had opposite effects under different conditions. Sometimes and in some places it might reinforce the rejection of violence by the Waldensians—"masters" and "friends" alike. Yet at other times, perhaps when the inquisitors and their supporting forces were few and a "popular insurrection"[65] might have some chance of success, the existence of persecution might become a catalyst for a violent reaction against it.

The upshot is that it is impossible to say that the experience of persecution at the hands of the Church was either a neces-

[63] Ibid., p. 187.
[64] Ibid., p. 180.
[65] Ibid., p. 186.

sary or a sufficient condition for the pacifism that ideally characterized the Waldensian movement. The "Constantinianism" of the Church—its involvement in secular affairs and its complicity with the secular authorities in authorizing holy war and religious persecution, as well as its emerging doctrine of just war—was thus a factor in what the Waldensians found repellent in this Church, but it still remains a category of interpretation belonging chiefly to the reflections of a later age. The pacifism of the Waldensians was, rather than a reaction against the "Constantinian" Church's use of violence, something inherent in the view of the Christlike life that Waldo and his heirs read out of the New Testament and believed was incumbent on all Christians. Their struggle against the allied secular and ecclesiastic authorities was a result of this intentional and conscientious nonviolence (amid other reasons for their being separated from the official Church), not the other way around. Indeed, although proponents of the anti-Constantinian theme seem not to recognize it, there is disagreement between the idea that the Waldensians became pacifists to be like Christ and the claim that they rejected force because of a revulsion against the official Church's use of force to coerce belief. If the first is true, the latter is no longer a necessary condition; if the latter is the main reason, then the pacifism of the Waldensians was not absolute but conditional on the behavior of the Roman Church. It is not possible to have this both ways.

There is, however, something to be observed in the fact that the Church and the secular authorities alike regarded the Waldensians as enemies to be opposed by inquisition and violence. In attempting to establish the Peace of God, the Church learned to rely on the secular sword and, in a masterful exercise of double-edged theology, supported the secular arm in rooting out private violence by declaring those who broke the temporal peace to be unfaithful to the teaching of the Church.[66] By inverting this latter logic, persons and groups declared unfaithful to the Church's teaching became enemies to the temporal peace and subject to chastisement by the secular

[66] See further Thouzellier, *Catharisme*, chapter III.

authorities. Thus, force might be rightly employed against those heretics who were not themselves making use of violent means—or even those who were conscientiously nonviolent, following the core doctrine of the Waldensians. We have here an example of the way in which the emerging just war reasoning was extended and twisted to justify religious coercion *as something in which the state itself had an interest*, since religious dissidence as such was a threat to the peace. This legacy took a long time to dissipate. In the fifteenth century the influential Spanish Schoolman Franciscus de Victoria could declare, "Difference of religion is not a cause for just war";[67] yet the following century was to experience some of the bloodiest and most fratricidal religious wars ever fought, and practically speaking it was not until the end of the Thirty Years' War that religious coercion by violent means was separated from reasons of state.[68]

The underlying problem is a real one: sometimes, in the interests of maintaining rights and values against those who threaten them, it may seem right to support the use of violent means. This was what the Church did early in the history of the Peace of God movement, and it is also implicit in the later just war reasoning (based on a reading of Romans 13:7) that a secular prince might act "in the stead of God . . . to punish evildoers" by force. At its extreme, this aspect of just war tradition might justify military intervention against a government guilty of grave oppression of its subject population. But such permissions can also be abused, and then the secular authorities in question might themselves cross over the line into unjust usurpation of rights and values. The radical-sectarian kind of rejection of force, coupled as it is with a rejection of involvement in the government of the world, avoids the dilemma by opting out of the conditions that tend to create it. Resistance to evil becomes, for the radical, not a matter for potential resistance

[67] Franciscus de Victoria, *De Indis et De Jure Belli Relectiones* (Washington, D.C.: Carnegie Institute, 1917), *De Jure Belli*, section 10.

[68] The Thirty Years' War began as a religious conflict but ended as a dynastic one. This set the pattern for the subsequent wars justified in dynastic, then nationalistic terms.

by force, but one to be dealt with individually (through taking on the burdens of persecution and martyrdom). It also calls for an effort to reconstitute society so that it will have no evil in it—as much an effort at social engineering as that undertaken by the "Constantinian" Church. The irony of radical sectarianism is that it points toward an involvement of the Church in society perhaps even more thoroughgoing and fundamental than that of the "Constantinian" Church. For this reason it is difficult not to suspect that the real difference was over means rather than ends; and this reminds us that, historically, the Waldensians were rejectors of society first—including refusal of the oath and of bearing arms—and the objects of persecution second.[69]

D. The Peace of the Heavenly City on Earth

1. *The Historical Context*

The thirteenth century had opened with the crusade against the Cathars and continued with persecution against the Waldensians; yet, not without paradox, this century was also the one in which just war tradition, as an effort to set limits to violence, took definitive shape in canon law and Scholastic theology as the normative doctrine on war of the Western Church.[70] More development was still to come for this doctrine, but it was already strongly consensual on the major elements of re-

[69] Waldensianism, because of a strong missionary impulse, spread its teachings throughout Europe, but especially in central Europe. Brock writes (*Pacifism in Europe*, p. 31): "[T]he Waldenses, even though most of them were country folk and their Christianity a simple discipleship, exercised through the purity of their moral impulse a considerable influence on the thinking of the radically minded theologians in Hussite Prague." Though the Waldensians' own pacifism waned in the late fifteenth century, their earlier impact on the radical-Christian movement in Bohemia is to be found in the pacifism of the Bohemian Brethren and, through them, in that of the radical groups of the Reformation era. See further Brock, p. 29ff.

[70] See further Russell, *The Just War in the Middle Ages*; Johnson, *Ideology*, chapter I, and *Just War Tradition*, chapter V.

straint: namely, its concept of who might rightly authorize use of the sword, what constituted just cause for such use, and under what conditions it might be possible to have recourse to the sword in the service of such just causes.

At the center of this coalescing doctrine was the assumption that force itself was an instrument, to be used for good or evil. The theory and practice associated with the just war idea sought to specify limits to the use of force so that the sword of authority could serve good against the threats posed by evildoers. The official interpretation of Romans 13:4 provided the rationale: the prince "is the minister of God to execute his wrath on the evildoer" (*Minister enim Dei est, vindex in iram ei qui malum agit*). Already present in the Peace of God and Truce of God movements in the tenth and eleventh centuries, this notion of the justified use of the sword to restrain and punish evil occupied a prominent place in both Churchly and secular thought on war and peace in the High Middle Ages.[71]

This was a time when there was a considerable yearning for peace, for an end to the strife that pitted not only secular noble against noble, monarch against monarch, and the forces of authority against criminal or dissident groups, but that also set church against state—especially in the wars between pope and emperor.[72] The chief problem of peace in this era was no longer private violence, as it had been in the tenth and eleventh centuries, when the Peace and Truce of God appeared, or the rising power of mercenaries, as it had been in the twelfth cen-

[71] See further Johnson, *Ideology*, pp. 27-32.

[72] Contamine writes (*War in the Middle Ages*, pp. 292-93): "At certain epochs, peace became a true political concept, an omnipresent point of reference. Alongside the literature on war, there was a literature on peace: *Le Livre de la paix* of Christine de Pisan, *Le Livre de paix* of Georges Chastellain and several discourses and sermons by Jean Gerson." These are all from the end of the fourteenth century and the beginning of the fifteenth. Had Contamine wished, he could have named several other works of the same sort without the word "peace" in their titles, and had he reached back earlier in this listing, he would certainly have had to add to his genre of "peace literature" Dante's *De Monarchia* (written in 1309) and the *Defensor Pacis* of Marsilius of Padua (completed in 1324). These two works are the major focus of the remainder of this chapter.

tury, when the ban on weapons used mainly by mercenaries had been issued. While criminality, rebellion, and private violence such as dueling between knights had not by any means been eradicated, the consolidation of the great kingdoms and duchies meant that these kinds of violence did not represent the threat to the whole of society that they once had. Now the principal form of threatening violence, which brought forth longing thoughts of peace and plans for achieving it, was war between great powers—war proper, not police actions against malefactors on the fringes of society.

For Dante and Marsilius of Padua, in the early fourteenth century, the immediate historical context was the struggle between pope and emperor being played out in Italy. A century later, for Christine de Pisan, Georges Chastellain, and Jean Gerson, it was the Hundred Years' War between France and England, periodic armed uprisings of commoners, and a struggle between factions of the royal family for control of the French throne.

Peace, as conceived in these two groups of works a century apart, is strongly reminiscent of the idea of peace in the classical philosophers. Even as the ultimate peace of the city of God had been a transcendentalized version of this earlier peace, so now in the thirteenth and fourteenth centuries (and continuing into the fifteenth century and beyond) the peace of heaven began to be secularized back into a possibility to be achieved in human history. It was no longer enough in this world to seek spiritual peace: there had to be a society in which temporal peace was the product of order and justice among men. Nor was this to be achieved as sectarian pacifists such as the Waldensians thought, by a private and corporate renunciation of violence; rather, according to the concept now being advanced, the sword would remain, but it would be in the hands of a just sovereign, who would need this power to maintain the peace and order of the society he governed against both external and internal threats. Thus began to emerge the vision of a utopian world order that became explicit in the Renaissance humanists and in later modern internationalism. Looking backward in time, however, we can see in this concept the continuation of that earlier impulse which had combined the rejection of private violence with the justification of violence on the part of higher authorities to keep order, ensure justice, and maintain peace. The emphasis now shifted to efforts to describe the ideal monarch or the ideal state, the character of which would include the establishment and preservation of peace.

Set against this kind of thinking, just war theory seems to represent a pause along the way. Both the new proto-utopianism and just war thought issued from the same roots; yet, in the effort to define who possessed the necessary authority to use force, just war thinking focused on the regional sovereigns and remained there. Later international law, building on this implicit principle in the modern era, ratified the rights of sovereign states to use force in order to keep internal order and defend themselves against external threats. The long-run implications of just war theory can well be seen in the development of international law, which through most of its history has defined its *jus ad bellum* through the category of *raison d'état*, accepted wars among established states as the practical shape of reality, and concentrated on developing *jus in bello* restraints on the actual prosecution of war. In the Middle Ages the highly stylized knightly combat of the Hundred Years' War already exemplified the tendency to stress the *jus in bello*, for the claims to justice and authority made by the belligerents in this conflict were so tangled as to make a definitive stance on the *jus ad bellum* impossible.[73] But for those who thought in loftier terms, restraint in war was not enough: complete abolition of fratricidal strife between equals had to be the ultimate goal. This is the common thread that unites the authors of the

[73] The English king was a vassal of the king of France by dint of holdings in certain parts of France; yet, at the same time, he had a claim on the French throne that was valid in English law but not in French. In addition numerous English nobles had possessions in French territory, some dating back to the time of William the Conqueror. As between the kings, who was the lord and who the vassal? Among the nobles, to which feudal liege was prior obligation owed, and how was it limited by the obligation to the other? Law and custom could not provide a settlement; hence the resort to arbitrament of arms.

"peace literature" from the fourteenth and fifteenth centuries, that ties them in turn to the utopian theorists of the Renaissance and to twentieth-century internationalists, and that makes them all able to be called "pacifists"—though in this tradition of thought "pacifism" means something quite different from what it means among the radical sectarians.

2. *Dante's* De Monarchia

In Dante's *De Monarchia* and Marsilius of Padua's *Defensor Pacis*, both from early in the fourteenth century, we find two different aspects of the early stages in the third major tradition of the Western quest for peace. Developing alongside sectarian pacifism and just war tradition, this line of thought will be carried on by Renaissance utopianism, the "perpetual peace" movement of the Enlightenment, and the internationalism of the nineteenth and twentieth centuries. In these medieval works, though, the tradition is only beginning to coalesce.

Set against the immediate background of the Guelph-Ghibelline struggle, *De Monarchia* is an explicitly proimperial tract; at the same time, however, and understood in the context of Dante's larger political thought, it is a concept of society and of sovereignty that transcended anything existing in Dante's Europe. This book is a minor work when laid alongside *The Divine Comedy*, and when Dante wrote it his political thought was still developing; yet, for our purposes, it serves well to illustrate the idea that peace is historically possible through the establishment and working of the right kind of society. One commentator writes:

> Ultimately the value of *Monarchy* is the insight it allows into the workings of a great mind at the very moment it becomes seized of a great ideal. And the hope of a stable, peace-making government was a great ideal. It had been an influence on European history since the beginnings of Europe, in the Empire of Constantine, of Charlemagne, and of the German Emperors. After taking many forms

> and being centered in very different courts, it seemed to have returned, a few years before Dante's birth, to its original centre in the Roman people.[74]

This concept of the "Roman people," *populus Romanus*, also makes clear Dante's indebtedness to classical thought concerning how a good society would establish and ensure peace; it is at once a symbol for the present and an interpretive vehicle for the past. The ideas Dante employed were hardly unique in an age when the "study of Roman Law and of philosophical Jurisprudence played a great part in the higher politics";[75] yet the specific political use to which he put the idea of the *populus Romanus* and other concepts from the classical period was entirely his own.

De Monarchia is divided into three books, organized so as to answer "three principal questions":

> The first is whether [a temporal monarchy] is necessary for the well-being of the world. The second is whether it was by right that the Roman people took upon itself the office of the Monarch. And thirdly, there is the question whether the Monarch's authority is derived directly from God or from some vicar or minister of God.[76]

The first book, which demonstrates the need for a temporal monarchy "or, as it is more commonly called, the Empire,"[77] proceeds by a series of arguments. These are somewhat repetitious, and it is possible to give their gist by way of some examples. Dante begins as follows: a family, a village, a city, a kingdom are all made up of many diverse parts having different functions but aimed at a single end, the well-being of the whole. Dante cites Aristotle, "the acknowledged authority," as positing that "when several things are directed toward a sin-

[74] Donald Nicholl, introduction to Dante Alighieri, *Monarchy and Three Political Letters* (New York: The Noonday Press, 1954), p. ix.

[75] W.H.V. Reade, introduction to Dante Alighieri, *De Monarchia* (Oxford: The Clarendon Press, 1916), p. xvi.

[76] Dante, *Monarchy*, book one, II, p. 4. Citations from this work are from the English translation in *Monarchy and Three Political Letters*.

[77] Ibid., V, p. 9.

gle end it is necessary for one of them to act as director or ruler and the others to be directed or ruled."[78] Thus each type of community cited must have its particular head, for otherwise disaster will result: as Dante says of the kingdom, without a king "its inhabitants will not only fail to achieve their end as citizens but the kingdom itself will crumble."[79]

Or again, taking another tack, Dante writes that "the human race is at its best and most perfect when . . . it is most like to God." But mankind is most like to God when it is most united, since God is the ground of unity. Therefore, "when mankind is subject to one Prince it is most like to God. . . ."[80]

A few sections later, after further arguments of similar abstract nature, Dante reaches the subject of peace. First, there is the necessity of having a single monarch if disputes are to be settled without strife. Otherwise, arbitration and final judgment between the claims of two rivals would be impossible. To have order in society thus requires one sovereign at its head.[81] Similarly the virtue of justice in society requires a monarch, for the only person capable of rendering each citizen his due (the classical definition of justice employed here by Dante) is a ruler "with perfect will and power"; that is, a monarch whose position is above petty passions and whose strength enables him to make sure that no usurpation of another's rights or property can take place. The result is peace, "the most powerful means" toward which is justice.[82]

The society Dante sketches in these arguments thus embodies the familiar triad of political virtues: peace, order, and justice. In this society all citizens are free to seek their highest goods[83] and are not hindered by others acting contrary to the common good, for individual and common ends will coincide. Society is united around one goal, but that goal is achieved by the various contributions of every citizen, each acting in his

[78] Ibid., p. 10.
[79] Ibid., p. 11.
[80] Ibid., VIII, pp. 12-13.
[81] Ibid., X, p. 14.
[82] Ibid., XI, pp. 15-18.
[83] Ibid., XII, pp. 18-20.

particular station. Ultimately it may be said that the monarch's power is what ensures they act as they should for their own good and for the good of all; yet, it is clear, Dante believes that ideally the monarch would rule not through force but through "bringing the best out of others."[84] Unlike Plato's ideal of the philosopher-king, it is not the personal virtue or intellect of the monarch on which Dante here focuses; rather, it is the *position* of monarch, which is so high as to be unaffected by the common passions of lesser men. This is a *structural* solution to the problem of how to create a good state: the monarch rules justly by virtue of being a monarch.

> Since the Monarch . . . can have no cause for cupidity . . . and in this differs from other princes, and since cupidity alone perverts the judgment and compels justice, it follows that the Monarch is in a perfect—or at least the best possible—condition for governing, because he surpasses all others in the power of his judgment and justice.[85]

In *The City of God* Augustine had laid out a remarkably similar concept, but it was of the community of mankind at the end of history, when God had totally transformed it away from the city of earth. Augustine had built on Cicero, arguing that Rome, which the latter regarded as ideal, was lacking in justice since God was not given his due in this *civitas terrenae*. Augustine's city of God was the model on which medieval Christendom came into being; more particularly, it remained the model on which papal claims to temporal supremacy were grounded, since the Church of Rome was represented as the city of God on earth and the pope, as the designated vicar of God, was head of that Church.

Dante's *De Monarchia* represents a turn back to the perfection offered by the earthly city. His immediate model was Aristotle, rather than Cicero, and the turn away from the Augustinian concept as it was employed in the late Middle Ages is marked. The temporal monarch, not the pope, is depicted by

[84] Ibid., XIII, pp. 20-22.
[85] Ibid., pp. 21-22.

Dante as the one who corresponds to the presence of God in the state; the justice of the monarch is "the best possible" there; the peace of the state is guaranteed by the power and good government of the monarch, and it is a temporal peace, not to be confused with spiritual blessedness.

In the remaining two books Dante grounds the claim to monarchy in the *populus Romanus*, a people chosen by God because of their innate superiority over other men, and identifies the proper monarch of this *populus* as the emperor, not the pope. Thus the empire emerges explicitly as the ideal state Dante is endeavoring to depict, and the emperor, as he already revealed in an aside in the first book, is the universal monarch he would see all princes—Churchly as well as secular—acknowledge as their head.

In the historical Europe of his time, Dante must have known, such an acknowledgment was most unlikely; thus, there is an unreal (if not yet to say utopian) quality to his mental construct of the ideal society ordered and governed by a supreme monarch. In the early fourteenth century, the geographic extent of the empire and the number of its population made it theoretically the preeminent state in Europe. Still, it was internally weak; and, in practice, the power of the more coherent principalities and kingdoms that lined the empire's western border was equal or more than equal to that which the empire had at hand in each region. Quite apart from the question of the emperor's rightful superiority over the pope as temporal monarch, there was the larger question, posed but not addressed in Dante's concept of the unified kingdom of mankind, of what might induce other temporal sovereigns to accept this one as their common overlord. *De Monarchia* laid out an idealized picture and argued for it by means of philosophically composed syllogisms. Thus, despite Dante's secularizing the goal of peace in his earthly city, this peace was in fact no more likely of historical achievement than that of the *civitas Dei*. The heavenly city is here brought down to earth; yet, its location is not the empirical empire but (though the word did not yet exist) utopia—"noplace." Renaissance humanism was to give further development to this idea of an ideal society, and with it the establishment of peace.

Before leaving *De Monarchia*, we need to note for one final time the relation between the power of the monarch and his ability to "bring out the best" in his citizens in regard to the guarantee of order, justice, and "the tranquillity of peace."[86] Looking from this treatise toward just war theory, we recognize the principle that the supreme ruler must have a final monopoly of power to ensure these goods for his society; this was also recognized in the classical concept of peace on which Dante built. It is implied, as well, by practical reflection on the real extent of such a monarch's authority and on how it might be enforced on those who do not accept it. One commentator writes that

> it is difficult to see how, in practice, [the monarch] is to impose his judgments upon the unwilling, unless he be aroused with force. But force must imply, either that [the monarch] is to be the head of an actual state more powerful than any other, or that he will depend upon the arts of persuasion and diplomacy for securing executants of his will. In either case the upshot will surely be that he whose highest function is to guarantee the peace of the world will not bring peace but a sword.[87]

Dante's monarch, however, also partakes somewhat of the medieval concept of God, a Neo-Platonic ideal of the good toward whom all creation is drawn by an innate divine magnetism. Dante treats this ideal as existing in the institution of supreme monarchy itself; thus, its very existence would form a goal toward which all mankind would be drawn to be and do the best possible for it. Here the heavenly city is intermixed with the earthly, and the utopian ideal with the reality of history. Dante simply left unresolved the implicit conflict between this side of his reasoning and the other, and the Renaissance

[86] Ibid., book three, XVI, p. 93.
[87] Reade in Dante, *De Monarchia*, p. xvi.

humanists who inherited his approach and his ideals did hardly any better.

3. *Marsilius of Padua's* Defensor Pacis

In 1324, when *Defensor Pacis* appeared, the immediate issues of church-state conflict were different from those which had motivated Dante, but the overall intellectual atmosphere was much the same. On the one hand, some maintained that the pope possessed "plenitude of power" in matters both secular and spiritual; on the other, some favored the primacy of the temporal ruler over the Church; and between them was a group that "argued simply for a parallelism of the temporal and spiritual powers without any intervention of either in the other's affairs."[88] Marsilius's work was an entry into this debate; yet, as with *De Monarchia*, our interest is not with this larger topic of church-state relations and spiritual versus temporal supremacy. It is rather with the concept of peace as it appears in *Defensor Pacis* and its relation to the secular state.

Marsilius, like Dante, wrote within an Aristotelian framework of thought; unlike Dante, who relied most directly on Aristotle's political thought, Marsilius drew also from the Greek philosopher's logic and his understanding of nature. This led Marsilius to make more of Aristotle's theory of causation than Dante had done. Within the Aristotelian conceptual system as Marsilius used it, peace is the more significant because it has a causal relationship to the state: peace in Marsilius's theory is, as Alan Gewirth writes, "the formal cause of the state, that is, the principle of the state's order or organization."[89] Marsilius explains this concept by an analogy with animals:

> For just as an animal well disposed in accordance with nature is composed of certain proportioned parts ordered to

[88] Alan Gewirth, *Marsilius of Padua: The Defender of Peace*, vol. I: *Marsilius of Padua and Medieval Political Philosophy*, vol. II: *The Defensor Pacis* (New York: Columbia University Press, 1951-1956), vol. I, p. 17.

[89] Ibid., p. 94.

> one another and communicating their functions mutually and for the whole, so too the state is constituted of certain such parts when it is well disposed and established in accordance with reason. The relation, therefore, of the state and its parts to tranquillity will be seen to be similar to the relation of the animal and its parts to health. . . . Health, . . . as the more experienced physicists describe it, is the good disposition of the animal whereby each of its parts can perfectly perform the operations belonging to its nature; according to which analogy tranquillity will be the good disposition of a city or state whereby each of its parts will be able perfectly to perform the operations belonging to its nature. . . .[90]

There was nothing radical or new in such a concept. Indeed, coming as it does near the beginning of the first of the three books of Marsilius's work, it is meant to establish the argument to be made in *Defensor Pacis* within the commonly held assumptions of an age of triumphant Aristotelianism. But, as with Dante's *De Monarchia*, there was more to this fourteenth-century intellectual penumbra than Aristotle. There was also the tradition on peace reaching forward from Augustine's *City of God*, according to which peace is, first and generally, the right ordering of everything in the universe as provided by God and, second and more particularly, the state of "concord" (*concordia*) among men.[91] Gewirth notes that "concord" in this sense meant more than "an external relation" among men; it was "a rapport of their hearts, based upon their common ordering by and to God."[92] Hence the peace of the state is, in Augustine's words, "the ordered concord of the citizens in commanding and obeying."[93] Order thus is essential to peace. But so is justice, which is established by

[90] Marsilius, *Defensor Pacis* I.ii.3. Citations are from the English translation in Gewirth, *Defender of Peace*, vol. II.

[91] See the discussion of Augustine in Chapter I, above.

[92] Gewirth, *Defender of Peace*, vol. I, p. 95; see Augustine, *The City of God* XIX.13, 14.

[93] Augustine, *The City of God* XIX.13.

God's love (*caritas*). Without *caritas*, the state—and all human affairs—will be ruled by *cupiditas*, fallen, inverted desire; and its order will be a perverted one, and its peace will be "false" and "imperfect," not "true" and "perfect."[94]

Now, to the papalists it was precisely this sort of reasoning that attested to the temporal as well as spiritual supremacy of the pope, God's vicar on earth. Their concept of order—and of power—flowed downward from God through a hierarchy of positions, and in this hierarchy the spiritual occupied a higher place than the temporal. Therefore, in their reasoning, precisely because of his spiritual position the pope possessed "plenitude of power" that was temporal as well as spiritual.

Marsilius, however, advanced quite a different argument. He was not concerned with the peace of the state as part of the grand order of things in the universe, as were the papalists; nor was he concerned with the Augustinian *concordia* or immanent rapport of human hearts. Peace, for Marsilius, "is entirely a secular political concept, a 'civil peace,' having no cosmological, theological, or other extra-political reference whatsoever."[95] It is, moreover, an *instrumental* peace, one resulting from having the internal relations within the state functioning smoothly together, and not a peace of *ends* as with Augustine, Aristotle, and the common wisdom of the fourteenth century; thus, the emphasis on the temporal is reinforced, that on the eternal left aside. "This treatise," wrote Marsilius in his concluding book, "will be called *Defender of Peace* because it discusses and explains the principal causes whereby *civil peace or tranquillity* exists and is preserved, and whereby the opposed strife arises and is destroyed."[96] As Gewirth comments, "For a state to be 'at peace' in Marsilius' sense means only that its parts are functioning properly and interacting smoothly; it does not mean necessarily that the state is 'at peace' with other states."[97]

How did Marsilius arrive at such a concept? *Defensor Pacis*

[94] Ibid., XIX.14; Gewirth, *Defender of Peace*, vol. I, p. 96.

[95] Gewirth, *Defender of Peace*, vol. I, pp. 96-97.

[96] Marsilius, *Defensor Pacis* III.iii; emphasis added.

[97] Gewirth, *Defender of Peace*, vol. I, p. 97.

opens with a classical reference, citing Cassiodorus on "the greatest good of man, sufficiency of life, which no one can attain without peace and tranquillity." Marsilius then passes quickly through several biblical references to being "at peace."[98] But his real concern begins to appear in the next paragraph, where the focus abruptly becomes more concentrated. The immediate problem, we discover, is the condition of Italy: fragmented, torn by strife, so that "the Italian natives are deprived of the sufficient life, undergoing the gravest hardships instead of the quiet they seek, and the harsh yoke of tyrants instead of liberty."[99] Marsilius continues: "Into this dire predicament, then, the miserable men are dragged because of their discord and strife, which, like the illness of an animal, is recognized to be the diseased disposition of the civil regime."[100] By contrast, "while the inhabitants of Italy lived peacefully together, they experienced those sweet fruits of peace which have been mentioned above, and from and in those fruits they made such great progress that they brought the whole habitable world under their sway."[101]

Dante had argued that it was the superior virtue of the *populus Romanus* which had enabled them to triumph over so much of the known world and to establish the *pax Romana* so broadly: in acting as they did, they sought not their own gratification but sacrificed themselves for the good of the others whom they came to rule.[102] Marsilius turns this idea on its head. Peace is required first, so that "sufficiency of life" (read, in classical terms, virtue as well as material goods) may be had; and the result may well be, as it was in the past, that if the Italians become so well ordered among themselves, they will again come to rule "the whole habitable world." But such a possibility is beyond Marsilius's immediate concern. Italy's internal civil discord is the problem at hand, for it prevents Italians from living the good (or sufficient) life. Peace, then, would be

[98] Marsilius, *Defensor Pacis* I.i.
[99] Ibid., I.ii.
[100] Ibid., I.iii.
[101] Ibid., I.ii.
[102] See, for example, Dante, *Monarchy* II.vi.

"civil happiness,"[103] the end of this internal discord—whatever might yet obtain for Italy's relations beyond the Alps.

The "singular cause" of the "civil discord or intranquillity" Marsilius has in mind should by now be no surprise. It is "the belief, desire, and undertaking whereby the Roman bishop and his clerical coterie, in particular, are aiming to seize secular rulerships and to possess excessive temporal wealth."[104] The claim to "plenitude of power" is false, and "no rulership or coercive judgment over anyone in this world" belongs to the papacy on the basis of such a claim.[105] Rather than the temporal rulers being inferior to the spiritual because of some clerical investiture of the former, history shows that originally the temporal sovereign invested the clerics in their office.[106] The way to restore peace to Italy, then, is to have a single consensual authority (the "faithful legislator") and allow the clerical claims to temporal power to "wither away."

As the end is peace, so should the establishment of such a legitimate secular authority itself be by peaceful means. It is at this point that the conciliarism for which Marsilius is best remembered shows itself plainly; for Marsilius, arguing that an elected government is superior to a nonelected one,[107] reasons as follows:

> It now remains to show the efficient cause of the ruler. . . . Taking up the question, then, let us say, in accordance with the truth and the doctrine of Aristotle . . . , that the efficient power to establish or elect the ruler belongs to the legislator or the whole body of citizens, just as does the power to make the laws. . . . And to the legislator similarly belongs the power to make any correction of the ruler and even to depose him, if this be expedient for the common benefit.[108]

[103] Marsilius, *Defensor Pacis* I.vii.

[104] Ibid., III.i.

[105] Ibid.

[106] This point is made in various places throughout book II of *Defensor Pacis*; see, for example, II.xi and II.xvii.

[107] Ibid., I.ix.

[108] Ibid., I.xv.1, 2.

The better to understand what Marsilius is positing, we need to recall what was said earlier about the Aristotelian framework of causation assumed by Marsilius—and by his contemporaries. Aristotle had posited that for every effect there can be identified four types of cause, which he termed the material, the formal, the efficient, and the final. The material, in this conception, is simply the stuff of which the phenomenon in question is composed; the formal is the proper shape or relation of its parts; the final is the end for which this phenomenon exists; and the efficient is that immediate agency which causes development or change.

Working within Aristotle's framework (in which the four causal types are discrete), Marsilius in his concept of the state drew its four causes together into two pairs. The way he did this is central to his concept of peace as an achievement of the state. For instead of sovereignty originating at the top of the state and mediating its power and authority downward, creating the goods of order, peace, and justice as the product of this downward flow, Marsilius's concept was one in which the authority and power to rule are mediated upward. The "material" of which the state is made is the people and their material surroundings; yet "the whole body of the citizens" makes up the "legislator," whose functions include both the designation and supervision of the ruler and the creation of laws by which the ruler must rule.[109] These are actions of *efficient* causation. Similarly, we have earlier noted that peace and tranquillity make up the form of the good state; in Marsilius's secular concept, the "sweet fruits" of peace and tranquillity are its end, or final cause, as well. So peace rises ideally out of the consent and cooperation of the citizenry, who as "legislator" make the laws that give their society the form or order which is peace. In this concept the ruler is reduced to "the instrumental or executive cause" who governs "through the authority granted him for this purpose by the legislator, in accordance with the form which the legislator has given to him. This form is the law. . . ."[110]

[109] Ibid., I.xv.3, 4.
[110] Ibid., I.xv.4.

Nevertheless, there remains the need of coercion within this society, and of provision for the sword:

> [S]ince among men thus assembled there arise disputes and quarrels which, if not regulated by a norm of justice, would cause men to fight and separate and thus finally would bring about the destruction of the state, there had to be established in this association a standard of justice and a guardian or maker thereof. And since this guardian has to restrain excessive wrongdoers as well as other individuals both within and outside the state who disturb or attempt to oppress the community, the state had to have within it something to resist these.[111]

The state, Marsilius proceeds, must provide for "certain common things, and different things in time of peace and in time of war," and so there must be "in the community men to take care of such matters."[112] In particular, the ruler must take care to keep the state functioning properly for the common good and to protect it against external dangers. To these ends he may—and Marsilius fully expects he will have to—employ coercion by armed force. "The Marsilian ruler," writes Gewirth, "is a coercive judge, dispensing what Aristotle called 'rectificatory justice.' "[113] Or, to use the terms we have employed in earlier connections, he is the agent authorized to use the sword in order to secure peace.

The state is necessary for the "fruits of peace and tranquillity" to be achieved; thus, it is absolutely necessary to avoid the destruction of the state. For the animal to be healthy, it must first be alive. One is tempted here to push Marsilius toward universalism; for the healthy animal that is frequently or continuously attacked or menaced by predators may be prevented from feeding, from sleeping, from breeding and caring for its young, and from engaging in other activities necessary not only to its continued health but to its continued existence and that of its species. This suggests that Marsilius's concept of the

[111] Ibid., I.iv.4.

[112] Ibid.

[113] Gewirth, *Defender of Peace*, vol. I, p. 106.

ideal state is, in fact, endangered if external military threats are admitted to exist. The internal peace of a society at war is not the same as that of one not at war. Carried out fully, this logic implies that the ideal can be reached only in a universal state, where there are no external enemies. Then the problem becomes that of *internal* coercion, which would seem to be unnecessary in a state founded on the consent and participation of its citizens in their own government; however, only if sin were no longer to be found among men would no coercion of evildoers in society be needed.[114] But this takes us closer to the city of God and to the Augustinian concept of *concordia* than Marsilius would go. His focus remains on the secular state, on the peace it is capable of establishing, and on the need to preserve that state from destruction if such a peace is to remain. This is a strikingly modern notion of the state and of its peace. Writ small, it points toward the autonomous state as conceived by Rousseau; writ large, it points toward utopian internationalism. In either case, it is a secular "peace on earth" that is to be established.

In both Dante and Marsilius we find a version of the idea that peace may be established and maintained by the sword, a concept prominent as well in the developing just war tradition, which in turn had inherited it from the experience of European society in the era of the Peace of God and the Truce of God. What distinguishes the thinking of these two fourteenth-century theorists from the penumbra of just war assumptions held by the canonists and theologians of their time is a reliance on the role of the secular state in establishing that peace. Though Dante and Marsilius differed importantly in how they conceived this state and its rulership, they agreed in bringing it and its peace down to earth. Whether the ideal was to be, as in Dante, a restored Roman Empire, a society that through its "superior virtue" would gradually bring the world under its sway, or only, as for Marsilius, a single state among many that because of its good ordering would experience peace within itself, the new state was no longer the transcendent ideal implied

[114] See further ibid., p. 124.

in the city of God tradition. Theirs was the city of God on earth, with its goods and its perfection to be found within itself. Thus, in spite of their significant differences, Marsilius and Dante both pointed ahead toward the concept of the Renaissance and the modern era. Again, though, there is an irony to be perceived in this movement. For when eschatological peace is secularized into something that is in principle able to be achieved by the state, then the state is itself in danger of becoming universalized and absolutized; and this in turn can represent an endangerment of peace.

E. Conclusion

While the medieval period is generally remembered by historians as a time when temporal life was permeated by spiritual concerns, the opposite is also true. It was an age when ideas and ideals rooted in the spiritual and applied to earthly life began—precisely because of this application—to lose their transcendental connections and to be recast as secular constructions of thought. The complement of sanctification, by which human values are raised to comport more closely with the divine, is secularization, the process whereby those values originating in the divine become so much a part of earthly life that they are no longer recognized as belonging to the transcendent. If sanctification implies the transformation of values upward so that, for example, human justice becomes more perfect when improved by the action of divine love,[115] then secularization also implies a transformation; and its product is a new reality in which the divine value has been reshaped and reconceived in accord with human needs and concerns. This process of change is strikingly exemplified in medieval approaches to peace.

The peace of God, "which passes all understanding," was

[115] This is Augustine's concept of the work of charity in history, expressed in *The City of God* and in other works; cf. H. Richard Niebuhr, *Christ and Culture* (New York: Harper & Brothers, 1951), pp. 206-218, and Paul Ramsey, *Nine Modern Moralists* (Englewood Cliffs, N.J.: Prentice-Hall, 1962), chapters 5-7.

present to the Middle Ages principally in the form of the ideal of the city of God. This was not, however, a literate age; so the ideal was communicated through the empirical presence of the Church and, in a more pointed way, by the existence of monastic communities, enclaves of the heavenly life on earth. We have seen how the earliest medieval "peace movement," that associated with the Peace of God and Truce of God, began as an effort by the Church to extend freedom from harm to innocent persons who were being preyed upon by brigands and bullying *milites*; yet we have also seen how quickly the Church had to ally herself with the temporal powers in order to put down such private violence. The Church's efforts were thus temporalized or secularized. Among the results were the Crusades and the use of the secular sword for religious persecution, but they also included a doctrine of just war whose criterion of "right authority" vested the right to use the sword in the position of the secular ruler and whose concepts of "just cause" (punishment for a wrong deed, recovery of something wrongly taken, and repulsion of an injury in progress) were overwhelmingly tied to the need of such a ruler to keep order and do justice in his realm and to protect it against foreign invasion. At the dawn of the modern era, medieval just war theory was easily and thoroughly transformed into a concept of international law based wholly in "nature" and patterns of human behavior. The reason this was so easily possible is that in the Middle Ages the primary components of this doctrine, while still connected to transcendent ideals, goals, and notions of authorization, were already defined in the language of this-worldly experience, needs, and concerns.

The other two faces of the medieval quest for peace, as we have encountered them here, represent a far more radical secularizing of the divine peace of the heavenly city than does just war theory in the Middle Ages. On the one hand is the pacifism of separation from the evil world, which attempts to set up the city of God on earth as an alternative form of human community according to which all humankind, in principle, can live. As noted earlier, this was the monastic ideal radicalized and extended, so that the community of those already living the life of heaven while on earth was no longer composed of small enclaves but, at least in theory, might expand to include everyone touched by the gospel. It is important to recognize radical sectarianism, whose medieval expression is exemplified in this chapter by the Waldensians and the Cathars, as *the secularization of a divine ideal*, for their concepts of how to live the godly life on earth were fundamentally conditioned by their open-ended attitude toward human moral perfection and their reaction against a particular form of secular human community (including a Church that was all too obviously involved in secular affairs). The result in each of these movements—and more generally, we may observe, the result of radical religious sectarianism as a form of social organization—was to create separated perfectionist communities based on particular understandings both of divine ideals and of human moral potential. Their pacifism, then, while anchored on the one hand in religious idealism, is also absolutely dependent on the belief that rejection of violence is within human moral possibility in history, not somewhere off at the end of time in a new age of grace.

The divine ideal of peace, when secularized, also took a second form, present in the development of state-centered hopes of an ideal society, which we have explored here through Dante and Marsilius of Padua. The secularization of the divine ideal here is quite explicit, and it turns on a considerable irony. When Augustine set out to define the city of God in contrast to the city of earth, he argued from Cicero's definition of the good state as one in which everyone receives his due. Good as it may be, Rome is not the *best* state, countered Augustine against Cicero, because not *everyone* receives his due in it; God does not receive *his* due in the city of earth.[116] In Dante and Marsilius this is turned on its head: the city of God, in the form of pretensions to temporal supremacy of the Church and its clergy, is not the best human society, because the disorder that results from these unwarranted pretensions impedes justice and the other supreme value in medieval political thought,

[116] Augustine, *The City of God* II.xxi.

peace. So the best human society is the temporal one, ruled by a secular ruler, organized in such a way as to produce *civil* justice, *civil* peace and tranquillity, and *civil* order. Dante located the necessary virtue of such a society in the *populus Romanus*, that is, in the citizens of a reconstituted empire; Marsilius located it in the structures of government he described, which he thought were such as to keep human evil from threatening the destruction of the state and thus the good of all. A century later, Christine de Pisan and, a century after her, Erasmus would argue that something more was needed—a virtuous prince, who would guarantee by the exercise of his own virtue the goodness of the state over which he ruled.[117] This was a last return to the classical model of the philosopher-king, and the tradition after Erasmus would again concentrate, as with Dante and Marsilius, on the way in which the *structure* of the good society would ensure peace.

In all these cases from Dante forward, however, it is *temporal* virtue (whether of the state or of its sovereign) that secures the *temporal* values associated with the state, and which are treated as primary for this earthly life. The virtues of the state thus conceived are also (apart from the moral ideal of the good ruler) *collective* rather than individual. The peace and tranquillity of such a state depend not on the personal virtue of nonviolence in individual citizens, but in society's good ordering and just direction, which promote the welfare of the citizens without their having to resort to private violence for their own ends, and in the state's own claim to a monopoly of violence to enforce the peacefulness of its citizens and to protect them against external aggression.

The pacifism of this city of God on earth, then, is not that of a personal moral rejection of violence, as with sectarian pacifists such as the Waldensians; rather, it is a relocation of the right of the sword so that it is vested solely in the sovereign power over civil society. So stated, this corresponds to the cen-

[117] See Christine de Pisan, *The "Livre de la paix" of Christine de Pisan* (The Hague: Mouton & Co., 1958); for a discussion of Erasmus see Chapter III, below.

tralization of authority to use force also achieved in just war theory; what is interesting about the secular city of God on earth, however, is the carrying out of the implications of this ideal of human society over the long term. In the modern period, just war theory has developed into a moral theory that accepts the inevitability of evil in history, the need for force to restrain that evil, and the further need that force employed to protect and preserve values should itself not flout and destroy those same values. At the same time, though, the concept of the ideal civil society has developed as a tradition of historical progressivism in which the use of force between nations is gradually pushed out of human history, leaving ultimately, in the universal state, no place for force except as a form of police action.[118]

War, in the final implications of this idea and in the highest achievement of human social perfection, thus has no place: it disappears from human history as the ideal civil society is achieved. If, to speak empirically, war has not yet disappeared, then there must be a reason, and the history of the modern development of the secular utopian ideal of the state is also one of the development of theories explaining why this ideal has not been realized. For Dante and Marsilius, the cause of discord and lack of peace in the state lay in the pretensions of the Church; for Christine de Pisan, who lauded the peace to be achieved by a virtuous ruler, war was the result of "cruelty";[119] for Erasmus (and for many later humanists) it was self-seeking under the guise of an ostensibly just claim;[120] for twentieth-century internationalism, it is the "state system" itself, a "war system" that must give way to a new world order if peace is to be achieved.[121] Opposition to violence in all these cases thus

[118] See further below, Chapters IV and V.

[119] Christine de Pisan, *The "Livre de la paix."*

[120] This is a frequent theme for Erasmus. See, for example, Desiderius Erasmus, letter to Antoon van Bergen, Abbot of St. Bertin (London, March 14, 1514), no. 288 in *The Correspondence of Erasmus, Letters 142 to 297* (Toronto and Buffalo, N.Y.: University of Toronto Press, 1975).

[121] Again, this is a common theme of the modern "world order" movement;

becomes tied to a particular vision of what would constitute ideal human society and the conviction that humankind is capable of achieving such a social order.

We return, then, to the ideal society of the radical religious sectarians and the pacifism to be found there. The contrast between the two perspectives could hardly be sharper: in the one, violence is rejected (along with much else that has to do with life in civil society) so that individuals may join the new community where violence is not practiced; in the other, the state forms itself as a collective and employs violence both internally and externally until its ultimate form is reached, when the need for armed coercion disappears and violence itself withers away. Along the way to this goal, individual violence is prohibited; but this is imposed, ironically, by the threat of violence from the state. Both sectarianism and medieval proto-utopianism exemplify the secularization of the ideal peace of the heavenly city of God, though in very different ways. Both sought after peace on earth and therefore, in the broad sense, were pacifist phenomena; yet, in them we discover two fundamentally different varieties of pacifism, both of which have helped to condition modern moral consciousness.

see, for example, Richard A. Falk, *A Study of Future Worlds* (New York: The Free Press, 1975), especially chapter 3.

CHAPTER III

THE POLITICAL USE OF FORCE IN THE RENAISSANCE-REFORMATION ERA

A. The Military and Political Context

In 1494, the year that Columbus returned from his second voyage of discovery to the New World, Charles VIII, king of France, invaded Italy with an army that included numerous trains of horse-drawn artillery. These cannon were mostly bronze, about eight feet in length, and by later standards were cumbersome; yet they revolutionized warfare in two ways: by being easily transportable (bronze cannon were stronger for their weight than cast iron and could be made light enough to be carried overland on a field carriage) and by being employed against armies in the field, not just as siege weapons.[1] A third revolution in warfare was already well under way by this time: armies that once relied principally on heavy cavalry made up of armored knights and men-at-arms now began to rely increasingly on foot soldiers drawn from the common class of men. These revolutionary changes (as well as others, including the new metallurgical processes that made militarily effective cannon possible) reinforced each other and brought rapid change to the practice of war in the early Renaissance era. Antoine Perrenot de Granvelle, bishop of Arras, who among other accomplishments as a statesman served for a time as Spain's regent in the Netherlands, in 1559 put the matter succinctly: "[T]he art of war is now such that men be fain to learn [it] anew at every two years' end."[2]

[1] John Ulrich Nef, *War and Human Progress* (New York: Russell & Russell, 1950), pp. 24-25.

[2] Quoted by Nef; ibid., p. 30.

The rapidly moving revolution in warfare thus flowed from changes of three sorts: in the manpower composition of armies, in the technology applied to the production of weapons, and in new tactics and strategies designed to make the most of the first two. Together they transformed the nature of war decisively from its late medieval model. Let us look briefly at each of these in turn.

The popular image of medieval warfare is that of knights in shining armor riding against one another with lances leveled, a concept of warfare that makes of it little more than a tournament. In fact, in the fourteenth and fifteenth centuries, the combat of knights in tournament and in actual warfare had somewhat converged; yet the charge of heavily armored knights on horseback and the splintering of their lances against one another was never the total reality of medieval warfare. In the first place, knights were not the only ones involved in such war: they were accompanied by squires (aspiring knights) and men-at-arms, also mounted but less heavily and richly armored, and by foot soldiers of various sorts (mainly bowmen and pikemen), as well as by siege trains on some occasions. It was in the nature of things for knights to be outnumbered by non-knights; and, in the case of the great battles, those who fought on horseback were often outnumbered by those who fought on foot. Often forgot in recalling the effectiveness of the Welsh longbowmen in the English armies at Crécy and Agincourt is the fact that they outnumbered the English knights decisively. In terms of raw numbers, the English armies at these two critical battles were forces of longbowmen, not of knights.[3] The knights, to be sure, looked down on the commoners who fought with them and against them; while defeated knights were given quarter and held for ransom, beaten commoners, worthless for ransom and not part of the chivalric brotherhood, were often massacred.[4] This does not, however, alter the basic fact that even in the Middle Ages military forces

[3] See further Delbrück, *History*, vol. III, pp. 453-70; Keegan, *The Face of Battle*. On archers generally see Delbrück, *History*, vol. III, pp. 385-98, 411, 424, 434, 458, 524.

[4] Oman, *A History of the Art of War*, vol. I, pp. 357-58.

depended more heavily than is generally admitted on common soldiers.

Sociological and technical changes that took place at the end of the medieval period and early in the modern era shifted the weight ever more decisively toward armies of common men. The knightly class, which had begun as warriors, evolved toward being a caste occupied in the management of wealth, government, and the church. Toward the end of the Middle Ages, those knights who did military service were already functioning somewhat like officers in modern armies, with their own bands of armed retainers, some on horse, others on foot. As the number of knights available for military service shrank, the numbers of non-knightly retainers tended to increase. When guns began to appear on the battlefield, and especially with the increased use of individual weapons such as the harquebus in the fifteenth and sixteenth centuries, these latter numbers rose accordingly; for only the rare knight would lower himself to fighting on foot with a cowardly handgun. The effects were not realized evenly, all across Europe and at the same time: English armies, always relatively deficient in knights, shifted toward commoners as early as the Hundred Years' War; French armies, always in the Middle Ages including knights to the point of superfluity, were later in realizing this transformation; Italian armies, even into the sixteenth century, still depended heavily on the mercenary forces of *condottieri*, who fought like knights even if not all of them were noble. My own choice as the first modern army of common men is that of the Spanish general the Duke of Parma, in the Netherlands during the sixteenth century, when the sort of Spanish nobleman who a century earlier might have gone to war was instead seeking his fortune in the New World, and when the availability of handguns was making new formations of infantry an effective military force.[5]

Early gunpowder weapons appear to have had more effect

[5] On the armies of common men, their impact on the nature of warfare, and the problems of restraint they posed, see further Johnson, *Just War Tradition*, pp. 179-87.

from the terror of their noise, flash of fire, and smoke than of any physical damage they did. John Ulrich Nef observes that, even though cannon began to be employed as siege weapons in the Middle Ages, the classical siege engines based on levers, balances, capstans, inclined planes, and so on were more effective than these early cannon.[6] (This did not prevent the latter from being used, however.) Even the bronze field cannon of Charles VIII, in their first battle (Fornovo, 1495), killed only ten men.[7] Subsequent technological development of such weapons included improvements to the accuracy of field artillery and to their means of aiming; it also brought the first harquebuses and muskets fired from the shoulder as well as a great expansion in the availability of all sorts of gunpowder weapons in the sixteenth century. Nef notes that at the Battle of Marignano, twenty years after Fornovo, "the French cannon actually killed and wounded a substantial proportion of the enemies' best soldiers."[8] As for hand-held guns,

> it was the general use of firearms by foot soldiers—particularly the use of the musket, introduced by the Spaniards in 1521 with telling effect in their Italian campaigns against the French, and widely adopted late in the sixteenth century by the French themselves—which made infantry the decisive striking arm in war.[9]

Both the new cannon and the new hand-fired guns required new classes of soldiers to serve them. The latter weapons produced a form of infantry and a style of fighting that lasted into the nineteenth century; the former brought technical experts—"mechanics," as they were called—into Renaissance armies. Behind the scenes, the new technology of warfare claimed more from the civilian sector, both in terms of the manpower that now had to be spent, mining metals and fashioning guns and ammunition, and in terms of the employment of civilian

[6] Nef, *War and Human Progress*, p. 28.
[7] Ibid., p. 24.
[8] Ibid., p. 25.
[9] Ibid., p. 34.

intellectuals such as Leonardo da Vinci in Italy and John Napier in England in the design of weapons and fortifications.[10]

Finally, military tactics and strategy changed significantly in the first century of the Renaissance era. War became more deadly. One reason was, perhaps, that common soldiers were not so valuable in the eyes of their generals as the knights of an earlier age had been; as a reciprocal of this, the new deadliness of war was a good reason for a young man of the knightly class to employ himself in something other than military service. Another reason was that the stakes were somewhat higher. Two of the most important battle theaters of the sixteenth century were the Netherlands and Italy, both centers of commerce and industry, and therefore foci of new kinds and quantities of wealth. Both these factors tended to make armies larger; the new military technology made them more destructive. Tactics had to change in order to make effective use of the larger armies of common men who fought on foot with guns; strategies had to change in order to take account of the greater stakes for which war was being fought.

An older style, which had developed out of the military realities of the late Middle Ages, was found in the warfare of the *condottieri* in Italy. *Condottieri* were mercenary captains; usually of the knightly class themselves, they employed fighting men of all backgrounds in the military units they created (whose services they sold to anyone who could pay the price), and they commanded those men in combat. Most of the warfare among the Italian city-states in the late fifteenth and early sixteenth centuries was among *condottieri* and their companies. It was in the interest of these men not to be killed for the glory or the mercantile interests of their employers, but to avoid being killed or wounded in combat—and yet to win, or at least to avoid being beaten by the enemy. Thus, war became a chesslike game of maneuver and position, with little actual fighting between opposing forces. An outmaneuvered captain knew enough about how the game was played to surrender

[10] On the war applications of all these developments in technology, see further ibid., chapters 2 and 3.

without having to resort to the arbitrament of arms; he and his men would live to be employed in a later war.

Against such a backdrop, the terrorizing effect of even unwieldy and inaccurate cannon amounts to something; yet the presence of an artillery train in an army like that of the French in Italy under Charles VIII necessarily committed it to a tactical style more plodding and static than that of the highly mobile *condottieri*. We have a new tactical style, one which in combat was highly effective. The only rational response the opponents of the French could make was to mimic this style, together with the force composition that made it effective, and then to seek to outdo it with innovations of their own. This led to the rapid changes in the art of war of which Bishop Granvelle spoke. It also meant, though, that by the latter part of the sixteenth century the armies in Italy—the French and their allies against the Spanish and theirs—were increasingly like each other and fought like each other, maneuvering ponderously and inflicting heavy casualties when they came to battle. What was true of warfare there was also true elsewhere in Europe.

A related matter is what happened to the art of the siege. In the Middle Ages much of warfare had been siege warfare, with pitched battles in the field (contrary to the popular image) few and infrequent. As fortifications grew more impregnable, the emphasis shifted, until in *condottieri* warfare sieges were rare and maneuver was king. Maneuver in turn disappeared with the coming of field artillery and of infantry armed with guns. For a time, though, the new effectiveness of cannon gave an edge to the offense in siegecraft, even as the ponderousness of an army with a large artillery train made sieges a more attractive form of war. But this state of affairs did not last long, for among the employments of intellectuals in the service of military ends during the sixteenth century was their design of new types of fortifications. From Leonardo to that great designer of fortifications the Marquis de Vauban (1633-1707), fortification became an art and then a science combined with art, more than keeping pace with the developments in offensive siege weapons. This meant, in general, that sieges were unprofitable unless the besieging force already enjoyed battlefield superiority. Thus battles, not sieges (and not maneuvers short of battle), became the focus of the art of war; and tactics aimed at bringing the opponent to actual battle and then beating him there became the order of the age. It is in battles, not sieges or maneuvers, that most men are killed and wounded; so this development in the technology and tactics of war meant that the number of casualties among soldiers would increase dramatically.

Finally, the late medieval–early Renaissance period was a time when the restraints on war that had evolved were less able to limit the new warfare and its greater destructiveness. Partly this was because of the effects of changes in war itself, but partly it was a result of the way people in this period were thinking about politics, law, and morality. This was the era in which, from Victoria in the sixteenth century to Grotius in the early seventeenth, just war tradition was moving from a base largely in theology to one entirely in natural law and from what was chiefly a moral consensus to a foundation of international law.[11] It was also a time when the internalized code of chivalric conduct of the knightly class had to be transformed into a somewhat rudimentary and externally imposed military discipline by which the new armies of common men could be guided and held in check; this took time to accomplish, and in the interim armies tended to fight with less restraint than either earlier or later.[12]

Taken together, these various changes made for a form of warfare that was at once more costly in both military and civilian resources, more destructive of lives and property, and more difficult to restrain. At the same time, the nature of European politics in this period tended to make for frequent wars—a continual state of war in some areas.

The political face of Europe at the birth of the Renaissance was, broadly speaking, that of a small number of politically stable and relatively powerful core states bounded by rela-

[11] Johnson, *Ideology*, chapters III, IV; *Just War Tradition*, chapters IV, VI.

[12] Johnson, *Just War Tradition*, pp. 179-87; Nef, *War and Human Progress*, pp. 136-39 On the problem of restraint see further Johnson, *Just War Tradition*, pp. 172-74.

tively weaker, though often valuable, areas of political instability. The major core areas were France, Spain, the Holy Roman Empire (to be counted with Spain during the reigns of Charles V and Philip II), and the Ottoman Empire. Less powerful centers of political stability were England and Sweden. The principal areas fought over were Italy, where France and Spain vied for control over the city-states; the Netherlands, where Spain fought against independence-seeking indigenous forces assisted by allies including France and England; and Eastern Europe, where the Holy Roman Empire and the Ottoman Empire were locked in a perpetual struggle. The shape of the political landscape dictated the nature of the military conflicts, which were over strategically valuable buffer zones that, in the case of the Netherlands and Italy, were also centers of great commercial enterprise and wealth. Warfare was thus more or less continuous among the major political players, with the less powerful ones becoming involved or dropping out of involvement as interest or will dictated.

Against this backdrop, though later than the efforts toward peace discussed further on in this chapter, came the religious wars of the Reformation era, raging in various parts of Europe from the latter part of the sixteenth century (the French Wars of Religion and the religious phase of the Dutch War for Independence) through the Thirty Years' War to the English Civil War. What differed with these wars was that they were largely or entirely internal to the political entities affected: they were civil wars; but far from being "civil" in execution, they were at times orgies of fratricidal destruction. "Who will beleeve that your cause is just," a fictional peasant queries of a soldier in a French account from the era of the Wars of Religion, "when your behaviours are so unjust?"[13]

I have elsewhere written at some length about war for the sake of religion and the peculiar problems such conflict poses for efforts to impose limits on its destructiveness;[14] the moral

[13] François, Sieur de la Noue, *The Politicke and Militarie Discourses of the Lord de la Noue* (London: T. C. and E. A. by Thomas Orwin, 1587), p. 225.

[14] Johnson, *Ideology*, chapter II.

developments to be discussed in this chapter all come before large-scale religious warfare appeared on the historical scene. In the next chapter we shall consider those efforts in the quest for peace which followed the age of religious war. So, for now, we are concerned with the quest for peace as it took shape in the early sixteenth century, when the transformation in the nature of war described above had begun to appear, but before war's destructiveness became further inflamed by religious ideology. All three of the traditions identified earlier can be found here: just war tradition as a broadly consensual cultural position, which by the end of the Middle Ages included both a *jus ad bellum* and a *jus in bello*; the humanistic utopianism of a superior international order in which the causes of war would disappear; and a sectarian pacifism of withdrawal from the world and its conflicts.

B. The Just War Inheritance

The climax of medieval just war thought was reached, not in the canonists and theologians of the twelfth and thirteenth centuries, nor in their contemporaries who worked at understanding and updating the secular *jus gentium*, but in the quasi-chivalric writings of people like Honoré Bonet in the late fourteenth century and Christine de Pisan early in the fifteenth.[15] Bonet is the more important example. A monk of the knightly class who lived and wrote during the Hundred Years' War, he expressed the synthesis reached by European Christendom in this period—a synthesis that united the theory of Church and secular lawyers and the theory of the theologians with the norms of knightly conduct contained in the chivalric code and the practice of warfare according to that code.[16] The synthesis he expressed, reflecting a broad cultural consensus across Christendom, remained intact into the modern era as an

[15] See Bonet, *The Tree of Battles*, see also Christine de Pisan, *The Book of Fayttes of Armes and of Chyvalrie*, trans. of *Les Faits d'armes et de chivalrie* by William Caxton, ed. A.T.P. Byles (London: Oxford University Press, 1932).

[16] See further Johnson, *Ideology*, pp. 64-80; *Just War Tradition*, pp. 131-50.

ideology for understanding the justification of war as well as its proper limits. This cultural understanding forms the intellectual context out of which—or against which—the theorists treated in this chapter thought and wrote.

It is an interesting historical fact that the major theorists of just war tradition in the Renaissance-Reformation era all come from the mid-sixteenth century through the first half of the seventeenth. This period begins with the Spanish Neo-Scholastics Victoria, Soto, and Molina and ends with the Puritan divine William Ames; in between, we find the Jesuit theologian Suárez, the legal theorist Alberico Gentili, and Hugo Grotius, both theologian and theorist of the law of war, as well as many lesser figures. All these efforts at consolidation within the just war tradition come after the strong pacifist currents set in motion by Erasmus and the radical Protestant sectarians discussed below. Earlier in the sixteenth century, the just war concept had simply been taken for granted; only after it is challenged—by pacifism on the one hand and by changes in the nature of war on the other—does a conscious theoretical effort emerge, aimed at restating the terms of this tradition for the conditions of the early-modern era.[17]

Having already devoted most of an earlier book to these figures from the late sixteenth and early seventeenth centuries,[18] I want here to concentrate instead on two men who employed just war reasoning early in the age of the Reformation: the Reformers Martin Luther and Ulrich Zwingli. James Stayer, writing of the Anabaptist doctrine on worldly power, argues that these two figures, together with the radical Thomas Müntzer, shaped a common set of attitudes in a "Reformation public" from which the Anabaptists drew and against which they reacted.[19] Zwingli also stands in an interesting relation to the pacifism of Erasmus. None of these Reformation figures is par-

[17] There is an almost Hegelian pattern in this. In any case, the moral traditions of the quest for peace have regularly influenced one another through history, and changes in the nature of war have also influenced all three traditions in each age.

[18] Johnson, *Ideology*, pp. 81-232.

[19] Stayer, *Anabaptists*, p. 27.

ticularly innovative or systematic in his thought on morality and war; indeed, precisely in this lack lies their testimony to the pervasiveness of the just war consensus as a way of thinking about war and peace in the early sixteenth century.

1. Martin Luther

The parameters of Luther's thought on war are set by four treatises: *Temporal Authority: To What Extent It Should Be Obeyed* (1523),[20] *Against the Robbing and Murdering Hordes of Peasants* (1525),[21] *Whether Soldiers, Too, Can Be Saved* (1526),[22] and *On War against the Turk* (1529).[23] Of these the most fundamental is the first, which establishes the general framework of Luther's political theory around the concept of the two "kingdoms" (that of God and that of the world) with their respective "governments" (the spiritual and the secular).

The distinction between the spiritual and the secular was passed on to Luther and his contemporaries from the common intellectual heritage of the Middle Ages. Luther, however, developed his own understanding of this distinction. More specifically, in *Temporal Authority* he defined an alternative understanding of these two realms, in opposition to the claim of the papalists of the late medieval period and his own time that the spiritual authority occupied a place superior to that of the secular. For Luther these two authorities occupied separate realms: neither had authority over the other outside its own realm, and within the other's realm each was subordinate to the other. In the worldly "kingdom," then, rightful authority belongs to the secular powers, extending even to the regulation of religion. Similarly, in the kingdom of God spiritual authority holds sway; yet this does not extend to any authority in worldly government. Each Christian, for Luther, is a citizen of

[20] Martin Luther, *Luther's Works*, 54 vols., ed. Jaroslav Pelikan and Helmut T. Lehmann (St. Louis: Concordia Publishing House; Philadelphia: Muhlenberg Press and Fortress Press, 1955-1976), vol. 45, pp. 123-29.

[21] Ibid., vol. 46, pp. 49-55.

[22] Ibid., pp. 93-137.

[23] Ibid., pp. 161-205.

both realms but has different responsibilities in each. The dialectic tension that Luther's concept sets up is intensified by his seeing in the world a disorderly, sinful state of being in which the responsibility of secular government is to "use force and punish those who are evil in order to protect the righteous."[24] This duty of the worldly authorities gives them the power of the "sword," in the term of Luther's day; yet there is no such power corresponding to it in the godly kingdom, for in this ideal realm evil does not, by the nature of things, exist. Nor, for the reasons already given, do the spiritual authorities have any say over the use of the worldly "sword."

This position of Luther's contrasts sharply with that framed by the medieval papalists around the doctrine of "two swords," one religious and one secular. This "two swords" theory was based on an allegorical reading of Luke 22:38: "And they said, Lord, here are two swords. And he said unto them, It is enough." This theory justified the use of military coercion by the Church, with implications for the persecution of dissenters and heretics, for the launching of crusades, and (not least) for the exertion of papal power over recalcitrant secular rulers. The Reformation generally, and both Luther and Zwingli in particular, rejected this "two swords" theory and its implications in favor of a doctrine of a single coercive power or "sword," that of the state.

This solved only part of the problem, however: what remained unresolved was whether the state could, on behalf of its understanding of true religion, use its coercive power to enforce belief. This question required a century of religious warfare to settle finally, in the negative. Thus the "two swords" idea was not laid completely to rest along with the argument that only the civil "sword" is legitimate. So long as religion and the state were closely interlinked (as they were in Philip of Hesse's Lutheran *regnum*, Zwingli's Zurich, Calvin's Geneva, Bucer's Strasbourg, England under both the Catholic Mary and the Protestant Elizabeth, and in all Catholic states

[24] Paul Althaus, *The Ethics of Martin Luther* (Philadelphia: Fortress Press, 1972), pp. 55-56.

throughout the Reformation period) the underlying issue remained substantially unchanged. Despite scholarly attempts to deny the use of the sword to enforce religious uniformity,[25] and despite the Reformers' denial of a legitimate use of the sword by Church officials for religious coercion, the state continued to enforce religious uniformity, uphold the prerogatives of the Church in its jurisdiction, and wage wars on behalf of religion (as justified by the ecclesiastical authorities in each secular jurisdiction).

This meant that one of the problems faced by religiously motivated pacifists in the Reformation era was to attempt to achieve the full implications of the doctrine of "one sword"—the civil—as declared by the magisterial Reformers on the basis of the classic just war text, Romans 13:4 ("For [the secular ruler] is God's servant for your good. But if you do wrong, be afraid, for he does not bear the sword in vain; he is the servant of God to execute his wrath on the wrongdoer"). As we shall see, the effort to do this is especially characteristic of Anabaptist pacifism, leading it ultimately to rejection of the authority of the state as well as of the established Church.

For Luther's own position on war, though, the single-sword doctrine is significant in a different way: it marks Luther's acceptance of the main line of just war thinking, according to which the secular government possesses "right authority" to employ military force according to the terms of the above passage from Romans. War proper is the extension of the state's authority to preserve domestic right into the international sphere. Government has the dual obligation to ensure justice for its citizens and to ensure their protection against injustice and violence imposed by others. At times it cannot fulfill this obligation without resort to military force. Hence Luther comments, in *On War against the Turk*, that "it is . . . a work of Christian love to protect and defend a whole community with the sword and not let the people be abused."[26] The obligation

[25] Cf. Desiderius Erasmus, letter to Paul Volz, in John C. Olin, ed., *Desiderius Erasmus: Christian Humanism and the Reformation, Selected Writings* (New York, Evanston, and London: Harper & Row, 1965), chapter V.

[26] Luther, *Works*, vol. 46, p. 121.

to provide such protection thus serves as the fundamental basis of the definition of "just cause," as in the just war tradition inherited by Luther.

In *Whether Soldiers, Too, Can Be Saved* Luther connects this explicitly to the cause of peace, again following the main line of the inherited just war tradition: "What else is war," he asks rhetorically, "but the punishment of wrong and evil? Why does anyone go to war except because he desires peace and obedience?"[27] Not only, then, should the Christian not avoid military service; it becomes a duty for him, as a way of ensuring peace, order, and justice in the kingdom of this world: "For the sword and authority, as a particular service of God, belong more appropriately to Christians than to any other men on earth."[28] Only they, in a world in which the majority of people are lost to Satan, have the understanding necessary to know and enforce righteousness. It is difficult to imagine a position more diametrically opposed to the sectarian-pacifist position we shall examine below.

Early in his career, in 1521, Luther had himself been accused of pacifism by the Dominicans of the University of Paris because of some comments he had made about war against the Turks. Luther had suggested that the Turks represented a scourge through which God was punishing Christendom.[29] Eight years later he continued to insist that war against the Turks should not be a crusade on behalf of Christian faith; such war was justified, nonetheless, out of simple self-defense. Fighting against the Turks should be done "simply," argued Luther, and "with fear and humility."[30] This is hardly a pacifist position, but rather one that accords with just war reasoning and those justifications of the Crusades that accord with such reasoning.[31]

[27] Ibid., p. 95.

[28] Quoted by Althaus, *The Ethics of Martin Luther*, p. 71, n. 135.

[29] See Walter F. Bense, "Paris Theologians on War and Peace, 1521-1529," *Church History*, vol. 41, no. 2 (June 1972), p. 170.

[30] See Althaus, *The Ethics of Martin Luther*, pp. 141-42.

[31] See further LeRoy Walters, "The Just War and the Crusade: Antitheses or Analogies?" *The Monist*, vol. 57, no. 4 (October 1973), pp. 584-94.

Finally, in a work some commentators regard as the low point in his career, *Against the Robbing and Murdering Hordes of Peasants*, Luther made essentially the same arguments we have identified above. It is the prince's duty to intervene against plundering mobs of peasants, Luther argued, in order to keep order, guard against injustice, and re-establish the peace. The rulers may not succeed; that is in God's hands. Yet their duty is clear, both from the nature of their office and from Scripture.[32] This treatise of Luther's was thus in a direct line of descent from the reasoning of the medieval Peace of God movement: the higher authorities should establish peace by using their military power to impose order. In this view (as with Dante and Marsilius in the fourteenth century) order comes first: only with order can justice be ascertained and established, and only then can peace be achieved. Just as the Peace of God bequeathed this idea to both just war tradition and the late-medieval theorists of a new political order, so Luther now drew on the heritage of this tradition to argue that the peasants' rebellion was a manifestation not of good, but of the evil that the secular authorities out of obligation ought to suppress.

2. *Ulrich Zwingli*

Though Zwingli was a contemporary of Luther, his position on worldly government and its relation to the Church anticipated that of Calvin and his successors instead of mirroring Luther's. Where Luther thought in terms of the preservation of order in a sinful world until Christ should come, Zwingli thought in terms of the creation of the best possible society. Where Luther counseled Christians to bear patiently the sufferings imposed by the world, Zwingli envisioned positive Christian involvement in worldly government to help it achieve as close as possible a conformity to the laws of the kingdom of Christ.[33] This significant difference over the nature

[32] See further Althaus, *The Ethics of Martin Luther*, pp. 140-41.

[33] See further Stayer, *Anabaptists*, pp. 49-51.

of government and the role of Christian faith in the world made for a difference also in Zwingli's concept of how the authority of the worldly government should be exercised through the sword.

Zwingli's position on these matters was, in fact, more directly influenced by humanist thought, particularly that of Erasmus, than was Luther's. As we shall see more fully below, Erasmus conceived of the ideal state not only in internationalist terms, as one expressing the unity of Christendom (a point Zwingli did not carry over into his own thought), but as one in which the ruler would govern according to Christian virtue. This was Erasmus's emphasis in *The Education of a Christian Prince*.[34] In Zwingli's hands, this idea was applied directly to the government of his own city, Zurich; and, in place of the humanist scholar offering instruction to a young prince, he had Reformed Church authorities offering their own advice to the secular magistrates of the city, including counsel on the use of the civil military authority.

This is, however, to get ahead of the story. Zwingli went through three main stages in his attitude toward the sword. First was his opposition to mercenary warfare, expressed in his earliest preserved work, *The Fable of the Ox*, written in 1510.[35] This was principally an ardent expression of Swiss patriotism. Swiss soldiers had long been hiring themselves out as mercenaries to the two main powers on either side of them, France and the Holy Roman Empire, and to the pope. Zwingli was especially opposed to the first two in his early years: these powers were an immediate threat to Swiss integrity, while the papacy was not. In Zwingli's view it would be better if Swiss soldiers stayed at home to defend Swiss nationhood instead of wasting themselves for money in the service of foreign powers.

A few years later, between 1514 and 1517, Zwingli fell

[34] Desiderius Erasmus, *The Education of a Christian Prince*, in Lester K. Born, *The Education of a Christian Prince by Desiderius Erasmus* (New York: Octagon Books, 1965).

[35] Ulrich Zwingli, *Huldreich Zwinglis Sämtliche Werke*, 13 vols., ed. E. Egli and G. Finsler (Berlin: C. A. Schwetschke und Sohn, 1904-1968), vol. I, pp. 1-22; cf. Stayer, *Anabaptists*, p. 51.

much under the influence of Erasmus's thought. This was the period when Erasmus was writing against war and in favor of universalistic political reform to bring peace. Zwingli, impressed by Erasmus's arguments as well as by his personal experience of war, became a pacifist.[36] In 1519 he addressed the following counsel to a friend, the schoolmaster in his home town:

> [S]eek out the pastors in your region and instruct them that they should be friends of peace and preach without ceasing about peace, harmony, and staying at home [from mercenary expeditions]. The blood merchants and wastrels cannot lead anyone away to the princes in a nation inclined to pleasant harmony.[37]

By 1519, then, Zwingli had brought together his nationalist opposition to mercenary service and his new, Erasmian humanist opposition to war. By this time he was a pastor in Zurich, and he joined his influence to that of others in supporting a 1521 decision of the city magistrates not to enter into an agreement with Francis I of France to supply mercenaries to him, and a further decision in 1522 not to supply mercenaries to any foreign prince or lord.[38]

The problem of mercenary service, though, as noted earlier, was not simply one that flowed from pacifist opposition to war; it was also implied by concern for Swiss independence. A profound Swiss patriotism was never far from the surface in Zwingli's thought on war. It was one thing to sell the military service of young Swiss manhood to foreigners; yet, by 1523, Zwingli was accepting that it was something else again for these same soldiers to bear arms in defense of the Swiss Confederation against Hapsburg power. This was not pacifism, that is, opposition to war; it was acceptance of the use of military force in self-defense along with opposition to mercenary service, two elements found in traditional just war thinking.

[36] See further Stayer, *Anabaptists*, pp. 52-56.

[37] Zwingli, *Sämtliche Werke*, vol. VII, p. 233.

[38] Stayer, *Anabaptists*, pp. 55-56.

Zwingli's own change of heart was also related to increased influence from Paul's writings in the New Testament; thus, that classic text justifying civil military power, Romans 13:4, moved closer to the center of his theological consciousness.

At this point we enter the arena in which Zwingli discussed the secular state and its relation to the realm of Christian faith. Zwingli, like Calvin later in his distinction between the "visible" and the "invisible" Church, distinguished between the "external" kingdom of God and the "internal" one. The laws of the former are, for Zwingli, the same as those given in the law of nature. Thus the secular authorities, who have an obligation to use coercion as necessary to enforce the laws of the state and natural law, are in the same measure helping to establish conformity with the requirements of the external kingdom of God. The secular ruler must keep the law of Christ before him, because it provides a yardstick by which to measure human justice: "all [the secular ruler's] laws are similar to the will of God, not exactly similar, but having something of the image of the divine law and will."[39] The authority of the state to employ coercion by the sword, though, extends only to the maintenance of the law of nature, the laws of the external kingdom of Christ; this authority stops well short of the coercion of belief, which has to do with the *internal* kingdom. There the state may not reach.

In Zwingli's thought, thus, we have several elements of the inherited just war tradition, along with the development of a "single sword" doctrine limiting the authority to use force to the civil powers. That authority, for Zwingli, is proved by Romans 13:4, a text used by just war theorists at least since the thirteenth century to establish the limits of "right authority" to make war. In the brief look we have taken at Zwingli, we have encountered two concepts of just cause, both central to the inherited just war tradition: self-defense (the defense of the Swiss homeland against foreign powers) and punishment of evil (the enforcement of the laws of the state and natural law). His acceptance of self-defense by military means was, moreover, as a

[39] Zwingli, *Sämtliche Werke*, vol. II, p. 478.

last resort—another just war concept. Finally, at least from his Erasmian period forward, the establishment of domestic peace was never far from Zwingli's mind, and his ultimate acceptance of war as the only remaining way to peace also manifests just war thinking.

3. *Similarities, Differences, and Implications*

It is an interesting phenomenon that the influence of just war thought in both Zwingli and Luther appears principally in *jus ad bellum* terms; that is, in terms of the authority to use force and the justifying reasons for such use. Neither of them has any *jus in bello* to speak of. Nor did Erasmus, and herein, I think, lies a clue to explaining why the Reformers did not develop this side of the inherited tradition. All these figures lived and wrote precisely at that time when the changes in the face of war described in the first section of this chapter were becoming manifest and when the inherited restraints on war's cruelty and destructiveness were losing their grip. This condition endured for more than a century, as noted, and the practice of war continued to deteriorate until the climax of cruelty and destructiveness was reached in the Thirty Years' War. Things were, though, presumably already bad enough in the second and third decades of the sixteenth century. We shall see how Erasmus characterized the practice of war in his time as so evil that it should be avoided by virtually any means; correspondingly, and contrary to late-medieval moral tradition and military practice, both Luther and Zwingli seem to have taken for granted that war has no limits. Luther thus counseled the princes of Germany to put down the peasant rebellions with bloody ruthlessness; and Zwingli, preaching on the evils of mercenary service in 1523, depicted war as plundering, burning, rape, and murder.[40] Given such a concept of the factual nature of war, it is perhaps the more remarkable that Luther and Zwingli held to the fundamentals of just war tradition on the rightness of employing the sword on behalf of order, jus-

[40] Ibid., vol. I, pp. 175-76.

tice, and peace. Erasmus, however, was persuaded differently, as we shall see.

Somewhat ironically, the Reformers' reasoning pointed toward a close alliance between church and state in Protestant lands, so that in practice the Protestant religious authorities could cause or influence the use of force by the political authorities. This was explicitly so in Zwingli's thought (and in that of the later Reformed tradition), and Luther did not succeed in completely erasing this possibility from his thinking. Whatever the theory, then, the results in fact mirrored the situation in Catholic areas. To persons of religious persuasions heterodox to both Catholics and Protestants, the use of state power to enforce religious belief (however much the Protestant authorities might insist it was not *belief* that was being coerced) might well seem satanic; this was the reaction that led many Anabaptists toward secession from the state and denial of all legitimacy for use of the sword, and we shall encounter it in the Swiss Brethren below.

To humanists envisioning a peaceful commonalty among states on the basis of shared belief, history and culture, the church-state alliance on both sides of the post-Reformation religious divide was enough to spell an end to their utopian dreams. Yet it was their theme, modified in accord with circumstances, that at the end of the religious wars was picked up again by Grotius and other theorists who sought to shape a new kind of international law without religious or ideological bias,[41] and by the new theorists of the "perpetual peace" movement in the following centuries.[42] But whereas the concern of the humanists of the sixteenth century was to limit recourse to war (since they saw war, once begun, as necessarily involving all kinds of inhumane and criminal acts), the focus of the humanistic theorists of international law during the following centuries was on defining restraints to the practice of war (since they thought rulers had a fundamental right to initiate war. That it was not possible to think in this latter way in

[41] See further Johnson, *Ideology*, pp. 208-56.

[42] See Chapter IV below.

the sixteenth-century context suggests a great deal about why such strong expressions of antiwar sentiment emerged then.

C. Humanistic Pacifism: Erasmus's Argument against War

The writings of Erasmus on which we shall focus here all date from a brief period in his life, 1514 to 1517.[43] His earliest writing specifically on war is the letter of March 14, 1514, to Antoon van Bergen, abbot of St. Bertin; the following year, an expanded essay on themes raised in this letter appeared in the form of a commentary on Pindar's adage, "Sweet is war to them that know it not" (*Dulce bellum inexpertis*). This essay was published separately as a pamphlet the same year and, in all, saw fourteen printings in various languages over the next few years. In 1516 Erasmus wrote his *Institutio Principis Christiani* [*The Education of a Christian Prince*], two chapters of which specifically dealt with peace and one with war. The fourth major contribution to this subject came the following

[43] For other related writings see Born, *Christian Prince*, pp. 1-26. In the extant literature on Erasmus his pacifism is most often discussed as a topic within a larger subject. For example, Olin includes in his edited volume (note 25, above) two letters bearing on war and peace from among the nine he advances as showing the connection between Erasmus (as a representative of Christian humanism) and the Reformation; yet, that these letters treat of pacifism is only incidental, as they are chiefly about other matters. The letter to Van Bergen, which is entirely on war, apparently did not meet the test of relevance for Olin's purposes. Similarly, in his introductory essay, "Erasmus and Reform," Olin gives less than a paragraph to Erasmus's opposition to war (p. 15). Erasmus's commentary on the adage *Dulce bellum inexpertis* is generally recognized as one of the most important of the large volume of such commentaries produced by Erasmus (cf. Margaret Mann Phillips, *The "Adages" of Erasmus: A Study with Translations* [Cambridge: Cambridge University Press, 1964]); yet this is only its due, since this particular commentary was published separately in numerous languages shortly after it first appeared, and it continued to be republished in succeeding centuries. Pulling together the different kinds of materials that express Erasmus's pacifist views has been left to the works on his political thought; and, of these, Born's on *The Education of a Christian Prince* remains, to my mind, the most useful introduction to Erasmus on peace and war.

year, 1517, when the *Querela Pacis* [*Complaint of Peace*] was published.[44] During these years Erasmus also wrote much on other matters, and the use of force was but one theme among many even in his political writings. As befitting one who saw himself as a citizen of Christendom, he began this period living in London under the patronage of Lord Mountjoy, the Archbishop of Canterbury, and Henry VIII, ending it under the patronage of Prince Charles (later Emperor Charles V), for whom the *Institutio* was written, and Philip, bishop of Utrecht, to whom the *Querela Pacis* was dedicated. During this period, England was at war with France and the latter's Hapsburg allies; so Erasmus had a personal stake on both sides in the struggle. (One of his complaints in the letter to Antoon van Bergen is that preparations for war were drying up the patronage on which he depended for a living.)[45] But Erasmus's concerns were also more general: common to all his writings on war is the conviction that war is an evil to be avoided at virtually all costs, an evil that outweighs all possible goods, an evil that affects all persons—regardless of guilt or innocence—alike. These concerns are first stated in the letter of 1514, and they recur in fuller, more polished form in the later, published works.

What, precisely, was the nature of Erasmus's pacifist objection to the political use of force? A kind of utopianism, already alluded to, certainly forms one element of this position. Roland Bainton writes of Erasmus, "Peace was necessary for his program of the reform of the Church and society through the

[44] See Erasmus, letter to Antoon van Bergen (Chapter II, note 120, above), lines 30-35.

[45] The letter begins with this complaint about Erasmus's financial state. He writes (lines 13-19): "By [a gift from the Archbishop of Canterbury] I hold a substantial income from a living, which I have resigned. To this my other Maecenas adds a similar sum from his private resources. A considerable amount of further support is given to me by the generosity of prominent men, and there could be much more if I were in the slightest degree ready to beg. But the war that is being prepared for has brought a sudden change in the character of this island. Here the price of everything is going up every day, while liberality declines. Why should not people give more sparingly after all those tithings?"

processes of education."[46] Allied to this reason for objecting to war was another factor already mentioned, Erasmus's own personal Pan-Europeanism. But these elements in Erasmus's advocacy of peace appear more strongly in other types of writings than those specifically on war; they must be read as a background for the works on war, not as positive arguments made there. In the works on war on which we are here focusing, Erasmus makes this point in two other ways: first, by an appeal to nature and to classical pagan practice; second, by an appeal to the common Christian faith of European society. These arguments appear in similar forms in all four of the writings mentioned above. Some examples will give the flavor of Erasmus's reasoning. "Not all dumb animals," he writes in the letter to Bergen,

> engage in combat, only wild beasts, and even they do not war among themselves but only with animals of other species. Furthermore they fight with the weapons nature has given them, not as we do with machines invented by a devilish science. Again, they do not fight on any kind of pretext, but only for food or in defence of their young, whereas our human wars are generally caused by ambition, lust, or some such disease of the mind.[47]

With respect to *Dulce bellum inexpertis*, expanding on the same theme, Erasmus observes additionally that it is obvious from nature that man should aim at peace, since he is not armed with horns like the bull, with claws like the lion, or with spines like the porcupine;[48] further, man is inherently social and dependent on others. Pursuing this thought further, Erasmus argues for peace as sowing in man the seeds of benevolence, "that what is most wholesome in him will also be sweet."[49]

We encounter here a foretaste of that vision of a noble and

[46] Bainton, *Christian Attitudes*, p. 131.

[47] Erasmus, letter to Antoon van Bergen, lines 30-35.

[48] Erasmus, *Bellum Erasmi* (London: Thomas Berthelet, 1533), p. 4. This is the earliest English translation of the commentary on *Dulce bellum inexpertis*.

[49] Ibid., p. 5.

peaceful state of nature which would later emerge full-blown in the "noble savage" idea of Rousseau and others. Erasmus in these allusions is not looking forward to the coming kingdom of Christian hope in which the lamb will lie down with the lion: in nature, as he knew it, this might still lead to disaster for the lamb. But the lion would not kill the lamb wantonly, none-theless—only to secure food. Men, not wild animals in the state of nature, are the creatures who kill without adequate reason.

Although the classical age, as employed by Erasmus, is not nature, it approaches that state more closely than had anything in his contemporary Christian society. Erasmus notes that Plato called it sedition, not war, for Greeks to fight with Greeks, "and if this should happen, he bids them fight with every restraint."[50] While Victoria a generation later and Grotius in the following century could apply the same restraints to wars among Christians, Erasmus clearly did not believe Christians of his own time could be so good. *His* example of a society in which the evils of war were limited is a classical one: though Seneca did not hold back from calling his soldiers "mad thieves," Erasmus writes, they "warred after a gentler fashion than we do, they were more faithful of their promise in war, [nor did they use such] mischievous engines in war, nor such crafts and subtleties, [nor did they make war] for such light causes as we Christian men do."[51]

If this were all that Erasmus says, then his utopianism—which might better be termed idealism—regarding the good of peace and the need to avoid war would amount to a yearning for a time or a state in human cultural development that is most like the natural order. Such restitutionism is a theme that ran throughout Renaissance humanism and Reformation thought alike; only the vision of the ideal varied. But this is not the only argument Erasmus employed to support the aim of peace: he also insisted that peace, not war, is fundamental to being truly Christian. Immediately following his reference to

[50] Erasmus in Born, *Christian Prince*, p. 251.

[51] Erasmus, *Bellum Erasmi*, p. 27.

the peacefulness of nature, in the letter to Bergen quoted above, Erasmus says:

> For us, who boast of naming ourselves "Christians" after Christ who preached and practiced naught save gentleness, who are members of one body, one flesh, quickened by the same spirit, nurtured upon the same sacraments, joined in union to a single head, called to the same eternal life, . . . how can anything in this world be so important as to impel us to war. . . ?[52]

Elsewhere in the same letter, Erasmus contrasts "the numerous utterances of Christ, of the Apostles, and of orthodox and highly respected fathers, on peace and on tolerating evils" with the supposed right of princes to make war upheld by "an already decadent Christianity, overburdened with earthly possessions."[53]

There are several faces to Erasmus's argument that genuine Christianity implies the rejection of war. A few years after he wrote these lines it would be possible for radical Reformers to read the passage concerning "an already decadent Christianity" as a denunciation of the post-Constantinian Church and an appeal for restitution of the primitive Church, with its rejection of the state and all it stood for, including the use of armed force. Erasmus clearly was looking over his shoulder at the primitive Church when he cited Christ and the Apostles as his witnesses for the rejection of violence; but it was *violence* he sought to reject thereby, not the state. And if he wanted to remove the Church from participation in worldly affairs, what he had in mind was certainly not something like the later Anabaptist model, but rather a concept modeled on his own life as adviser and friend to rulers, yet not himself a ruler. Erasmus's backward look at early Christian teachings was also balanced by his references to the Christian hope for a new life. If the Bergen letter makes this hope appear too other-worldly to

[52] Erasmus, letter to Antoon van Bergen, lines 38-44.

[53] Ibid., lines 131-34; cf. Erasmus, *Bellum Erasmi*, pp. 21-25, *The Education of a Christian Prince* (Born), pp. 265-66.

have ethical moment, then it is more than offset in *The Education of a Christian Prince*, where Christian principles and examples are laid alongside classical ones to describe how the prince should act so as to govern best.[54] His point was not that Christians should seek escape from the world, but that they should transform it by acting according to the best wisdom of Western cultural tradition—Christian and classical alike. This transformed society would be one of peace, and paramount among the means to it would be advocacy of peace and rejection of war.

Alongside this idealism or, in Bainton's word, utopianism about the need to reject war, Erasmus laid a particularly vehement denunciation of war as he knew it—inherently vicious, tending to destroy the best in men and bring out the worst, giving license to criminal behavior, destroying religion, and causing slaughter and bereavement to friend and foe, guilty and innocent alike. The evil in war is war's violence itself, brought on by the judgments of princes who have been misled by bad motives or who have not sufficiently thought through the proportions of good and evil that war will bring:

> Consider [war's] instruments, I pray you: murderers, profligates devoted to gambling and rape, and the vilest sort of mercenary soldier to whom pay is dearer than life. . . . Think, next, of all the crimes that are committed with war as a pretext, while good laws "fall silent amid the clash of arms"—all the instances of sack and sacrilege, rape, and other shameful acts, such as one hesitates even to name. And even when the war is over, this moral corruption is bound to linger for many years. Now assess for me the cost—a cost so great that, even if you win the war, you will lose much more than you gain. Indeed what realm . . . can be weighed against the life, the blood, of so many thousand men. Even so the worst evils fall upon those who have no stake in the war, while the blessings of peace

[54] Cf. Erasmus, *The Education of a Christian Prince* (Born), pp. 265-66.

affect all. In war, for the most part, even the victors mourn.[55]

Erasmus simply does not credit what Victoria and Grotius after him could conceive as possible: that war might be fought within limits so as to satisfy justice and not do more harm than good. He also clearly believed that wars are generally fought for trivial causes: "The Jews fought by the commandment of God; we make war to avenge the grief and displeasure of our mind";[56] "there exist princes who first make up their minds what they want and afterwards search for a specious pretext to cover their action."[57] Can a war ever be just, then? The answer is, in the *jus in bello* sense, never; and Erasmus moves extremely close to denying the possibility of *jus ad bellum* justice as well. At one point he concludes a sentence scornfully, "if there really is any war which can be called 'just' ";[58] at another he asks rhetorically, "[W]ho does not think his own cause just?"[59] In still another he gives his own judgment, "[E]ven if there are some [wars] which might be called 'just,' yet as human affairs are now, I know not whether there could be found any of this sort."[60]

Erasmus supported his denial of the possibility of a just war in two ways: by citing the evils perpetrated by war and by alluding to the bad motivation of some princes—a great many, he implies, though naming no names. Like his contemporary Machiavelli, Erasmus depended on the generosity of princes for his own livelihood; yet Erasmus, with respect to the view princes should take regarding war, is at an opposite extreme from Machiavelli. For the Italian, the wise prince is one who notes the possibilities for his own advantage in a dispute and chooses to wage war, or not, according to such advantage; for Erasmus, it is exactly this sort of self-interested machination

[55] Erasmus, letter to Antoon van Bergen, lines 47-63.

[56] Erasmus, *Bellum Erasmi*, p. 28.

[57] Erasmus, letter to Antoon van Bergen, lines 84-86.

[58] Erasmus, *The Education of a Christian Prince* (Born), p. 248.

[59] Ibid., p. 251.

[60] Ibid., p. 252.

that is to be deplored in the conduct of princes, as leading to unjust government and popular enslavement and misery. Yet for all his plain antipathy to what his English contemporaries called "policy" (Machiavellianism) in government, the anti-violence theme is the more fundamental and stronger one in Erasmus's denial of the justice of making war. In just war terms, the impossibility of justice *in bello* meant also the lack of justice *ad bellum*.

It is at this point that the essential pacifism of Erasmus's position most clearly emerges. It is possible to interpret his writings on war as defining a kind of just war stance.[61] But while it is correct that he employed just war language and more than once turned just war reasoning to his own ends, his assumptions about war are so unrelievedly negative and his alternatives to war so decisively preferred that he establishes himself in the tradition that attempts to deny the political use of force rather than that which accepts some such use as justified and seeks to set criteria for it.

For Erasmus anything was preferable to war, and the crescendo of his rejection of war grew the more he tuned his arguments. In his letter to Bergen, amidst descriptions of the evils caused by war and the speciousness of the justifying causes alleged by princes, he called for arbitration by Church authorities: "It is the proper function of the Roman pontiff, of the cardinals, bishops, and abbots, to settle disputes between Christian princes."[62] In his commentary on the adage *Dulce bellum inexpertis*, published the following year, he had extended his denial of the use of war to include war with the Turks as well.[63] Another year later, in *The Education of a Christian Prince* (first published in 1516), he denied the right to go to war against Christians and Turks alike, renewed his call for arbitration, and in addition urged the good prince to seek to tolerate affronts to his rights, avoiding war at all costs.

[61] Cf. Bainton, *Christian Attitudes*, p. 131: "As for the traditional ethic of the just war, Erasmus subscribed to it." True, he did use the language of just war tradition; but that is quite different from "subscribing" to it.

[62] Erasmus, letter to Antoon van Bergen, lines 94-96.

[63] Erasmus, *Bellum Erasmi*, p. 34.

"Those who are wise sometimes prefer to lose a thing rather than to gain it, because they realize it will be less costly," he reasoned, adding the example that Caesar would rather have given up his rights had he known what would befall him; a few lines later, his examples are the friend who gives in to another to maintain the friendship and the husband who makes a concession to his wife for the sake of harmony.[64] These admonitions refer to relations between Christians, but to make his point a general one Erasmus states flatly a few pages later, "Not even against the Turks do I believe we should rashly go to war."[65]

There remains in Erasmus's rejection of war a lingering and grudging admission that self-defense may sometimes be necessary and legitimate.[66] This is for him the closest approach to the just war requirement that resort to war be a last resort. But the tone of this admission simply does not compare with the passion of his pleas for toleration of harm done, for giving in to the demands of another, for positive measures aimed at improving relations between princes. Alongside such pleas stand his repeated and detailed descriptions of the calamities caused by war and the needless combativeness of many princes. Even his call for objective, third-party arbitration of disputes, stated with considerable vigor in 1514, was by 1516 a minor note alongside the much more forceful charge to the Christian prince: to accept harm done or threatened, to give up rights rather than fight to protect them, to consider the costs of war and count how they always exceed the costs of giving in to maintain peace. There is nothing in Erasmus on war that speaks of the need to protect legitimate rights even by force, nothing to suggest that he takes seriously the notion that common people may sometimes deserve protection by princely force, nothing that attempts to spell out the possible conditions under which a prince might legitimately as a last resort undertake war. Despite some use of just war arguments and

[64] Erasmus, *The Education of a Christian Prince* (Born), p. 253.

[65] Ibid., p. 256; cf. Erasmus's argument to Volz on this point in Olin, *Christian Humanism*, pp. 112-115.

[66] See Erasmus, *The Education of a Christian Prince* (Born), pp. 249, 256.

terminology, Erasmus's position on war was a pacifist one—not unlike that of present-day pacifists who cite the horrors of war, the inevitability of mass destruction in any nuclear war, and the bellicoseness of contemporary heads of state as reasons for rejecting the possibility of just war, while calling for unilateral concessions, third-party arbitration of disputes, and the creation of an international atmosphere of mutual trust to replace what is commonly called the "war system."

The pacifism of Erasmus flowed in part from his vision of a new world order that corresponded somewhat to his own experience of cosmopolitan life as a citizen of Christendom; and it flowed in part from his convictions about the essential evils of war, including the inadequacy of the causes for which princes fought and the overwhelming disproportion between the costs of war in blood and inhumanity and the benefits allegedly secured by war. The former may not quite have been a utopianism, since Erasmus thought the new society could realistically be achieved by princes acting on Christian principles, but it was certainly a strongly idealistic vision of a new world. Clearly he rejected violence as such as a means to protect human values. Together these theses defined a form of pacifism that stands generically apart from that of the Anabaptists of the Schleitheim Confession, to which we now turn.

D. Pacifism in Radical Religious Reform: The Anabaptists of the Schleitheim Confession

Not all the movements in the broad and diverse left wing of the Reformation—the movements George Williams has collectively labeled the "Radical Reformation"[67]—were Anabaptist, and not all were pacifist. Indeed, a crusading apocalypticism appeared again and again—most notably in Thomas Müntzer, the preacher of the Peasants' War, and in the beliefs of the Melchiorite movement as realized in the abortive Münster Kingdom, but also in the teachings of other individuals such as

[67] George Huntston Williams, *The Radical Reformation* (Philadelphia: The Westminster Press, 1972).

Hans Hut. One Anabaptist preacher, Balthasar Hubmaier, held an essentially just-war position (in his case close to Zwingli's), as did the Socinian movement in Poland.[68] But the embracing of a pacifist position with respect to the use of political force, together with varying degrees of rejection of the state and a personal practice of nonresistance that often led to martyrdom, have become the lasting marks by which a continuing tradition of Christian radicalism identifies itself. These marks first appeared in the earliest group of Anabaptists, who came to be known as the Swiss Brethren, in the 1520s. We will approach them through the document they produced known as the Schleitheim Confession (a term subsequently applied to a text entitled "Brotherly Union of a Number of Children of God concerning Seven Articles") of 1527.[69]

Though the geographical distribution of the Swiss Brethren extended to Strasbourg on the north (Michael Sattler, regarded as the principal author of the Schleitheim text, was himself for a time leader of a congregation there), the course of the Reformation in Zurich had a much more direct and deeper impact on the development of the Brethren. Zwingli's thinking on the shape of the Reformed Church, civil government, and church-state relations defined a Christian role in the state that admitted no dissent, religious or political. Ironically, as noted above, he was much influenced by Erasmus's thought and was himself a pacifist in an early stage of his career, particularly opposing the use of mercenaries in warfare. But as we have also seen, both his theological convictions and his political situation changed, the former becoming more dependent on Paul and the latter focusing on the military needs of the Swiss Confed-

[68] For a discussion of these movements and individuals see Stayer, *Anabaptists*, and Williams, *The Radical Reformation*, passim. The Socinian movement in Poland also went through a pacifist phase; see Stanislaw Kot, *Socianianism in Poland* (Boston: Starr King Press, 1957), passim.

[69] See further Brock, *Pacifism in Europe*, chapter 2; Williams, *The Radical Reformation*, chapters 6-8; Stayer, *Anabaptists*, chapters 5-6; Yoder, *Michael Sattler*. On the earlier influence by Conrad Grebel on this group's pacifism see Brock, pp. 59-62.

eration to defend itself.[70] By the time of the rise of the Anabaptist movement in his area, Zwingli was every inch a defender of Christian involvement in the use of political power to secure order and to defend the state against harm—a position he defined in essentially just war terms in two writings from 1523, his sermon "Divine and Human Justice" and his *Exposition* of sixty-seven theses of religious reform. When the Anabaptist movement began, he saw no inconsistency in the use of civil power to enforce religious conformity, with the result that in 1527, when the Schleitheim synod was convened, the Swiss Brethren were suffering persecution from Zwinglian Protestants and Catholics alike.

It is against this background of rejection and persecution by the established order, whether Catholic or Protestant, that the position of the Swiss Brethren on civil society and its use of the sword may best be viewed. One scholar[71] characterizes the Brethren's position as "separatist nonresistance"; an important fact for understanding this position was that neither the separatism of the Swiss Brethren nor their nonresistant pacifism was developed in a political or social vacuum. They became separatists in part because of the persecution suffered at the hands of civil authorities backed by magisterial Reformers and Catholics; separation from the affairs of these regimes was thus an attempt to distance themselves from the evil use of power that was, in part, directed toward them. They became nonresistant pacifists for similar reasons: since the sword of the civil societies they knew was experienced as evil (having been used for their own persecution), and since they had not themselves the military power to resist it, they separated themselves spiritually by rejecting all resistance to the civil authorities and by rejecting for themselves the use of the sword.

There is, of course, much more to be said. In particular, the religious convictions that accompanied these political decisions must be examined to produce the full picture. Further, it must be noted that while the influences that shaped the posi-

[70] See further Stayer, *Anabaptists*, pp. 57-60.

[71] Ibid., p. 117 et passim.

tion taken by the Swiss Brethren included an important ingredient from the political context, their *justifications* of that position were always put in religious terms. Still, the same can be said of the position taken by the magisterial Reformers. The point remains that, from the first, the particular type of pacifism characteristic of the Swiss Brethren—and ultimately of the entire movement—was not purely religious; it was also a practical result of interaction with their political and social environment. Stayer writes:

> [T]he evidence is fragmentary, but it seems that Zurich radicals considered the whole range of Protestant teachings on the Sword before settling on extreme apoliticism. The basic problem was that they were confronted in the Zurich Council by what appeared to them to be an un-Christian government.[72]

Similarly Bainton comments on Anabaptist apoliticism generally:

> Appeals to princes . . . were deemed fatuous, and plans for world peace were considered futile. The Anabaptist could not, like Erasmus, write an *Institute of the Christian Prince*, because there could not be a Christian prince. The true Christian could do no other than withdraw from all political life—and in the sixteenth century the Anabaptists were compelled to withdraw from all social life. Survival was possible only by accommodation or withdrawal.[73]

Implicit in such judgments as these is the possibility that matters *might have been otherwise*—as in fact they were in the teachings of such other radicals as Thomas Müntzer, Hans Hut, and Melchior Hoffmann.

The political ingredient in the pacifism of the Swiss Brethren was, however, inextricably mixed with the religious. Sattler could call the established government a *civitas diaboli*, and in

[72] Ibid., p. 98.

[73] Bainton, *Christian Attitudes*, p. 156.

Article IV of the Schleitheim Confession, treating of separation, a form of Christian dualism rules:[74]

> Now there is nothing else in the world and all creation than good or evil, believing and unbelieving, darkness and light, the world and those who are [come] out of the world, God's temple and idols, Christ and Belial, and none will have part with the other.
>
> To us, then, the commandment of the Lord is also obvious, whereby he orders us to be and to become separated from the evil one. . . .
>
> Further, he admonishes us therefore to go out from Babylon and from the earthly Egypt, that we may not be partakers in their torment and suffering, which the Lord will bring upon them.

A list follows of all those "abominations" the believers should shun: "popish and repopish works and idolatry, gatherings, church attendance, winehouses, guarantees and commitments of unbelief, and other things of the kind"; then, concluding the article, comes a separate paragraph on the use of the sword. This is the first reference to the renunciation of violence in the Confession, and it is placed in the context of a general rejection of life in civil society:

> Thereby shall also fall away from us the diabolical weapons of violence—such as sword, armor, and the like, and all of their use to protect friends or against enemies—by virtue of the word of Christ: "you shall not resist evil."

In Erasmus, we recall, government in itself is a good (only some princes are bad) and offers a means to a perfect society, one characterististic of which is the absence of war. The violence of war, by contrast, is held up as evil in itself, an evil so plain that, Erasmus believes, anyone of good will and common sense must reject it out of hand. But in the Schleitheim Confession matters are different: it is the government and civil society that are evil, belonging to the realm of sin, and that must be

[74] Yoder, *Michael Sattler*, p. 38.

utterly rejected as applying "within the perfection of Christ"; violence is shunned as a part of the evil, un-Christian world from which Christians must separate. This theme, first introduced in Article IV of the Confession, appears centrally again in Article VI, which treats specifically of "the sword."[75] Article VI begins as follows:

> We have been united as follows concerning the sword. The sword is an ordering of God outside the perfection of Christ. It punishes and kills the wicked, and guards and protects the good. In the law the sword is established over the wicked for punishment and for death, and the secular rulers are established to wield the same.

"But within the perfection of Christ," the article continues, "only the ban is used . . . without the death of the flesh. . . ." No Christian may wield the sword or serve as a magistrate passing sentence "in disputes and strife about worldly matters," even "against the wicked for the protection and defense of the good, or for the sake of love." The reasoning is that Christ, by teaching and by example, showed Christians they should do otherwise. But even this appeal to Christ is put in the dualistic terms of rejection of the world: "[Christ] Himself . . . forbids the violence of the sword when He says, 'The princes of this world lord it over them, etc., but among you it shall not be so.' " The concluding paragraph of this article is devoted to this same theme of the evil of the world versus the righteousness of Christians: magistrates have their citizenship and houses in the world, Christians have them "in heaven"; the weapons of government are "carnal and only against the flesh, but the weapons of Christians are spiritual, against the fortifi-

[75] Ibid., pp. 39-41. Note here the peculiar tension of the Schleitheim Brethren's position on the sword: with the magisterial Reformers they accepted the need for the sword in the hands of the political authorities, so that order could be maintained in a sinful world; yet, despite this, they held that Christians may not participate in the use of the sword and, accordingly, they themselves refused to do so. Not only the Zurich government but *all* "the princes of this world" represent a way of life that the true Christian must avoid, even at the cost of a separation from the larger society.

cation of the devil"; worldly persons "are armed with steel and iron, but Christians are armed with the armor of God, with truth, righteousness, peace, faith, salvation, and with the Word of God."

This statement on the use of the sword explicitly rejects the use of violent force for Christians, even if defended in just war terms ("against the wicked for the protection and defense of the good, or for the sake of love"),[76] but it does not anywhere reject violence as such apart from the rejection of the world. Rather, the sword is "an ordering of God outside the perfection of Christ." In this fashion the Schleitheim Brethren attempted to make their peace with the divinely ordained use of the sword in the Old Testament (a point emphasized by the magisterial Reformers), while rejecting the possibility of an apocalyptic crusade like that accepted by Müntzer's followers as well as the possibility that Christian magistrates might employ the sword for the sake of peace, as Zwingli taught.

There is a utopian vision here, but it is not that of Erasmus, in which government itself was to be the instrument of bringing about a new society. Rather, the new society of the Swiss Brethren could be formed only in separation and isolation from existing civil society, which forever remains evil no mat-

[76] Were the Schleitheim Anabaptists opposed to violence as such, in a way similar to Erasmus? They certainly had reason to be from their own experience, for they had the pain of violence directed at them, while Erasmus only observed the effects of violence on others. Most present-day interpretation from within the Anabaptist tradition holds that the Swiss Brethren rejected violence because of its inherent evil. This view is also supported by some of the Brethren's use of Scripture. Yet the evidence is not, I think, persuasive. My interpretation is that we find in the Schleitheim Confession a type of divine-command reasoning where Christian use of the sword is concerned. In this view, nonviolence becomes evil for Christians only because of the nonviolent example found in Christ and because of such of his commands as "Do not resist evil" and "Turn the other cheek." In Erasmus, by contrast, we have a version of natural-law reasoning: as he says in so many words, anyone of common sense can recognize the evil of violence just by looking at it. As much as anything, this disparity reveals the difference between Erasmus and the Swiss Anabaptists, a difference that is fundamental in spite of the intellectual links that are sometimes drawn between them by modern commentators (cf. Williams, *The Radical Reformation*, pp. 10-12).

ter how much reformation it might receive. It is this disbelief in the possibility of transforming "the world" that forms the religious reason behind the antipathy of Sattler and the other Swiss Brethren toward attempts to create the kingdom of God through force, not only an antipathy toward force itself or its effects rooted in the example of the meekness of Christ.[77] The argument concerning the sword in the Schleitheim Confession consistently links the evil of the use of force to the evil of the world,[78] and rather than making the sort of argument often made by pacifists in other periods (including the present) that violence is to be avoided because it is evil in itself, the Confession instead links the need for Christians to avoid violence to the command of Christ "to be and to become separated from the evil one."[79] That is, rather than beginning, as Erasmus does, with the evil of violence, the Anabaptists of the Schleitheim Confession begin with the command to separate from the sinful world and to be like Christ. Avoidance of violence is one aspect of this, as is not serving as magistrates (Article VI)[80] and not taking oaths (Article VII).[81] We encounter here a difference between the humanist perspective on violence as evil in itself and the Anabaptist perspective on it as evil because Christ abstained from using force and commands Christians to do likewise.

Yet the rejection of the state and of violence justified in such dualistic terms in the Schleitheim Confession was, as noted above, reinforced by the political powerlessness of the Swiss Brethren and their own personal experience of martyrdom for their faith. They knew the power of the sword to be evil not only because Christ told them so, but because they personally experienced it as evil in the imprisonments, tortures, and deaths inflicted on them by the civil authorities.[82] Yet this experience was treated (as in Sattler's speech in his own defense

[77] Yoder, *Michael Sattler*, p. 40.

[78] Ibid.; cf. pp. 38-40.

[79] Ibid., p. 38.

[80] Ibid., p. 40.

[81] Ibid., pp. 41-42.

[82] See, for example, ibid., pp. 75, 77-78.

at his trial for heresy, sedition, and rebellion) as the result to be expected when Christians confront the world of "the flesh."[83] Christ, after all, suffered similarly. Once again, it is not the violence but the world that is, in the first place, evil.

E. Conclusion

It has not been the purpose of this chapter to attempt to survey and analyze the entire scope of pacifist argumentation and practice during the Renaissance-Reformation era. Rather, we have sought to identify two different and typical forms of pacifist opposition to the political use of force as they took shape in the early sixteenth century and to set them in context alongside contemporaneous developments in the nature of war and in just war tradition. These two forms of pacifism appeared within the frameworks of Renaissance humanism and Anabaptist sectarianism, but each of them is part of a longer tradition in the historical quest for peace. Indeed, with these two positions we can say that these traditions have now coalesced more definitively than they had earlier in history. From this point on, the lines of influence and development are much clearer and more readily acknowledged.

We have, in Erasmus and in the Anabaptists of the Schleitheim Confession, two distinct and differentiable types of pacifist rejection of the political use of force. Erasmus focused on the evils caused by force as such, and his pleas for peace returned again and again to the destruction, death, and misery caused by war. He accepted some of the reasoning of just war tradition but used it to reject that tradition's conclusion that war could, under some circumstances, be justified. For Erasmus, the perceived fact that war meant unrestrained violence was sufficient argument (on the basis of proportional reason) that seldom if ever could a just cause be found for war. In rejecting violence, though, Erasmus exalted the idea of the state and good government, holding up to view an idealistic vision of a new society governed by Christian princes in which all

[83] Ibid.; cf. pp. 72-73.

would be at peace and in which even the lowliest member of civil society would benefit and prosper.

In sharp contrast, the Swiss Brethren focused on civil government as part of the evil world of "the flesh" and, though they had from personal experience far better reason than Erasmus to regard violent force itself as evil, rejected "the sword" only as an element in their general rejection of "the world." Their attitude toward the ideas of just war tradition was also shaped by their dualism: while no true Christian may use the sword even for good, to protect innocent persons, or out of love (all prominent justifications for Christian use of force from Augustine forward), the sword itself was "an ordering of God," albeit "outside the perfection of Christ." In other words, the just war idea is not applicable to Christians, but it expresses God's will for the governing of civil society. The goal of a new society as conceived by the Swiss Brethren meant their own separated, apolitical,[84] nonresistant fellowships; this was not a goal they expected to be realized in society generally, and they had no place in their concept of the Christian life for efforts to bring in the kingdom of God through force, as in the teaching of Müntzer, or by social or intellectual transformation, as in the teaching of the magisterial Reformers or that of Erasmus and other humanists.

That each of these positions led to a rejection of political use of force must be granted, but the two positions are quite different in their roots, their justifications, and their political implications. They originated from different premises, different experiences of the world, different visions of the possibilities of human life, and different concepts of how God might reward the faithful. Erasmus argued for a vision in which good princes, ruling on Christian principles, could bring in a world

[84] The term "apolitical" is Stayer's (*Anabaptists*, passim) and, I think, well expresses what the Schleitheim Anabaptists conceived themselves and their movement as being about. But their efforts at separation were certainly not regarded as apolitical by the magisterial Reformers; as noted earlier, Zwingli accused them of a clandestine subversiveness, and Bucer, on the edge of the geographic region where the Swiss Brethren lived, found in Anabaptist separatism a threat to the state.

of universal peace; for the Swiss Brethren, peace was possible only in "the perfection of Christ" and was not granted to be possible for the world at large, which remained trapped in sin. Erasmus sought to influence rulers, and his lifestyle in dialogue with men of power as well as the arguments of his writings pointed toward the enhancement of a universal Christendom. The Anabaptists of the Schleitheim Confession, by contrast, regarded the magistracy as part of the unredeemed and unredeemable world, and they explicitly denied that a Christian could serve as magistrate. (The implication that magistrates were un-Christian particularly galled Zwingli and Calvin, both of whom seized on this point in their criticisms of the Confession.)[85]

These positions develop further in subsequent eras[86] and have parallel positions in the contemporary world, where pacifist conclusions are supported, on the one hand, by religious apoliticism and visions of the kingdom of Christ as separate from the affairs of nations and, on the other hand, by visions of nuclear holocaust, rejection of war on the basis of the evil caused by violence itself, and "world order" efforts aimed at transforming society so as to eliminate the "war system." As in the sixteenth-century context, these two contemporary kinds of pacifism are foundationally and thematically different, in spite of possible coincidence on specific political issues in the current debate. Understanding this difference, both historically and in the present debate, might help to clarify and advance such issues as what connections may exist between just war and pacifist ideas and what unique contribution moral tradition on the quest for peace can make to public discussion.

[85] See Richard Stauffer, "Zwingli et Calvin, Critiques de la confession de Schleitheim," in Marc Lienhard, *The Origins and Characteristics of Anabaptism/Les Débuts et les caractéristiques de l'Anabaptisme* (The Hague: Martinus Nijhoff, 1977), pp. 140-42.

[86] In particular, the Mennonite movement, including the more radically separatist Amish tradition, is the most direct descendent of the Swiss Brethren; see Hershberger, *War, Peace, and Nonresistance*, pp. 81-86.

CHAPTER IV

"PERPETUAL PEACE" AND LIMITED WAR

A. The Coalescence of Pacifist Tradition

The Renaissance and the Reformation bequeathed to the modern period two significantly different, if related, approaches to the rejection of war and, more generally, of violence. Neither was genuinely new: both humanistic and radical-sectarian pacifism had, as we have seen, medieval predecessors, and their deep roots reach even into the classical age. Yet, up to the Renaissance-Reformation era these lines of thought are not continuous. Afterward, though, this changes; and because of this new continuity it becomes possible to begin to speak of pacifist tradition—or rather traditions—for the first time.

So far as the development of pacifism is concerned, a major reason for the significance of humanistic utopianism and radical sectarianism is precisely in their *lack* of newness, in their connections with intellectual movements that had occurred earlier. In geometry it is necessary to have two points in order to define a line; to define a moral tradition, though, it is not enough to have similar ideas or practices occur at different times in history, for they must be connected by bonds of influence. In just war tradition, for example, it is true that Augustine first stated the main elements of what in the Middle Ages became the Church's doctrine of just war; yet it is also true that these ideas were forgot or ignored for seven centuries after Augustine committed them to paper. To speak of just war *tradition*, we must begin with Gratian's recovery of Augustine on war in the twelfth century and follow the rather clear lines of connection and influence that developed after this. Similarly, while it is undoubtedly true that elements from classical and early Christian thought were taken up by proto-pacifists in the Middle Ages, these elements, too, had lain fallow for centuries by the time they were rediscovered; and when they were recalled and employed, it was for the secondary purpose of bolstering concepts more fundamentally determined by the historical context of the twelfth or fourteenth century.

For a moral tradition to form, there must be cultural coherence and continuity; these conditions were met for Western culture only from about the twelfth century forward. Despite divisions over religion and the rise of the role of the nation-state, they have since abounded, and the development of pacifist moral tradition has prospered accordingly. The quest for peace is common to all cultures and to all periods of history; but pacifism, as commonly understood today, is a phenomenon of Western moral experience and reflection in the modern era.

Nonetheless, one of the difficulties of studying pacifism remains its diversity. The British historian Martin Ceadel, whose work we shall examine more closely later on, has identified three distinct varieties of pacifism in Britain between the World Wars;[1] the Mennonite theologian and historian John Howard Yoder, as noted in an earlier chapter, defines no fewer than seventeen types of religious pacifism;[2] another contemporary theologian, Stanley Hauerwas, insists on a sharp distinction between Christian pacifism as he understands it and the "ecological" type of nuclear pacifism represented by Jonathan Schell;[3] others differentiate pacifisms of "witness" and "prophetic protest";[4] and so on. This diversity must be recognized

[1] Martin Ceadel, "Christian Pacifism in the Era of Two World Wars," in W. J. Sheils, ed., *The Church and War* (Oxford: Basil Blackwell, for The Ecclesiastical History Society, 1983), pp. 391-92. Also see Martin Ceadel, *Pacifism in Britain, 1914-45* (Oxford: The Clarendon Press; New York: Oxford University Press, 1980), pp. 1-8.

[2] John Howard Yoder, *Nevertheless: Varieties of Religious Pacifism* (Scottdale, Pa.: Herald Press, 1971).

[3] Stanley Hauerwas, "On Surviving Justly: An Ethical Analysis of Nuclear Disarmament," in Jill Raitt, ed., *Religious Conscience and Nuclear Warfare* (Columbia: University of Missouri Press, 1982), pp. 1-20.

[4] See Shannon, *War or Peace*, pp. 99-102.

and taken seriously. In my own division of the waters, there is a difference between those we might call the "broadeners," who would remove the prospect of war by expanding the bounds of human society so as to abolish the kind of conflict that flows from the rivalry of multiple sovereign states, and their opposite, the "narrowers," who would remove themselves from the state and its violence to live in their own radically constricted communities, where violence is repudiated. There is further a difference between those who reject the phenomenon of violence as such and those who are primarily concerned with the social structures that, in their view, foment and support violence.

It is important to admit and identify such distinctions: pacifism *is* a multifaceted phenomenon. To stress the differences, though, would be to imply that there is nothing more to be found than a group of phenomena, connected only accidentally if at all, and that would be going too far. The history of pacifism has been one of shifting emphases, lines of influence, and coalitions; it is one in which there has been a periodic alternation between the making of common cause among pacifists of different stripes and their separation, perhaps along different lines than were present earlier. Ceadel recognizes this pattern and seems to be somewhat puzzled by it; in any case, he is not surprised when his three kinds of pacifists have a falling out at the beginning of World War II.[5] Hauerwas, too, cannot abide the coalition of Christian pacifism, which ought to leave the "fate of the earth" in God's hands, and the secular progressivists represented by Schell.[6] Still, such alchemical unions of opposites have regularly come to pass: they are part of the phenomenon of the "peace movement," as pacifists of various sorts began collectively to call themselves in the nineteenth century. It helps us to understand the overall phenomenon to be able to recognize the distinctions that obtain; yet, if we are to understand the various kinds of pacifism that may be

[5] Ceadel, "Christian Pacifism," pp. 395-408.
[6] Hauerwas, "On Surviving Justly," pp. 8-13.

identified, it is also helpful to recognize that they are parts of a larger phenomenon.

B. The "Perpetual Peace" Ideal

Geoffrey Best, whose *Humanity in Warfare* is an admirable historical treatment of the development of the modern humanitarian law of war, speaks of an "Enlightenment consensus" on war and peace.[7] Would that he were correct. In fact, though, the era of the Enlightenment was a period in which two rather distinct kinds of consensus took shape, one around the ideal of a universal and lasting abolition of war—a "perpetual peace"—and the other around the ideal of limited warfare fought according to the dictates of humanity. In examining these, we may see further how the just war ideal and pacifism have tended to become separate currents in the quest for peace.

Best's concern lies with the limited war idea, and his prime exemplar of this line of thought is the Swiss jurist and diplomat Emmerich de Vattel. This is also the main line of development of the just war tradition during this period; and, understood more broadly, this brand of consensus also includes the theory and practice of limited war as it developed in the eighteenth century. Since I have already discussed this topic in some detail in other books,[8] here I will limit myself to whatever is useful in shedding light on the other line of consensus, which emerged alongside it.

Our primary focus in this chapter, then, will be on the ideal of "perpetual peace," one that is both linked backward to the utopian and "superstate" theorizing of earlier eras and connected forward to the internationalist pacifism of the nineteenth and twentieth centuries. More specifically, though not exclusively, I will discuss the "perpetual peace" ideal in Kant and Rousseau, two figures who (albeit mostly by dint of their

[7] Geoffrey Best, *Humanity in Warfare* (New York: Columbia University Press, 1980), chapter I.

[8] See particularly Johnson, *Just War Tradition*, chapter VII, and *Ideology*, pp. 240-53.

other writings) have had enormous impact on later Western thought on morality, politics, and the shaping of society for good.

Indeed, as I remarked above of pacifist tradition generally, what these two authors wrote on the "perpetual peace" concept is most interesting precisely because it was not particularly original, but instead built on ideas that had been in existence for some time. The story begins in the seventeenth century, at the end of the age of religious wars. Exhausted by war, intellectuals began to dream of an enduring peace. Disgusted by the connections they discerned between rivalries among nations and the occurrence of wars, they projected this peace in terms of a new international system in which national sovereignty would be severely restricted and the right to use force relocated in the new corporate community, where it would either function in a police role or wither away entirely. Some of these ideal projections sought to be truly universal, embracing not only Europeans but the Turkish Empire, Persia, Muscovy, China, and India—in short, the major political units of the world as they knew them—as well. Others were more limited, embracing peace only among Europeans or among Europeans and the Turks. Erasmus was clearly an immediate intellectual inspiration for some of this thinking: twenty-eight editions of his writings on peace were published during the seventeenth century, and eight more during the eighteenth, besides those contained in the editions of his *Works*.[9] Erasmus's new order, we recall, built upon the community of ideals and relationships existing in Christian Europe, but it was also to include the Turks.

The "perpetual peace" ideal developed through a canon of works from the early seventeenth century through the end of the eighteenth. First in this canonical listing stands Emeric Crucé's *Le Nouveau Cynée ou Discours d'Estat*, published in 1623; next comes *Le Grand Dessein de Henri IV*, written by his minister Sully and published in 1638. Crucé proposed a federation of states possessing sufficient power to enforce

[9] See Bainton, *Christian Attitudes*, chapter 11, n. 3.

peace, by arbitration if possible but by force if necessary, against any unruly member. He drew on the ideal of common humanity, setting it against differences that are "only political." The latter are the cause of hostility and conflict; the former offer a way to peace.

> Why should I a Frenchman, wish harm to an Englishman, a Spaniard, or a Hindoo? I cannot wish it when I consider that they are men like me . . . and that all nations are bound together by a natural and consequently indestructible tie which ensures that a man cannot consider another a stranger. I will say the same as regards the religions which so arouse men's passions and set them against one another. . . .[10]

Such Erasmian universalism was perhaps made more urgent by the religious and dynastic warfare going on at the time of Crucé's writing. Reflections on the common humanity of all mankind appear regularly throughout the "perpetual peace" writings, but it is worth noting that they could be used to argue a very different case. In the developing consensus represented by Vattel, for example, the same reasoning was employed not to argue against war but, accepting war, to argue for observation of noncombatant immunity and other *jus in bello* measures of humane military conduct.[11]

By contrast with Crucé's work, Sully's was more narrowly focused and more pragmatic; its international community stopped at the borders of Christendom. Nor did it depend on the good will and free choice of princes for its establishment. It depended, as one commentator puts it, on "an acceptance, so far as possible, of the *status quo*, and an appeal to the innate selfishness of man."[12] Henri IV was himself to be the principal

[10] Emeric Crucé, *The New Cyneas of Emeric Crucé*, ed. and trans. Thomas Willing Balch (Philadelphia: Allen, Lane & Scott, 1909), pp. 84-86.

[11] Emmerich de Vattel, *The Law of Nations; or, The Principles of Natural Law*, trans. Charles G. Fenwick (Washington, D.C.: Carnegie Institution, 1916), book III, sections 146, 153, et passim.

[12] David Ogg, introduction to Maximilien de Béthune duc de Sully, *Sully's*

agent of change, undertaking to redistribute and balance European power by changing boundaries. Austria was to be driven out of the Netherlands, Italy, and Germany; Switzerland and the Netherlands were to be restored to autonomy and stengthened; Germany was to become an elective empire; and so on. French power was to be the agent for these changes; but, to demonstrate its disinterestedness, France was to gain no new territory thereby. A "Christian Republic" was to be the end result, presided over by a "General Council" of delegates (four from each great power, two from each of the others), which would have authority to make decisions binding on all the member states. War within Europe would thus be abolished, for the council could impose binding arbitration in all disputes. Perhaps equally important, Sully saw in the projected balance of power a way to eliminate international rivalry, envy, and fear—the roots, as he saw it, of war. To Sully himself it was all so reasonable:

> For what did [Henri IV] . . . require of Europe? Nothing more than that Europe should promote the means whereby he proposed to stabilize Christendom. . . . What they would gain by it, besides the inestimable benefits arising from peace, would greatly exceed all the expenses they would incur. What reason could any of them have to oppose it? and, if they did not oppose it, how could the house of Austria support itself against powers who would have risen as open and secret enemies in the hope of depriving it that strength which it had only used to oppress them?[13]

This idea of a parliament of nations appears again in William Penn's *Essay toward the Present and Future Peace of Europe*, published in 1693. Penn's argument against war followed the same lines as that of Erasmus: war caused great and indiscriminate harm and loss of life and property; its course

---

Grand Design of Henry IV, The Grotius Society Publications, no. 2 (London: Sweet & Maxwell, 1921), p. 10.

[13] Sully, *Grand Design*, pp. 29-30.

and outcome are always uncertain; its cost, both directly and in terms of lost trade opportunities, outweighs any benefits that might be claimed. Since intra-European war was not the only problem, Penn would have included the realms of the czar and the Turks in his parliament; yet his chief focus was to undercut the roots of war among the European states, and his solution did not much differ from Crucé's or Sully's—or, for that matter, Erasmus's. He did not propose the imposition of new borders; rather, the international status quo was to be recognized through a weighted system by which, for example, Germany would have twelve votes, France ten, Italy eight, and England six. But, like Sully, Penn proposed that national sovereignty in international affairs be surrendered to the parliament (home rule would obtain in domestic matters), and that only the parliament as a whole should have the right to invoke the use of force. Though Penn was a Quaker, he did not in this work take an absolute pacifist position; rather he accepted, in principle, the existence of an international military force that would function to police the peace against threats from unruly member states. At the same time, however, he suggested that such a force would never be needed. Justice would remove the motivation for war; the abolition of all national armed forces would mean that the international army would never need to use its arms.[14]

The next significant work in our "perpetual peace" canon is the one that immediately influenced Rousseau: the Abbé de Saint-Pierre's *Projet de traité pours rendre la paix perpetuelle en Europe*, published in 1713. This work (usually known as the *Projet de paix perpetuelle*) was also the one that brought the phrase "perpetual peace" into currency. Saint-Pierre's scheme appeared in the same year as the signing of the Treaty of Utrecht, which ended the War of the Spanish Succession, and would have frozen the boundaries of Europe as they were in that year. It did not include extra-European powers. Ac-

[14] William Penn, *An Essay toward the Present and Future Peace of Europe* (Philadelphia: Peace & Service Committee, Friends General Conference, 1944); on Penn's plan see further Bainton, *Christian Attitudes*, pp. 178-80; cf. Hershberger, *War, Peace, and Nonresistance*, pp. 158-59, 177.

knowledging his debt to Sully, Saint-Pierre argued as Sully had for a union of the states of Europe based on their common culture. While the new entity was in the process of formation, force might have to be used against noncooperating states; but once the union was in place, Saint-Pierre believed, internal peace would be established, no use of force to police the member nations would be necessary, and a general internal disarmament, disbanding of armies, and destruction of fortified borders could follow.[15]

The next work in the development of a "perpetual peace" canon was Rousseau's extrapolation from Saint-Pierre, titled *Extrait du Projet de paix perpetuelle de M. l'Abbé de Saint-Pierre*, published in 1761.[16] Previously, some time between 1753 and 1758, Rousseau had written a connected essay, *L'État de guerre*.[17] Before examining what Rousseau had to say on war and peace, though, we might well reflect back on the fortunes of the "perpetual peace" idea up to this point.

The proposals of Crucé, Sully, Penn, and Saint-Pierre all had in common that they envisaged the abolition of war, once and for all, through the establishment of a permanent league of powers. They differed in detail over how this league should be constituted and in how many powers should be involved—that is, whether non-European states should be included, and if so, which ones. All of them, though, agreed with one another—and, looking further back, with Erasmus, who is the link with still earlier versions of this same concept—more fundamentally than they disagreed. A common feature in their analysis

[15] Saint-Pierre published several versions of this plan. His own abridgment, *L'Abrégé du Projet de paix perpétuelle inventé par le roi Henri le Grand*, appeared in 1729 and again in 1738; a shorter version appeared in 1747. See C. I. Castel de Saint-Pierre, Abbot of Tiron, *Selections from the Second Edition of the Abrégé du Projet de paix perpétuelle*, The Grotius Society Publications, no. 5 (London: Sweet & Maxwell, 1927); see, also, Gilberte Derocque, *Le Projet de paix perpétuelle de l'Abbé de Saint-Pierre*(Paris: Librairie Arthur Rousseau, 1929), pp. 55-57.

[16] Jean-Jacques Rousseau, *L'État de guerre and Projet de paix perpétuelle*, with introduction and notes by Shirley G. Patterson (New York and London: G. P. Putnam's Sons, 1920).

[17] Ibid.

is a perceived connection between the existing state system and the occurrence of war. Ironically, with the exception of Sully, they assume that there is sufficient justice and virtue in states as they exist for them to be motivated to join in the proposed international union; even with Sully, *one* state—France—possesses such virtue. On the one hand, then, states as they exist are to be mistrusted, as conflicts among them are perceived to be the source of war; on the other hand, it is assumed that the interests behind these conflicts will not prevent states from coming together in the new union of nations.

These are all fundamentally eschatological proposals, though their authors did not realize it. The new structure of international relations will produce an inevitable and enduring peace; in these analyses it is the *structure*, with the means for adjudication of conflicts it provides, that causes this result. Yet without a *previous* change in the attitudes and perceptions of states and their rulers, it is impossible to see why they would enter the proposed new order. The nations would have to relinquish some sovereignty once in this order; that is a common plank in these "perpetual peace" platforms. Yet, in fact, they would have to relinquish that sovereignty *as a condition of entering the union in the first place*, and this is the change that is not seriously analyzed in such proposals. The most realistic one turns out to be Sully's, who would establish a *pax Gallicana* by the sword, just as the *pax Romana* had earlier been established; yet why should French disinterest be taken seriously by the other European states in Sully's time—or by us?[18]

In short, the problem with these seventeenth- and early-eighteenth-century expressions of the "perpetual peace" idea is twofold. First, they emphasize the elements of community among nations and the benefits of union without granting the force of those values and interests which support the separateness and distinctiveness of the existing national states. Wars, according to these proposals, are rooted in frivolous conflicts, and they create only evil, never good. Second, they assume the

[18] Cf. the reasoning of Dante and Marsilius in the fourteenth century; see above, Chapter II.

state of affairs they purport to be trying to create. The breakdown of state sovereignty that brings an end to war is in fact not a *result* of the new international systems proposed; it is a *precondition* for states to enter such a union. The arguments are thus circular, and they offer little help as to how to get on the circle.

The perception of war as rooted in frivolous conflicts and as always producing a net effect of evil was also, as we saw in the previous chapter, Erasmus's position; in the seventeenth and eighteenth centuries, it became a central feature of the new moral tradition defined by the ideal of "perpetual peace." This perception of affairs received literary expression in Swift's *Gulliver's Travels*, where the conflict between the empires of Lilliput and Blefuscu is described as having originated in an argument over which end of an egg to break in order to eat it (frivolous cause) with the result of, among other things, a three-year war in which Lilliput has lost "forty capital ships, and a much greater number of smaller vessels, together with thirty thousand of our best seamen and soldiers; and the damage received by the enemy is reckoned to be somewhat greater than ours" (results that are only evil).[19] If there were any other reasons for the conflict, they are not revealed; if there have been any positive results, they are not mentioned. Erasmus is no different. Nor are Crucé and Penn; nor, as we shall see below, is Rousseau.

Indeed, the same kind of analysis turns out to surface throughout this tradition of pacifist thought. It is, in fact, less an *analysis*, a word that implies objectivity, than a statement of a *myth*, defined as in Swift through exaggeration and irony but nevertheless expressing one kind of fundamental moral perception of war. Paul Fussell finds similar expressions in the reactions of British soldiers to World War I: war is nothing more than senseless destruction, lacking real reason, directed by no control to no purpose moral or not, producing evil far out of proportion to any claimed good.[20] The same perception

[19] Cited by Bainton, *Christian Attitudes*, pp. 175-76.

[20] Paul Fussell, *The Great War and Modern Memory* (New York and Lon-

can also be found in many of the first novels and autobiographical books of Vietnam veterans such as Philip Caputo and Michael Herr.[21] Fussell forthrightly uses the term "myth" for the understanding of war he is exploring. Yet he argues that this is a *new* perception, replacing an older one that represented war as heroic, and urges further that it is the controlling myth of war in the twentieth century. One wonders. In another book, I insisted that, if Fussell is correct about the newness of this perception, it began to appear much earlier—not with World War I, which Fussell regards as the first of the modern-style wars, but with the American Civil War or perhaps even the Napoleonic Wars, conflicts that were totalistic in nature and fought by popular armies of nonprofessional soldiers.[22]

Now I am inclined to go still further. The presence of this same sort of perception of war in the advocates of "perpetual peace," before that in a Renaissance humanist such as Erasmus, and before that in a late-medieval proto-humanist such as Christine de Pisan, suggests that instead of being something new—whether in the twentieth century, or the nineteenth, or the eighteenth, seventeenth, sixteenth, or fifteenth—the myth of war encountered here is one that runs throughout history. Alongside it we would expect to find other myths based in other perceptions: a myth of war as the crucible for self-realization and heroism, as found in classical writers such as Thucydides, medieval writers such as Honoré Bonet (and Christine de Pisan, too, who employs it as a remedy against the horrors of war), and the memoirs of professional soldiers in all ages; or a myth of war as capable of being employed with due restraint in the service of justice and the defense of other human values, as in Clement of Alexandria, Augustine, the Peace of God movement, Gratian, and the just war tradition generally. The seventeenth- and eighteenth-century works describing in various ways the ideal of "perpetual peace" are thus the expres-

---

don: Oxford University Press, 1975); see further my analysis in *Just War Tradition*, pp. 30-38.

[21] Philip Caputo, *A Rumor of War* (New York: Holt, Reinhart & Winston, 1977); Michael Herr, *Dispatches* (New York: Alfred A. Knopf, 1977).

[22] Johnson, *Just War Tradition*, pp. 33-34; cf. chapter IX.

sion of a unique way of looking at war, its roots, and its results; we may term it the pacifist myth of war. Given the assumptions, its conclusions are the only ones reasonable; yet may not the same thing be said about the competing myths of heroic war and just war?

We turn now to Rousseau, beginning with his perception of war in *L'État de guerre*. This is a comparatively brief work of fewer than 4,500 words, likely a fragment of some larger uncompleted project, and was never published by Rousseau. In that brief space, though, Rousseau wrestles with three main themes: a rebuttal of Hobbes on the state of nature, an argument for a necessary connection between the state and the existence of war, and the horrors of war itself. The work is at the same time grandly optimistic about the peacefulness of man in the state of nature and deeply pessimistic about man in civil society. Rousseau does not here essay a remedy to war, but he prepares the way by laying out the nature of what is to be remedied if war is to be abolished.

Rousseau begins with an argument against Hobbes, with which we may quickly deal. Hobbes had posited a "war of all against all" in the state of nature. Rousseau replies that such a view is absurd: if all warred against all, the result would have been a fight to the last man, and then this man would have found himself in a totally undesirable situation. "Can his stomach devour all the fruits of the earth?" demands Rousseau ironically. "To whose eyes will he show off his power?" What good are riches with no one else in the world to appreciate them?[23] Rather, man in nature is fundamentally peaceful. It may occasionally happen that quarrels may arise there, and even that a man may sometimes kill another over such disputes. But this is far from a permanent state of war. Indeed, such a permanent state presupposes constant relationships among men; in fact, though, human relations in the state of nature are "in a continual flux which unceasingly changes relationships and interests."[24]

[23] Rousseau, *L'État de guerre and Projet de paix perpétuelle*, p. 3.
[24] Ibid., pp. 4-5.

Whence, then, does the phenomenon of war come? Rousseau answers, from the state. When civil societies are established, their interrelations are precisely what Hobbes erroneously assigned to man in the state of nature. *Here* is where a settled state of enmity is to be found, Rousseau argues, for it is of the nature of the state to live in hostility with other states. He makes this argument in various ways, but most fully by comparing the "artificial body" of the state to the human body. The latter is characterized by limits set by nature: man has limited strength, limited faculties, limited years, and limited ability to enjoy riches, indulge his passions, and seek his pleasures.[25] By contrast, the state "has no determinate limits; its proper grandeur is [always] indefinite; it can always augment itself; it perceives itself as feeble if there is one stronger than itself."[26] The result is that the state must always seek to expand its being by expanding its power and its rule: "Its surety, its conservation demand that it make itself more powerful than all its neighbors."[27] The state that is not on the move, Rousseau remarks further on, is already as good as dead.[28] This is characteristic of all states; yet, in a world where all mankind belongs to one state or another, a given state can grow only at the expense of one or more of the others. Such, then, is the root of war, and it is a necessary and permanent feature of life in civil society: "I thus call war of Power against Power the effect of a mutual disposition, constant and obvious, to destroy the enemy State, or at least to enfeeble it by all available means."[29]

There appears in this discussion an idea also present in *The Social Contract*: war is between states only, not between their peoples.[30] In both contexts this is meant to bolster the distinction between the populace of a country and their sovereign, of whom Rousseau treats in *L'État de guerre* as the virtual equiv-

[25] Ibid., p. 8.
[26] Ibid., p. 9.
[27] Ibid.
[28] Ibid., p. 10.
[29] Ibid., p. 12.
[30] See Best, *Humanity in Warfare*, pp. 56-57.

alent of the state when at war. In a larger context, especially as stated in *The Social Contract*, it was also intended to support the concept of noncombatant immunity as applying to the general populace in an age when wars were generally fought by professionals. But, as Geoffrey Best points out, Rousseau was in fact making an artificial distinction, one already out of step with his times and even more at odds with the structures of the postrevolutionary societies of America and France not many years later. Best cites the language of the Declaration of Independence: "When in the course of human events it becomes necessary for *one people* to dissolve the political bands which have connected them with another. . . ."[31] The enemy was not just King George III: so far as the British people were concerned, the Declaration continued, "We . . . hold them, as we hold the rest of mankind, Enemies in War, in Peace Friends."[32] Best's point here is exactly the opposite of Rousseau's: that in fact "the people" have much to do with the fortunes of their state, an interpretation bolstered by the historical fact that in the late Enlightenment increased popular political participation was becoming a reality as well as being a major theme of political theorists—Rousseau himself included, ironically enough. Rousseau's distinction between people and state as concerns enmity in war simply does not fit this larger context very well. What it does fit is the developing myth of war already established in Erasmus: the concept that war is the result of some defect in the state, but that the bonds of community among humankind, which transcend artificial state borders, can offset that defect and bring in an enduring peace.

Rousseau's enmity toward the state as he perceived it extended as well to existing patterns of international relations and schemes of international law, including those limits on war from just war tradition as expressed by jurists of his day. These have nothing to do with reality, he concludes, characterizing the peace they define thus: "It is the tranquillity of the

[31] Ibid., p. 57; emphasis is his.

[32] Ibid.

companions of Ulysses closed in the cavern of the Cyclops." Reality lies outside the cave:

> I lift my eyes and look into the distance. I see fires and flames, deserted fields, pillaged villages. . . . I hear a frightful noise; what a tumult! what cries! I approach; I see a theater of murders, ten thousand men slaughtered, the dead heaped into piles, the dying trod on by the feet of horses, everywhere the image of death and agony. There is the fruit of these pacific institutions.[33]

Such is war. The words echo those of Erasmus two centuries earlier. They also, however, presage the words of the *Marseillaise*, the anthem of the French Revolution: "Do you hear, in the fields, the bellowing of the ferocious soldiers? They are coming almost into your arms to butcher your children, your companions." But this is a call to arms, not a tortured outcry against war. The "ferocious soldiers" in the fields are those who fight under the "bloody standard of tyranny," and to resist them the anthem raises the call, "Aux armes, citoyens"—"To arms, citizens." The sentiment is very much Rousseau's: it is tyrants, the sovereigns of the *ancien régime*, who cause wars with all their depredations. Yet, not without irony, in the *Marseillaise* the implication is not to move toward peace but for the people as a whole to take up the sword—a *levée en masse* against the threatening forces of the monarchies that sought to undo the revolution of 1789.

With the view of war and its causes expressed in *L'État de guerre* as background, it is natural to expect that Rousseau's position on the "perpetual peace" idea would follow the precedent laid down by his predecessors, all the way back to Erasmus. Actually, however, Rousseau's two brief pieces on Saint-Pierre's *Projet* convey a profound ambivalence, alternating between idealistic optimism and an almost cynical skepticism.[34] The former attitude is that of the *Extrait du Projet de*

[33] Rousseau, *L'État de guerre and Projet de paix perpétuelle*, p. 15.

[34] On Rousseau's position see further Stanley Hoffmann, *The State of War* (New York, Washington, D.C., and London: Praeger, 1965), chapter 3: "Rousseau on War and Peace."

paix perpetuelle de M. l'Abbé de Saint-Pierre, the latter that of the companion work, *Jugement sur la paix perpetuelle*, both dating from 1761.

There were two principal versions of Saint-Pierre's plan, the original having twelve provisions and a later abridgment (1748) having five. Rousseau takes this latter scheme over into his *Extrait*, developing his own ideas in the form of supporting commentary around them. In summary form, these five provisions serve to review the main line of thinking in what we may now call the "perpetual peace" tradition of the seventeenth and eighteenth centuries, differing only in their particulars. 1) The contracting sovereigns—all the nations of Europe plus Russia—would establish "a perpetual and irrevocable alliance" and create "an assembly or permanent congress" that would regulate and settle all differences among the contracting powers by "arbitration or judgment." This would be the first article of the proposed treaty. 2) The second article would concern housekeeping matters: who would be invited to participate, how the presidency of the assembly should rotate among the members, how contributions to pay for common expenses should be assigned. 3) The status quo would be established as the basis of the proposed alliance and any future decisions of the assembly regarding disputes among its members. 4) "The fourth article would specify the cases in which any ally who infringes on the treaty would be put under a ban by the rest of Europe and proscribed as a public enemy: that is to say, if it refuses to execute the judgments of the great alliance—whether by making preparations for war, negotiating treaties contrary to the confederation, or taking up arms either to resist it or to attack any one of the allies." 5) Another housekeeping provision, this article would give the delegates of the contracting parties the authority to make rules for the alliance as a whole; it also lays out the minimum requirements for adoption of these rules.[35]

[35] Rousseau, *L'État de guerre and Projet de paix perpétuelle*, pp. 41-43. English citations here and below are from a translation by Jinx Roosevelt in her Columbia University doctoral dissertation, now in progress.

As compared with Erasmus's vision of a united Christendom, this one is far closer to the form of a legal covenant among nations such as that of the League of Nations or the United Nations; that is to be expected of an age when the work of the publicists and the interactions of nations were moving progressively in the direction of establishing a positive international law. The parallel between Saint-Pierre/Rousseau's construct and that of Erasmus is on the more general level of assumptions, expectations, and hoped-for results. There is the evil of war: adding to what he said earlier in *L'État de guerre*, Rousseau writes here of "the perpetual dissensions, brigandage, usurpations, revolts, wars, and murders which daily lay waste to this respectable abode" of European society. There are the causes of war, to be found in the divisions between states and their rivalries: "Let us agree then that the relative state of the powers of Europe is properly speaking a state of war, and that all the partial treaties between certain of these powers are but temporary truces rather than true forms of peace." And yet, contrarily, there is the bond of unity that exists among Europeans, rooted in their common land—"more evenly peopled, more consistently fertile, better united in all its parts than other continents"—and even more fundamentally in the common culture forged by centuries of "blending of interests" by trade, marriage, art, industry, religion, and other forms of interaction. Peace, then, lies in the political formalizing of this subpolitical unity; once achieved, it will be a "perpetual" peace both because all will find it their common interest to maintain it and because the formal structures will provide for sanctions against those who reject it.[36]

If this were all Rousseau had to say, it would mark him as just one more visionary of a lasting peace that would be achieved by the expansion of human community and the creation of a new political agency superior to the sovereignty of the individual state. Yet Rousseau's pessimism about the empirical state itself, already expressed in *L'État de guerre*, emerges also in his *Jugement* on the "perpetual peace" idea.

[36] Ibid., pp. 30-31.

The problem is the sovereigns themselves, who will fear the loss of their rights and powers. "[T]he same princes who would defend the European Republic with all their might once it existed would now be opposed even to its being set up, and they would infallibly prevent it from being established with just as much energy as they would prevent it from being destroyed."[37] No prince, Rousseau later comments ironically, "would support without indignation the idea of seeing himself forced to be just."[38] Nor will any one of them voluntarily submit to a higher power for arbitration of differences when he is convinced he can secure a more favorable judgment by force of arms. Good will and the excellence of the result are not sufficient reasons for the establishment of the European Republic as proposed by Saint-Pierre.

The idea, Rousseau continues, is nonetheless "not mere fantasy." The problem lies in assuming that this republic can be brought about by voluntary consent. He introduces the example of the "first author" of the scheme, Henri IV, and his minister Sully, the former "no fool" and the latter no "visionary." Henri was well on his way to establishing such a Europe when death came to him; he was on his way to "a war which would end all wars . . . to make way for immortal peace." Rousseau comments: "The same blow which ended the days of this good king plunged Europe back into eternal wars which she can no longer hope to see come to an end. Nevertheless, those were the elements which Henri IV combined to form the same enterprise that the Abbé de Saint-Pierre claimed to create with a book."[39] The conclusion sounds more like Dante or Marsilius—or perhaps Machiavelli—than it does Erasmus, Penn, or Saint-Pierre:

> [W]hatever is useful to the public must be brought by force—seeing as special interests are almost always opposed to it. Doubtless perpetual peace is at present a project which seems absurd; but were we to be given a Henri

[37] Ibid., p. 63.
[38] Ibid., p. 65.
[39] Ibid., pp. 70-76.

> IV and Sully, perpetual peace might become a project which once again would seem reasonable. Rather, let us admire such a fine plan, but be consoled that we will never see it come about, for that can only happen by means which humanity might find violent and fearful.
>
> We will not see federative leagues establishing themselves except by revolution; and, on this principle, who would dare say whether this European league is to be desired or to be feared? It would perhaps cause more harm all at once than it could prevent for centuries to come.[40]

Rousseau's conclusion is thus fundamentally pessimistic, yet curiously prophetic; for, before long, the French Revolution was to shake the structures of the *ancien régime* whose sovereigns Rousseau regarded with such cynical skepticism, and Napoleon was to come closer to establishing a united Europe—albeit by a *pax Gallicana* imposed by force of arms—than Henri IV or any of the philosophers of "perpetual peace" ever did.[41]

What, then, is one to make of this movement? Its immediate intellectual inspiration in the seventeenth century appears to have been Erasmus, who envisioned the unity of European society coming about because of existing ties of community and good will. The *Realpolitik* of Henri IV and Sully aside, this vision runs throughout the "perpetual peace" tradition right up through Rousseau's *Extrait* based on Saint-Pierre's work. But the deeper inspiration for this line in the quest for peace, as we have seen, is in such late-medieval political thinkers as Dante and Marsilius and popularizers such as Christine de Pisan, whose concepts—from a later perspective if not from their own—have a darker, more totalitarian cast. The problem is that of all utopias: they carry in them the seeds of corresponding dystopias. Rousseau saw this, in an involuted way: his negative view of sovereign princes led him to see that they would

[40] Ibid., p. 76.

[41] This is not to say that such a united Europe, however brought into being, would have been Rousseau's own ideal; see Hoffmann, *The State of War*, pp. 80-82.

effectively prevent the establishment of the utopian ideal, and it also led him to flirt with the idea that one such prince (if strong enough and clever enough, but also if altruistic enough) could create the desired unity by force of arms. But, ever doubting the power of war to create more good than evil, he recoiled from this idea in turn.[42] That left him, lacking further insight, with making the best of the status quo; for rejecting the grand war to end all wars meant attempting to live with the seemingly perpetual little wars of the eighteenth-century sovereigns. This was where others had been all along; this is the consensus exemplified by Vattel and cited by Best. Before we examine it, though, we need to look briefly at one figure after Rousseau in the "perpetual peace" tradition of the Enlightenment, Immanuel Kant.

Kant's *Zum ewigen Frieden* (literally "To Eternal Peace"; known in translation as *Eternal Peace* or *Perpetual Peace*) was published in 1795, thirty-four years after Rousseau's *Extrait* and *Jugement* had appeared and in the sixth year following the French Revolution. The skepticism found in Rousseau also appears here: the title itself, Kant reveals in his opening sentence, was borrowed from the signboard of "a certain Dutch innkeeper . . . on which a graveyard was painted"; the theme of skepticism continues throughout, as Kant warns his readers that he is a "mere theorizer" and not a "practical statesman."[43] Yet the idealism found in Rousseau motivates Kant, as

[42] The result is more like Marsilius than it is like Dante; the ideal state of the *Defensor Pacis* (as we saw above, Chapter II) is not the international superstate, but the local state whose composition has been transformed so as to manifest order, justice, and peace. It will have nothing to fear from other states because of its own internal strength and unity, which will deter potential aggressors from attacking. Simultaneously, this ideal state will stand as an example to all its neighbors, who will be motivated to emulate it in order to have the same virtue and prosperity. Compare this to Rousseau's vision of "small, essentially self-sufficient republics, endowed with civic pride but no national vanity and equipped with purely defensive militias" (Hoffmann, *The State of War*, p. 78; see further pp. 73-82).

[43] Immanuel Kant, *The Philosophy of Kant: Immanuel Kant's Moral and Political Writings* (New York: Modern Library, 1949), chapter XII: "Eternal Peace." See p. 430; cf. passim.

well: he is one of those "philosophers who are dreaming that sweet dream of peace" to whom he refers.[44] The new element in Kant's contribution to the "perpetual peace" theme is the union of this skepticism and idealism in the same work. He will lay out the goal, but he does not expect it to work; he knows the "worldly-wise statesman" will look down upon his "impractical ideas," knowing at the same time that they "can bring no danger to the state, since the state must be founded on principles derived from experience."[45] This is irony, of the sort already found aplenty attaching to the utopian, pro-superstate tradition of "perpetual peace"; the difference is that here the irony is recognized by the author himself and does not wait to be perceived by his critic.

The result is, as Bainton puts it, a work with "ambiguities,"[46] and it is probably fairer to Kant and to the tradition of thought on peace within which he stands to let those ambiguities remain. Bainton himself probably goes too far toward a typical modern pacifist argument when he cites Kant's reflection on the maxim "Let justice be done, though the earth perish" (*Fiat justitia, pereat mundus*).[47] "But it will not perish," counters Bainton, going on to give Kant's own words in reply: "The universe would not totter if there were fewer wicked men in it."[48] Kant, though, was responding to his own commonsense rendering of the maxim: "Justice shall prevail, even though all the rascals in the world should perish as a result."[49] In correct context, Kant's later remark (the sentence quoted by Bainton), is simply a comment on the earlier one; together these two sentences do not at all amount to the combination Bainton provides: "Let justice be done, though the earth perish." "But it will not perish." Whether Bainton intended the connection or not, this tone is often adopted by contemporary pacifists whose purpose is to establish the reasonableness and

[44] Ibid.

[45] Ibid.

[46] Bainton, *Christian Attitudes*, p. 182.

[47] Ibid., p. 181; Kant, *Moral and Political Writings*, p. 467.

[48] Bainton, *Christian Attitudes*; Kant, *Moral and Political Writings*, p. 468.

[49] Kant, *Moral and Political Writings*, p. 467.

efficacy of nonviolent schemes of national defense.[50] The kind of immediate connection envisaged here is far from what Kant has in mind: the bad, he says, is "self-destructive," but while it thus "yields to the moral principle of the good," it does so only "in a slow progression."[51]

It is also incorrect to find in Kant's *Eternal Peace*, as the late nineteenth-century English writer James Farrer did, an example of going "straight to the point of trying to stop war altogether."[52] Insofar as Kant did this, it was in the realm of the ideal only, and Kant was too much a realist to expect the "worldly-wise statesmen" of his day to make much of it. Geoffrey Best, though, may err too much in the opposite direction, making Kant fit within the "Enlightenment consensus" Best exemplifies by Vattel.[53]

Rather than attempt to fit this work (and Kant himself) into some other pattern, a better course is simply to recognize the ambiguity that is present here, to reflect further that in a thinker of Kant's power it is almost certainly intentional, and then to ask what to make of that. The clue to answering this question, I suggest, is partly to be found in the ambivalence exhibited by Rousseau and partly in the nature of the text of *Eternal Peace* itself.

Kant's own skepticism as to the possibility of any fulfillment of the ideal of "perpetual peace" in the short term is but the next step after Rousseau's. In terms of Kant's own abilities, his treatment of this ideal is that of a far more self-assured philosopher, one more at home with ideas in the mind. Kant was perhaps able to expect less realization of the ideal in the short term because he was so convinced of its triumph in the long term. The result is a kind of detachment that Rousseau, a quite different personality, did not possess.

The "perpetual peace" idea had seemed possible of realization to each of the major contributors to its expression during

[50] Cf. Yoder, *What Would You Do?* (Scottdale, Pa., and Kitchener, Ont.: Herald Press, 1983), pp. 26-32.

[51] Kant, *Moral and Political Writings*, p. 468.

[52] Quoted in Best, *Humanity in Warfare*, p. 37.

[53] Ibid.

the seventeenth and eighteenth centuries—until Rousseau, who called it into question as a practical possibility. Kant begins at this point: eternal peace is not (unless in the graveyard sense) likely to be taken seriously or achieved by the work of practical politics in the short run; yet the principles for establishing it are universal and themselves eternal, and in the end peace itself may be expected to triumph. Kant's positive purpose, then, is to lay out the definitive general principles for establishing such a peace. This accounts for the difference between these principles as he states them and those of earlier "perpetual peace" authors; the similarity of content is owing to the fact that, withal, Kant stands in the tradition of thought that these earlier thinkers created. He is, though, with Rousseau, at a point of pause and consolidation. The nineteenth and twentieth centuries would develop this ideal somewhat differently from their predecessors.

Kant's *Eternal Peace* includes two different kinds of articles: "preliminary" and "definitive." The former are more connected to practical statecraft and the developing consensus on the limitation of war as it had taken shape in the eighteenth century; yet these are also the more immediately reflective of the previous "perpetual peace" tradition, which sought concreteness in such a recommendation as we find here:

1. No treaty of peace shall be held to be such, which is made with the secret reservation of material for a future war. [This would be "a mere truce," comments Kant.]

2. No state having an independent existence . . . may be acquired by another state through inheritance, exchange, purchase, or gift.

3. Standing armies shall gradually disappear.

4. No debts shall be contracted in connection with the foreign affairs of the state.

5. No state shall interfere by force in the constitution and government of another state.

6. No state at war with another shall permit such acts of warfare as must make mutual confidence impossible in time of future peace. . . . [Kant mentions using assassins or poisoners,

violating articles of surrender, and instigation of treason in the enemy state.][54]

The "definitive articles" are more general in nature:

1. The civil constitution of each state should be republican.
2. The law of nations should be based upon a federalism of free states.
3. The Cosmopolitan or World Law shall be limited to conditions of universal hospitality.[55]

These articles and their accompanying discussion are, however, only a bit more than a third of the whole of *Eternal Peace*. Kant provides two "additions" and an "appendix." The latter is specifically philosophical and concerns "the disagreement between morals and politics."[56] (It is in this section, not that of the articles, that the maxim on justice cited by Bainton appears.) The first "addition" discusses nature as offering a "guarantee of eternal peace."[57] It also makes clear, though, that the guarantee applies only to the long run of history; it is eschatological, and offers no real encouragement to the efforts of those who would bring in "perpetual peace" in the short term. The second "addition" is more immediate in focus: a "secret article" in the treaty on eternal peace requiring that "the maxims of the philosophers concerning the conditions of the possibility of public peace shall be consulted by the states which are ready to go to war."[58] This, writes Kant, means that the state will solicit the advice of philosophers

> *silently* (by making it a secret) which means that it will *let them talk* freely and publicly about the general maxims of the conduct of war and the establishment of peace (for they will do it of their own accord, if only they are not forbidden to do so).[59]

[54] Kant, *Moral and Political Writings*, pp. 431-36.
[55] Ibid., pp. 436-48.
[56] Ibid., pp. 457-76.
[57] Ibid., pp. 448-55.
[58] Ibid., p. 455.
[59] Ibid., p. 456.

This provision does not really belong to the tradition on "perpetual peace"; for, before Kant, the writers in that tradition stress the actions of good rulers acting in their own and their peoples' self-interest, not the need for philosophers to guide their thoughts and actions. Rather, it fits the model of just war tradition, already to be found in the Middle Ages but stated explicitly by Victoria (in the sixteenth century) and Suárez (in the early seventeenth): the sovereign should, before making war, consult the opinion of various sorts of advisers, including those able to assess the morality of the enterprise. We do not find this in Grotius or his publicist successors, including Vattel. Thus, it is all the more striking when it appears in Kant, albeit in a new form well suited to the republican state that is Kant's ideal—and, incidentally, to the empirical modern liberal democracy: grant freedom of speech and do not suppress public discussion, but pay attention to what is said by people of wisdom. It is not clear that this will always, in the short run, produce the choice to avoid war; yet Kant clearly believes that, over the long run, it will aid the cause of a lasting peace.

With Kant, then, the Enlightenment concept of "perpetual peace" reaches a new level of statement and, as a practical political ideal, begins to metamorphose into another form. Understood as a stage in the development of a broader tradition of pacifist thought, seeking an enduring peace through the creation of a new order superior to the state, the "perpetual peace" movement is a link between the utopianism of Erasmus and the internationalism through which this tradition has expressed itself in the nineteenth and twentieth centuries. At the same time, though, as we see in Rousseau, it provides a reminder that utopian goals have a tendency to resolve themselves into dystopias, and as we see in Kant, the ideal may not be expected to realize itself in history for a long time to come.

C. The Limitation of War in the Enlightenment Era

There are many ironies in the development of moral thought on war, and not least of them is that the very same period which saw so much intellectual energy spent on laying out the vision of "perpetual peace" and describing plans for its achievement was the classic age of limited warfare in Europe. The first two of the "perpetual peace" authors treated above, Crucé and Sully, lived at the end of the era of religious warfare that followed the Reformation. These wars of religion were often terrible in their impact on the ordinary people of the regions where they were fought, and it is understandable that many persons began to think of the ideal of a lasting peace and the restoration of fraternity and community among all the citizens of a splintered Christendom. Most nourished such thoughts while reading the works of others, such as Erasmus, whose commentary on the adage *Dulce bellum inexpertis* was reprinted in various languages numerous times during this period. Crucé and Sully went further, reformulating the ideal of an enduring peace for themselves.

After the Thirty Years' War ended in 1648, though, a new atmosphere prevailed. Ideological hatred and mistrust rooted in religious difference, which had marked warfare, both civil and international, through the previous century, had dissipated. No one wanted to go to war for religion any more, if the result was to be such bloody and exhausting conflicts as the one just ended. Moreover, with the demise of Christendom came a corresponding rise in the power and autonomy of the nation-state. This shift had already taken place during the Thirty Years' War, which was, during roughly its last half, more a dynastic than a religious struggle. In any case, the Peace of Westphalia ratified the new reality, and from the time of its signing until the beginning of the French Revolution in 1789 the wars of Europe were of a sort that reflected this reality. They were, as one writer calls them, "sovereigns' wars,"[60] wars engaged in by the ruling princes of the various nation-states for dynastic or national-interest reasons, fought by relatively small, compact, and highly trained armies of professional soldiers, financed with the limited resources of the sov-

[60] J.F.C. Fuller, *The Conduct of War, 1789-1961* (New Brunswick, N.J.: Rutgers University Press, 1961), chapter I.

ereigns themselves, and carried out in an increasingly stylized fashion. The aims of these wars were limited, the resources used to fight them were limited, the impact on the civilian population in the theater of war was limited: this was "limited war" in its classic form.[61]

The moderation of war in the resolution of conflicts and the pursuit of peace was thus given practical expression in military practice during this period. Yet, beneath this, there was a growing body of opinion, legal thought, and diplomatic tradition that pointed in the same direction. The irony, then, is that all this was contemporaneous with the flowering of the "perpetual peace" tradition in Penn, Saint-Pierre, and Rousseau; it was not entirely gone even by the time of Kant's *Eternal Peace*. In developing the ideal of "perpetual peace" these authors rejected the moderation of war as a means toward real peace. The horrors of war depicted by Rousseau (or by a writer like Swift) were not the depredations of the early period of the Thirty Years' War; they reflected instead the practice of limited war in the post-Westphalian era. Those killed were not noncombatants impaled on pikes or burned in their homes, but paid soldiers who met death on the battlefield while opposing the enemy. But such moderation was not enough for the advocates of "perpetual peace." Although the reason for fighting was no longer difference of religious confession, this was no gain in the eyes of the "perpetual peace" theorists, to whom the new reasons for war were only trivial and silly. These writers would thus not have recognized anything ironic in their opposing the "sovereigns' wars," however much it may seem so in a longer historical perspective. For them, limited war was at best only a halfway measure toward peace—defined as the cessation of *all* war. They wanted such a peace, and nothing less.

Yet, for a writer such as Grotius, contemporaneous with Crucé and Sully, or John Locke, writing later in the same century, or Emmerich de Vattel, whose major work was published in 1758 (about the same time as Rousseau's writing on the evils of war and the ideal of perpetual peace), the moderation

[61] See further Johnson, *Just War Tradition*, chapter VII.

of war represented the most realistic and best way to achieve peace. This did not necessarily preclude the kinds of international congresses called for by the "perpetual peace" advocates, but these were not conceived of by writers such as these as miracle drugs that might cure the whole range of causes for war.[62]

It should, perhaps, be stressed that these writers were utterly serious about the positive effects they expected to result if nations acted according to the proposals they made. They were not in any way apologists for war. The effect of their thought was to reconceive and recast just war tradition so as to derive its provisions entirely from natural law and the customary behavior of nations. They and others like them defined a new tradition, international law, that carried forward into a secular age the fundamentals of the broader just war tradition. As Bainton says of Grotius, the goal was "to repristinate the just war theory—to make war again the servant of law, the instrument of justice, and the tool of peace."[63]

Several features run throughout this newly forming consensus. First and most fundamental, as already noted, is the reliance on the law of nature and the customary behavior of nations (or "law of nations," as it is most often called, after the old Roman and medieval concept of *jus gentium*). The requirements of just war were not, in this concept, tied to Christian morality—a reflection of the demise of a united Christian religion in Europe—but came from the nature and structures of nations and their interrelationships. That nature is regarded not as ineffably venal, as the tradition from Erasmus to Rousseau generally had it, but as capable of good as well as evil. Relations among nations are not inveterately hostile, as Rousseau believed, but depend on trust and reciprocal behavior. All in all, this new version of the just war idea perceived the state and international relations with a blend of optimism and pessimism. Its proponents believed that this system could produce justice and reduce the level of armed conflict to a minimum,

[62] See further Johnson, *Ideology*, chapter IV.
[63] Bainton, *Christian Attitudes*, p. 178.

but they did not believe an everlasting condition of peace among nations could be achieved.

Second, the sovereign state is simply taken for granted as the basis of relations among nations, and as a result the inherited *jus ad bellum* of just war tradition takes on a *pro forma* cast. In the time of Gratian and his successors in the twelfth and thirteenth centuries, one of the most fundamental questions in the restraint of violence was the establishment of responsible and just government; accordingly, right authority, just cause, and the other *jus ad bellum* concepts were at the center of concern. Only after the issue of sovereignty and authority to use force had been settled did the focus shift to incorporate fully the *jus in bello* concerns for the protection of noncombatants and the general regulation of force levels. Still, in the late-medieval consensus on just warfare, these two kinds of interests were held in balance—a state of affairs that obtained right through the great Neo-Scholastic just war theorists of the sixteenth and early seventeenth centuries, Franciscus de Victoria and Francisco Suárez.

With Grotius, though, the balance shifted decisively toward the *jus in bello*, a condition characteristic of the next three centuries of development in international law. (Only in the twentieth century, through the League of Nations Covenant, the 1928 Pact of Paris, and the United Nations Charter, has some sort of recovery of a *jus ad bellum* in international law begun; yet what has been restored remains only a truncated version of the *jus ad bellum* idea of just war tradition as a whole.)[64] The problem of limiting violence was no longer, as it had been in the early Middle Ages, how to root out private violence by insisting on duly constituted, responsible authority behind every use of the sword; now the overriding issue was how to regulate violence among such "right authorities" themselves. Every sovereign ruler was accepted as possessing the necessary competence to judge the justice of his cause, weigh the costs, and consider the interests of his people; if all else failed, he had the required authority to wage war. With no superior power to

[64] See further Johnson, *Ideology*, pp. 265-72.

settle disputes by fiat or impose binding arbitration, war might be the only means to a conclusion. In accepting what would later be called the *compétence de guerre* of the sovereign ruler of each nation-state, the nascent theories of international law in the seventeenth and eighteenth centuries subtracted from the ability of the *jus ad bellum* of the inherited tradition to limit recourse to war. With this limitation for practical purposes gone, they concentrated instead on the restraints to be observed in the prosecution of war, and here they were by no means inclined toward tolerating excess.

Faced with the same historical state of affairs, the advocates of "perpetual peace" did just the opposite. Convinced of the overwhelming evil of war as such and discounting any possibility of limiting it meaningfully, they sought instead to establish a power superior to the national sovereigns; this new power would be the only one with the necessary qualifications to judge the rightness of the use of force and to authorize such use. In effect, the "perpetual peace" plans took the road of trying to establish the end of war by emphasizing the *jus ad bellum*, believing nothing important could come from the *jus in bello*. Conversely, the new theorists of international law, having for practical purposes given up on the possibility of limiting recourse to war through the *jus ad bellum*, instead saw new possibilities in a *jus in bello* connected explicitly to nature, *jus gentium*, and the mutual interests of nations and their sovereigns.

That the newly secularized law-of-nature-and-nations version of just war tradition had real teeth can be seen through Vattel. He limits the state's right to make war to that which is necessary to "repulse aggressors, secure its rights, and render it everywhere respectable."[65] Men and nations alike are obliged to "assist in the perfection of others" and are forbidden to "increase their imperfection." Vattel continues:

> This general principle prohibits all nations every evil practice tending to create disturbance in another state, to foment discord, to corrupt its citizens, to alienate its allies,

[65] Vattel, *The Law of Nations*, book I, section 20.

> to sully its reputation, and to deprive it of its natural advantages.[66]

A sovereign may not go to war lightly. Besides the moral responsibility imposed by the above considerations, when the sovereign assumes the power to judge his own cause and the authority to wage war, he also implicitly takes onto his own shoulders the guilt for an unjust war. For Vattel, the ruler who goes to war unjustly may be held solely responsible for it and forced to pay all its costs.[67] There are thus some quite real restraints, rooted both in natural morality and self-interest, on the casual initiation of war. The state's power to wage war, for Vattel, extends to its self-preservation; it does not include the right to threaten the lands or wealth of another. What has been given the ruler in *compétence de guerre* is thus taken back, at least in great part, by a doctrine that finds justice only in wars of defense of one stamp or another.

Vattel, like the consensus he helps to form and express, assumes that, in spite of all, there will be wars; in his view, every belligerent has the duty to seek to restrain the destructiveness of war. Vattel takes up the inherited tradition on noncombatant immunity, states it in terms of secular values, and elaborates it into a newly broadened *jus in bello*.

The immunity of noncombatants from the ravages of war follows from their remoteness from the guilt of war. Noncombatants are those persons whose social functions do not involve them in warmaking. Those most closely associated with the sovereign implicitly share in any guilt he may bear, but others, even though supporting his designs through obedient citizenship, are to be regarded as innocent. Such persons—including the classic noncombatant categories of women, children, the sick, and the aged—"are members [of the enemy society] which make no resistance, and consequently give us no right to treat their persons ill, or use any violence against them, much less to take away their lives. . . ."[68] Peasants on the land

[66] Ibid., section 177.
[67] Ibid., section 187.
[68] Ibid., book III, section 145.

are likewise to be treated as noncombatants, but not just because of their social function: "by protecting the peaceable inhabitants, keeping the soldiers in strict discipline, and preserving a country, the general procures an easy substance to his army, and saves it many losses and dangers."[69] The reasoning here is clearly based in a belligerent's self-interest, and behind it lies a veiled threat—that harshness against the people of the land will be repaid in loss of substance to the army and perhaps, though Vattel does not say so explicitly, in guerrilla activity. Indeed, a theme of self-interest seems to run throughout Vattel's development of the argument for noncombatant immunity: no army can engage in generalized rape and murder without fear of reprisal; no army can do such things and even remain a disciplined fighting force, rather than armed rabble. It is not altruism, then, which dictates protection of noncombatants: nature sets the first limits, and self-interest adds its own large measure of restraint.

Subsequent positive international law on war embodies exactly the same sort of reasoning as employed here by Vattel. Noncombatants deserve protection in their own right, out of natural justice; yet, a further element of protection is rendered by provisions that allow reprisals of sorts not otherwise allowed when noncombatants are treated in unlawful ways.

What Vattel had to say on the *jus in bello* was not, however, limited to his recasting of the inherited tradition on noncombatant immunity in terms of natural law and mutual self-interest. Civilization itself is to be protected from the ravages of war. Vattel explicitly condemns needless violence directed toward an enemy's lands and cities: there should be no uprooting of vines or cutting of fruit trees, for to render a country desolate for many years in this way can be dictated only by "hatred and fury," not wisdom;[70] there should be no bombardment, burning, spoliation, or other defacement of "fine edifices" that "do honour to human society, and do not con-

[69] Ibid., section 147.
[70] Ibid., section 166.

tribute to the enemy's power."[71] The immunity of noncombatant status thus extends to the conditions of civil living: the sources of food and wealth in a society, its cultural expressions, its public buildings. War, when fought, is to be fought between *armies*, not whole populations.[72]

Finally, war is not to be conducted in such a way as to endanger the peace that is to come. Classic just war thought had included in its *jus ad bellum* the requisite that war not be fought except for the end of peace. Part of the new consensus expressed by Vattel was an effort to give force to that concept, though in the context of the *jus in bello*, not that of the *jus ad bellum*. The provisions mentioned above were measures toward that end; yet there were more.

As Geoffrey Best remarks, "[a] large part of the modern law of war has developed simply as a codification and universalization of the customs and conventions of the vocational/professional soldiery."[73] What this meant in the context of eighteenth-century warfare was fighting according to the generally accepted conventions. While the popular concept of warfare dwells on great battles between opposing forces in the open field, the truth of most eighteenth-century warfare is that it was predominantly a contest of position, fought over the various fortified places ("magazines") possessed by the belligerent powers. The typical forms of war were thus maneuver and the siege, not battle in the open. Not only were such battles far too costly in trained men and materiel to be entered into lightly, but no commander in an army of this period could entirely trust that the soldiers they had enrolled with the promise of regular pay would stay in the ranks when confronted by the prospect of death. Harsh discipline was the answer to the latter concern: all European armies used flogging and the firing squad as punishment for indiscipline; also (and perhaps with more practical results) in the typical order of battle, noncom-

[71] Ibid., section 169.

[72] This was not only theory but the practice of eighteenth-century war; see, for example, Jay Luvass, ed. and trans., *Frederick the Great on the Art of War* (New York: The Free Press; London: Collier-Macmillan, 1966).

[73] Best, *Humanity in Warfare*, p. 60.

missioned officers were placed behind their men with orders to turn back or kill any who tried to flee. Still, even such Draconian measures could not always be depended on at the extreme; for one army always had to break—or be annihilated—if there was to be an end to a battle. There remained in any case the first reason for avoiding battle: the exorbitant cost, together with the risk it posed of losing all. So armies in the "sovereigns' wars" tended, instead of seeking battle, to march around attempting to achieve superior position and to lay siege to fortified places left inadequately defended by the enemy.[74]

"Not much ordinary fighting," comments Best, would go on during a siege; rather, "fighting might be avoided altogether if a capitulation were signed at the appropriate moment: i.e., when a 'practicable breach' had been made in the fortifications."[75] Such were the conventions, not written down in any rulebook but known by all professional soldiers. Capitulations, on this form, were not surrenders but "prudent agreements between a force that seemed certain to win and one that seemed certain to lose."[76] The aim was to win without any more loss of blood than absolutely necessary. So long as both sides in a war observed these tacit rules, and so long as the formal conventions of capitulation, safe-conduct, truces, and the like were honored and not used in an attempt to gain unfair advantage, a war could be concluded without indiscriminate slaughter and such mutual hatred and distrust that no real peace between the belligerent nations could ever be achieved.

Going beyond the accepted conventions, Vattel sought also to limit the use of weapons that had the effect of increasing the destructiveness of war. His explicit example was the use of red-hot cannon balls for bombardment of fortified cities; these

[74] That is, they followed a strategy of attrition (wearing down the enemy) rather than one of annihilation. These terms are originally those used by Hans Delbrück in his *History of the Art of War*; for their application to eighteenth-century warfare, see Russell F. Weigley, *The American Way of War* (New York: Macmillan; London: Collier-Macmillan, 1973), p. xiv, n. 10, and chapter I.

[75] Best, *Humanity in Warfare*, p. 61.

[76] Ibid.

were "an extremity."[77] A century after Vattel, Francis Lieber, author of the first manual of the law of war for United States forces (*General Orders No. 100* of 1863), argued just the opposite way. Calling Vattel "Father Namby Pamby," Lieber himself was fascinated with new weapons that, while increasing the destructiveness of war, thus gave promise of shortening wars. For him the best wars were the briefest, and implicitly whatever shortened a conflict should be approved.[78] Lieber, of course, lived long before the advent of nuclear weapons, and it would be unfair to him to suggest that he would have supported a nuclear holocaust lasting only a few minutes over a lower-level limited war lasting perhaps years. But even in his own time, the "miracle weapons" (e.g. one of his favorites, the exploding rifle bullet) caused additional suffering without measurably shortening the overall progress of the war in which Lieber was immediately involved, the American Civil War. Vattel and the professional soldiers of the eighteenth century[79] thought in diametrically opposite ways, as did their sovereigns—not how to increase the pain of war so as to end it quickly, but how to secure a state's interests without needless bloodshed and without ensuring the hatred of an enemy population (and reprisals against one's own) by extreme measures that widened the war.

When one lays the "perpetual peace" literature alongside that expressing this consensus on the proper aims and limits of war, it is hard to believe that the authors are talking about the same phenomenon at all. The difference of perspective between the pacifist and just war approaches expressed here are no longer as close as they had been in the late Middle Ages. Indeed, they appear to be almost mutually exclusive. One of

[77] Vattel, *The Law of Nations*, book III, section 169.

[78] Francis Lieber, "Addenda and Notes for Inclusion in Lieber's *Code*," ms. and other materials in the Lieber Collection of the Huntington Library, San Marino, Calif. (Huntington Library index no. LI 182).

[79] This was also true of such generals as Henry Wager Halleck, for a time the Union Army general-in-chief during the American Civil War, reflecting the training he had received at West Point; see further Johnson, *Just War Tradition*, pp. 284-89.

them looks at war and sees the savage butchery of countless numbers of hapless souls; the other looks at war and sees a stylized chess match, to be conducted with the least possible loss of valuable personnel and equipment. One side sees wars fought for the frivolous whims of the sovereigns, with the people bearing the losses; the other sees wars fought for serious interests, with the sovereigns themselves taking the greatest risks. I spoke earlier of competing myths of war, each representing reality according to its own perspective; here the competition and difference of perspective are starkly obvious. In fact, "sovereigns' wars" were never so stylized or restrained in their prosecution as the ideal; otherwise, there would have been little motivation for Vattel to put the proper limits down in writing. Yet the "perpetual peace" myth was even more off the mark. Its concept of the destruction inherent in war fitted better the scope of the religious wars (particularly the Thirty Years' War) or that of the wars of the Napoleonic era still to come than it did the dimensions of eighteenth-century warfare. Whether the sovereigns who authorized and paid for wars in that century were being frivolous is harder to answer; yet if, in their own concept of their interests, they were in fact being frivolous, it is difficult to imagine that their ambassadors, convened in a supranational parliament, could be much different, as the history of the League of Nations and the United Nations suggests.

These reflections are not intended to suggest that the one perspective on war is universally to be trusted over the other; in the era of the wars of religion or in the wake of the trench warfare of World War I, an objective judgment on the actual nature of war would likely tilt the other way. As to the solutions offered by these competing myths, it may be enough to say that neither offers the whole truth. Perhaps it is necessary for both myths—and the perspectives they reflect—to persist together in history. The most fundamental moral goal in the quest for peace, then, would be to bring them into dialogue with each other.

CHAPTER V

THE QUEST FOR PEACE IN THE AGE OF MODERN WAR

A. Abolition, Restraint, or Total War

Both the idea of "perpetual peace" and the quest for peace embodied in the theory and practice of limited war were dealt a crushing blow by historical circumstance beginning in the last decade of the eighteenth century. The shock was from the effects of the French Revolution on the accepted order, both in politics and in military practice. As to "perpetual peace," the 1789 Revolution threw to the winds the possibility of a peaceful coming together of the European powers into a cooperative league aimed at establishing peace. In place of the idealism that fueled this vision it set a new idealism, defined ideologically by the goals of the revolution and politically by French nationalism. If peace through unity was henceforth to be obtained in Europe, it was to be on French terms; and it would be imposed by French arms, not achieved through mutual cooperative agreement among the powers. As to the character of war, this was fundamentally transformed from that of the earlier period of "sovereigns' wars." The military conflicts of the *ancien régime* had been limited affairs which, while frequent, were fought by a relatively small segment of society, the professional soldiers, over dynastic and territorial claims. The new style of warfare produced the concept and reality of "the nation under arms," eroding the distinction between combatant and noncombatant; the goals by which it was justified included the establishment of high ideals such as "the rights of man," which tended to justify greater losses to achieve them. As a result, this new warfare was notably harsher than that of the previous period, both on the civilian populations of Europe and on the soldiers themselves. Let us look at these two major developments in greater detail.

1. A New Kind of Idealism

The idealism of the French Revolution offered a notably greater challenge to established political verities in European society than had the American Revolution not many years earlier. Then the conflict had been a relatively minor one, centered in a colonial land three thousand ocean miles away, affecting continental Europe hardly at all and, indeed, directly involving only a comparatively limited segment of the English population. The ideals for which the Americans fought were represented not as a challenge to those of the mother country, but rather as rights possessed by freeborn Englishmen in which the colonials should share. While George III was represented to be a tyrant in the revolutionary rhetoric of the 1770s, this was not a general challenge to monarchy itself, only a response to the bad rule of one particular monarch. The establishment of the new American nation on a republican foundation had great symbolic value for European society, but the English nation itself continued as a monarchy—indeed, as a monarchy under King George III, despite his obviously failing mental powers.

The French Revolution, by contrast, took place at the heart of European society. It directly involved the most populous and arguably the most powerful single nation in Europe. The "Declaration of the Rights of Man" went beyond freedoms possessed by the French people at the time and tapped into a vein of transcendent ideals whose previous expression had been limited to the works of political philosophers. "Liberty, Equality, Fraternity" meant far more than the claim by American revolutionaries that they should have the same kind of parliamentary representation as they would if they happened to live in England itself, or that they should pay no taxes levied by a Parliament in which they had no elected representatives.

This new idealism of the French Revolution was focused on values held as *ultimates*; the political ideology these values defined was more like religious belief than anything found in the continental European states since the age of the religious wars two centuries earlier. The French Revolution, moreover, directly assaulted the institution of monarchy, and it carried this assault through to the point of regicide—again, a political act not seen in Europe since the beheading of Charles I in England a century and a half earlier. Finally, it sought complete acceptance of its aims by the French people at large, and where propaganda was not enough, there was the power of the state; where high-principled hortatory language failed, there was the fear inspired by the Reign of Terror.

For our purposes, the important results of these radical developments are those that affected the ideal of European unity—expressed by the advocates of "perpetual peace" in terms of a "parliament of Europe" or a supreme confederation of states that might even include polities with different cultural roots, such as the Turkish Empire. This was the ideal that was dealt a devastating blow by the French Revolution. We can see this in four major respects.

First, the revolution's challenge to monarchy in the name of republicanism undercut the fundamental political similarity among European states that was a significant element in the overall cultural commonalty stressed throughout the "perpetual peace" literature. The Pan-European parliament, which was a regular feature of the vision of the path to peace defined in this literature, depended upon the institution of monarchy. Kings were to send ambassadors to such a parliament, and these ambassadors were to possess authority to act in the name of their kings. Agreements reached in the parliament were in effect to be agreements among the principals who had empowered their ambassadors to act for them. In terms of the political concepts current in the seventeenth and eighteenth centuries, and as Rousseau specifically puts it in his *Extrait* from Saint-Pierre, these agreements would be contracts personally binding on the contracting sovereigns.[1] The challenge to the project of "perpetual peace" on this level was simply *anarchical*, in the fundamental meaning of the term: without order. Who, in a re-

[1] See Rousseau's first provision: Chapter IV, at note 35, above.

publican government, could be counted on to speak for the state in the way a sovereign of the *ancien régime* could? With what person or persons in a republican government could a personally binding contract be made? Even if this were settled, who was to be held accountable should the person who had made the agreement later leave the government?

It is difficult to imagine with sufficient vividness, in an age when republican government has become the norm in Western society, how seriously such questions were felt when the normative governmental form was monarchy and the new French Republic represented a step into largely unknown political territory. Perhaps the most important loss was the ideal of personal accountability, with all this implied when attached to the concept of monarchical government. The connection between the two was ancient and pervaded existing political assumptions in the eighteenth century. An international treaty between two states was still in theory a compact between two sovereigns. War, as we have seen, was still conceived of as a struggle between rulers, who were expected to make war largely out of their own resources. A soldier, as in Roman and medieval times, swore fealty to a person, the sovereign, not to the state that sovereign headed. At the end of a war, as Grotius had maintained following a much longer tradition, and as Vattel had echoed hardly a generation before the onset of radical republicanism, the ruler and those closest to him were to be held responsible for making up the costs of the war, and they incurred personal guilt for any depredations committed by their armed forces during the war.[2] This personalization of international relations even extended to that most fundamental of social institutions, marriage; for, just as in the Middle Ages and in more ancient times, political alliances in the age of Enlightenment were concluded by strategic marital unions.

Now, the striking thing is how deeply this personal concept of rule was attached to the ideal of "perpetual peace." Erasmus had set the tone, envisioning a Europe in which peace and tran-

[2] Grotius, *Of the Rights of War and Peace*, book III, chapters xii-xiv; Vattel, *The Law of Nations*, book III, sections 183-87.

quillity would be achieved through the cooperation of virtuous princes who took seriously their Christian faith; this was the ideal in *The Education of a Christian Prince*. The other side of his vision was, of course, a view of war as caused by the personal decisions of venal princes. Both themes run through the literature of the "perpetual peace" movement from Sully to Saint-Pierre and on to Rousseau. So much was invested in this concept of politics that the introduction of a radically different idea of the state and its government, in the form of French republicanism, meant a fundamental challenge to the vision of a lasting peace built upon the good will of monarchs who, operating through their personal ambassadors, could create a new form of universal government that might transcend the conditions that caused wars to occur. The idea of a parliament or congress of Europe was but a new structured form for the older vision of a brotherhood of Christian princes, cooperating in the interests of peace, harmony, and the greater good of all. Republican government in one of the largest, most populous, wealthiest, and most powerful states in Europe destroyed the possibility of such a union of monarchs, and with it the seventeenth- and eighteenth-century concept of the way to achieve "perpetual peace."

Ironically, though, the French were, both implicitly and explicitly, offering an alternative vision; this alternative was the second challenge to the older "perpetual peace" ideal. The firebrands of the revolution, who were now also the leaders of the French state, were committed to the universal overthrow of monarchy. While in the short run this meant war, in the long run it meant a vastly increased opportunity for achieving a lasting universal peace. For the revolutionaries accepted the Erasmian view that strife among nations stemmed from the venality of princes: this was but a natural extrapolation of their understanding of the same sovereigns' role in oppressing their own people within the state. Like Rousseau, the revolutionaries could conceive no possibility of these same monarchs uniting in the cause of peace, for no one of them, put to the test, would sacrifice his self-interest in the necessary ways.

The *people*, on the other hand, could by cooperation achieve such a universal peace, for their collective self-interest would be served by that achievement. The ideals of the French Revolution thus pointed toward a vision of peace which was much like that of the "perpetual peace" literature and yet critically different. The old vision had been one of peace achieved from the top of societies down, through the cooperation of monarchs. These individual rulers would form a union among themselves—actually never a full union in political terms, but at best only a confederation, since each component part retained its autonomous existence. In the concept implied by revolutionary republican ideals, on the other hand, the union to be achieved was one of peoples, and the necessary structural linking of governments was but a formal means of effecting the will of the people as a whole—just as in the republican ideology the government of a state was but a formal structure to manifest and implement the popular will for the popular good. This would be peace from the bottom up. The *ancien régime*'s hereditary monarchs and monarchical government could have no part in such a vision, for these rulers were felt to be by their very nature self-interested and incapable of truly serving the will or the good of the people they governed.

This new vision, however, required not only the removal of the monarchs, but a reconceptualization of the fundamental political structures defining the nature of the state and the possibilities of relations among states. It was one thing to construct these in terms of the revolutionary ideology, quite another to work out all their implications for governmental praxis in detail, and still another to bring about the almost religious conversion necessary for this vision to take hold throughout European culture. For the monarchs and their supporters were far from willing to admit that their governments did not serve the public good and did not flow from the public will. Indeed, in England one of the ironic results of an earlier experience of revolution, parliamentary government, and regicide had been the restoration of the monarchy; and the Calvinist doctrine that allowed lesser magistrates to correct and depose kings when they ruled unjustly had metamorphosed into a system of government in which the very limitation of kingly autarchy by Parliament made the institution of monarchy in that nation one of the strongest in Europe.

The problem of political reconceptualization was, put briefly, how to shift the understanding of government from the *personal* to the *structural* or *institutional*. For one state to do business with another on the republican model, it was inappropriate to focus on the personalities of the leadership of the two states: at least in theory, a republican leader did not impose his own personality (in the form of self-interest) on his acts and decisions on behalf of the people; in practice, moreover, the individuals occupying leadership roles in a republic could be expected to change over time. What was necessary was to insist on institutional coherence and continuity, so that whoever occupied given governmental offices, agreements made by those offices in the past would continue to be honored. Within the state, moreover, government had to be structured so that personality mattered little and personal aggrandizement of power would be inhibited or prevented by the nature of the institutions themselves. Erasmus had confronted the problem of the venality and pettiness of princes and thought to solve it by describing how to make princes virtuous; the Enlightenment tradition of "perpetual peace" projects built on this model, describing how the enlightened self-interest of monarchs would lead them to join in a parliamentary confederation. Skeptics such as Rousseau denied even the possibility of such a definition of virtue and thus denied the possibility of this route to peace; the revolutionaries of 1789 agreed with him. Faced with the venality and pettiness of princes, they sought a new structure of political life in which princes had no part: the republic.

The magnitude of the problem of reconceptualization this implied is suggested by the fact that even today much of the language of international law and international relations employs the terminology of the age of monarchy: the sovereign state has replaced the sovereign prince; the state is now the international "person," as in the *ancien régime* the monarch had been; the notion of responsibility in war that once attached to the prince has been carried forward in the concept of guilt defined in Nuremberg law. Similarly, the course of a particular nation at a given moment is often described in popular parlance by reference to its leader: differentiating De Gaulle's France from Mitterrand's is a way of symbolizing a difference in policy; so we speak also of Thatcher's Britain, the United States under Carter or Reagan, the Soviet Union as directed by Stalin, Khrushchev, Brezhnev, Andropov, or Gorbachev. There is a subtle but strong temptation thus to reduce national policies to the personality of the nation's leader, even when the ideology of republicanism is quite the opposite.

We have, of course, already in this book encountered other efforts to resolve the problems of bad government by the creation of new structures. The "perpetual peace" idea was itself one such effort: once in place, the new universal congress would by definition remove the causes of war formerly found in the rivalries of princes. Before that, a similar vision appeared in Dante's *De Monarchia*, where the institution of monarchy was described as ensuring order (and, in turn, justice and peace) just by being what it was, regardless of the personality of the monarch. This sort of vision is intellectually powerful, offering a chesslike solution to the problems of politics, whether the ideal structures are those of monarchy, republicanism, or whatever. Would that the problems of good government and a lasting peace were so easy to resolve!

The third type of problem posed for the "perpetual peace" vision by the French Revolution had to do with the concept of war itself. For the "perpetual peace" intellectuals, war between nations was invariably bad; but use of military force within the proposed union of nations would be to a good end, because such force would be employed only to put down a rebellious aggression by a member state. Such a policelike use of force would be a protective reaction of the many, united into a whole, against the one. It never seems to have occurred to the proponents of the "perpetual peace" schemes that matters might have looked different to the state that was the object of such coercion. In the aftermath of the revolution, though, this was precisely the role in which France was placed, as the monarchical powers collectively sought to undo the revolution by military invasion. Thus war against other states became, for France, not a self-indulgence but a necessity, not an evil but a glorious good, the protective reaction of the one against the tyranny of the many. The new state of affairs turned the model of the "perpetual peace" plans on its head.

Finally, we must mention the effect of the French Revolution on the balance of power that had obtained in Europe throughout the period from the end of the Thirty Years' War until 1789. This balance was both static and dynamic, with an ongoing pattern of national rivalries at its core but with minor adjustments accomplished through shifting alliances among the other states. The balance was maintained not only by diplomatic means, but also and importantly by war. Both the frequency of wars during this era and their limited character served to help maintain the overall balance. While the advocates of "perpetual peace" would never have admitted these results as any kind of virtue, they in fact assumed the good of a power balance for achieving and maintaining peace: their vision of the international order in which lasting peace is attained is one in which the balance of power lies decisively with the central authority symbolized by the parliament or congress of nations. Once the system of union had begun to be established, all nations would seek to become part of it, because all would wish to be on the side of the preponderance of power.

This was, however, only an ideal. With the French Revolution, France was effectively removed from the political equations employed to calculate the actual balance. A new set of equations was immediately generated by consensus on both sides of the republic/monarchy divide: it was republican France against the rest of Europe, ruled by monarchs. This was, as already noted, the sort of situation envisioned in the "perpetual peace" plans when justified military force might be employed against the disturber of the common peace; yet, as also noted, who was the aggressor and who the defender depended on one's perspective. From the standpoint of beleaguered revolutionary France, the enmity between the monarchies and the République Française was likely to remain until the former were all put down by force of arms. Thus, ironically, the French revolutionaries generated their own vision of "perpetual peace" in Europe: the universal republican society discussed above. Here, too, the balance of power would all be one way, but it would be all on the side of the republicans. Once in place, it would be static, for no single dissenting power could effectively challenge it. France, admittedly no longer republican by that time, almost achieved this goal under Napoleon; whether the peace thus achieved would have been "perpetual" is another matter. But the vision of the ideal is remarkably similar to that found in the "perpetual peace" literature, even though its terms are reversed; the one is the positive, the other the negative of the same picture. For neither was the balancing act performed by the shifting alliances and frequent limited wars of the *ancien régime* any kind of ideal. Thus, not without irony, the circle closes in the unity of these two seeming opposites, the "perpetual peace" movement and the radicalism of the French Revolution. The latter, however, was to bring in the place of limited war not universal peace but, as we shall see next, a new age of total war.

2. *The New Shape of War*

The French Revolution began in an age of limited war; yet the effect of the revolutionary wars and the following era of the Napoleonic Wars was to displace the restraints of the previous age and to make war more nearly total. The changes did not all occur overnight or all at once, and in some respects—notably, the weapons used, the tactical formations, the problems of supply, and the fact that war could not be easily fought in winter—the Napoleonic Wars were much like those of Frederick the Great and other European monarchs of the previous century. The changes that did occur, however, were fundamental: they transformed the shape of war in their own time and for our time as well.

These wars of the revolution and its aftermath were the first modern wars—motivated by ideology, involving large numbers of men under arms, tending to dissolve the traditional barrier between combatants and noncombatants, and hence terribly destructive in their scale. They would likely have been more destructive had technology allowed, but the French and their opponents still fought under the technical restraints that had helped limit the wars of the *ancien régime*. Later, when the Industrial Revolution provided mass-produced, breechloading rifles, long-range, large-caliber artillery, and the machine gun, and when the railroad and the truck made it possible to supply armies and keep them fighting year-round, the stage was set for the slaughter which was World War I. Technological change has continued apace, and the powers of destruction available to a contemporary superpower dwarf those of 1914-1918.

Yet it is a mistake to identify the problem of modern war with such growth in the potential destructiveness of weapons. The armies of the eighteenth century did not always use even what they could have used: the Swedes refused to employ the bayonet (except against the Poles); the Russians and Louis XV rejected an improved form of gunpowder because it was too destructive of human life.[3] Similar decisions might well have been made in the nineteenth and twentieth centuries as new weapons became available. So the problem does not lie in what is at hand but, rather, in how people think about using what is at hand. It lies in the basic ideological, attitudinal, and social changes that have come to define war as the occasion for inflicting the worst possible damage on an enemy, even perhaps at the cost of enormous suffering on one's own part. This was the change in war brought by the French Revolution and its aftermath, and it has greatly affected the course of the quest for peace in the modern age. Thus, we need to examine the elements of this change more closely. I have singled out four main aspects of it.

First, the armies of revolutionary France fought for the nation, not the sovereign. They were the forces of *France*, not of the Directorate or even, later, of Napoleon. This change did not immediately affect the armies of the monarchies aligned

[3] Noted by Bainton, *Christian Attitudes*, p. 186 (citing Nef, *War and Human Progress*, pp. 118, 122, 252, 260).

against the French, but by the end of the Napoleonic period this new nationalism had spread widely and taken root. The Spanish *guerrilleros*—or, as we would call them today, guerrillas—who harassed the French occupying army during the Peninsular Campaign were not fighting for the weak and remote monarchy that then was the nominal sovereign of Spain, but for freedom from domination by the French. While the idea of a Spanish nation would have been an abstraction foreign to most of these country and hill people, fighting for their own homes and property (and, as they must have seen it, for their customs and Spanish identity) meant a new perspective on war: a struggle of peoples, not of sovereigns and their mercenary armies.

Rooted in the same spirit, yet with a nationalism that was closer to consciousness, were the reflections of the sixteen-year-old Francis Lieber as he marched with a Prussian force against Napoleon before the Battle of Waterloo. Lieber later emigrated to the United States, where he became a professor of international law and, as we have seen, the principal author of the United States Army's *General Orders No. 100*. Reflecting back on his youthful experience of war, Lieber wrote in terms of being a Prussian, of defending his homeland against Napoleon—not of serving his king.[4] Interestingly, he cites Napoleon by name as the enemy, revealing that same personalization of the evil author of war that we find in the Erasmian tradition. But Lieber is clear in depicting his own motivations in terms of the newly emergent nationalism, and in assigning the same motivations to the other forces opposed to Napoleon.

Related to this development is a second factor, the enlargement of the military forces of the state so that the quest for manpower reached deep into all aspects of society. For one thing, there was the *levée en masse*, used by the French early in the revolution as the only realistic hope of holding back the invading counterrevolutionary armies of the monarchies, and

[4] Francis Lieber, *Lieber's Miscellaneous Writings*, vol. I: *Reminiscences, Addresses, and Essays* (Philadelphia: J. B. Lippincott & Co., 1881), pp. 151-75, "Personal Reminiscences of the Battle of Waterloo"; see particularly pp. 151-54.

later employed somewhat less effectively by the Prussians against the forces of Napoleon. The *levée en masse* was provided for in existing concepts of international law, but seldom employed. It was a version of the *levée de troupes*, the process undertaken at the beginning of a war to add new men to the forces that had been maintained under arms during peacetime (or, during a war, to replace men killed or wounded in combat). The difference was that the *levée en masse* called on every able-bodied man to rise up in arms to oppose the invasion in progress. These might or might not have regular weapons, might or might not be formed into tactical units, might or might not have trained, responsible leaders, might or might not fight according to the rules of war accepted by regular soldiers. The roots of the *levée en masse* went to the concept that individuals had an absolute right to protect their persons, homes, and property against an army, even when that army may have had the just cause in the larger dispute between states.[5] By extension, the ideal would perhaps be that each peasant would guard his own holdings and protect his own household. But the French quickly transformed this into an effective and large-scale *levée de troupes*, organizing a peasant army of disproportionately large size relative to the population of France, when compared with the ratios of the armies of the monarchies to the populations that supported them. Thus, the *levée en masse* was the precursor of a national army based on a wide-reaching military draft. With this latter development we enter the age of the large standing army of citizens, fed by conscription and by requisite service in reserve units, as it became a standard feature in continental European society during the last half of the nineteenth century and on into the twentieth.

These new-style armies were not so distinct from the general population as were those of the *ancien régime*, and this leads us to the third major aspect of the new shape of war introduced by the French Revolution: the erosion of the distinction between combatants and noncombatants. This was, in the first

[5] Cf. Grotius, *Of the Rights of War and Peace*, book III, chapter xxvi.

place, a matter of the practical difficulty in distinguishing between these two classes of people under the conditions of the *levée en masse*; later, the same difficulty was experienced by the French themselves in the guerrilla warfare of the Spanish Campaign. But the erosion of this distinction was also a product of two other factors: a new ideological bias that broadened the concept of "enemy" and a new national policy that, again extrapolating from the *levée en masse*, involved the civilian population in supporting the military in ways they had not during the era of "sovereigns' wars."

As to the ideological factor, Geoffrey Best comments as follows:

> "Liberty" and its revolutionary accompaniments "equality" and "fraternity" were goods it could seem a duty and pleasure to extend to others. So self-evidently good were these principles that, when they failed at once to catch on in neighbouring countries, surprised French revolutionaries ran rather quickly to explain the failure in simplified terms of conspiracies, oppression, and wickedness."[6]

In other words, if the people of any liberated territory seemed less than positive toward the high goals of the French Republic, they were enemies of the revolution as much as if they carried arms. In the name of "humanity" the French armies soon found themselves occupied in forcing the noncombatant populations of conquered territories to become free! Consider the following, from a proclamation designed to be read to each new group of "liberated" people:

> Brothers and friends, we have won our liberty, and we shall keep it; our unity and our power guarantee it. We offer to help you too to enjoy this inestimable good, which has always been your right, denied you by your criminal oppressors. We came to chase away those tyrants; they have fled before us; *show yourselves now to be truly free,*

[6] Best, *Humanity in Warfare*, p. 85.

and we will guarantee to protect you from their vengeance, their plotting, and their return. . . . [7]

As generous as this offer of protection sounds, its reverse side held an ominous threat: anyone who did not show himself to be "truly free" was an ally of those "tyrants" against whom the forces of the revolution were implacably opposed. This was a profound and real, if subtle, shift from the reasoning of Vattel, who had observed that while all the citizens of an enemy nation are called enemies, there are some who do one's own nation no direct harm, and these should not have harm done to them.[8] This is an application of the criterion of functionality,[9] which has been one of the main sources of noncombatant immunity in Western moral tradition. But when "doing direct harm" ceases to mean bearing arms and comes to mean ideological or political disagreement, an important threshold has been crossed in the denial of noncombatant rights. The revolutionary armies crossed this threshold, but their political leaders had obscured it already by their rhetoric.

Along with this threat to the combatant/noncombatant distinction came the new factor of the total mobilization of society to support the war effort. The phrase *la nation armée* (usually translated "the nation in arms") well symbolizes this changed reality. So thoroughly has this concept entered into the common consciousness that this is now how war is expected, by its nature, to be. Yet there is nothing "natural" about it. Limited warfare has always taken place without much impact on the noncombatant population of the belligerents, and still does. But there is no denying that total wars mobilize belligerents' entire populations for the war effort; on the "home front," civilians undergo rationing, knit gloves and sweaters for their "fighting men," and work in munitions factories. Such was the experience, with differences only in particulars, of the Western nations in the two World Wars, of the

[7] Quoted ibid., p. 86; emphasis added.

[8] Vattel, *The Law of Nations*, book III, sections 145, 146; see further Johnson, *Ideology*, pp. 246-48.

[9] See Johnson, *Just War Tradition*, pp. 132-33.

South in the American Civil War, and of the French people in the wars of the revolution and the Napoleonic era. It is, broadly speaking, a characteristic of ideological war; and ideological war is almost inevitably total. Such implicit broadening of involvement in the war effort by people who, in struggles conceived in less ultimate terms, would be noncombatants is the direct corollary of what happens to conquered people who must show themselves to be "truly free" by wholehearted support of their "liberators."

Finally, in fourth place, the new shape of war was defined by strategic aims that could be satisfied only by total victory. This, too, was a direct consequence of understanding the stakes of the war between the revolutionaries and the monarchies in terms of ultimates. Monarchies might have their disagreements, their supporters could admit; yet they could live together nonetheless. Everything being equal, so might the revolutionaries have argued about republics. But both sides agreed that republics and monarchies could not share the same world in peace, and herein lay the trouble for the limited model of warfare. With this perception added to the emergent nationalism and the mobilization of the "nation in arms," we have the basis for total war. Now, neither the French nor their opponents could in fact wage total war in the sense of the two World Wars of the twentieth century: they did not have the technology. But as the technology emerged, there was now a conceptual image of war that it could be made to serve, and the World Wars were the result.

Taken together, these changes posed enormous problems for the quest for peace. On the one hand, the stakes were much higher, and the secular state, which had been merely a political fact, now became the focus of a utopian idealism that tended to justify great sacrifices. This represented a direct challenge to the ideas of "perpetual peace," whose idealism had focused on the utopian vision of a brotherhood of nations sharing a common culture and common form of government, joined together in a Pan-European congress formed to protect and preserve peace. If there had been problems concerning how such an end was to be achieved in practical terms, these were nothing compared to the problems of how monarchies could be expected to coexist with republics, and vice versa. Nor was the goal of a parliament of Europe, made up of the ambassadors of monarchs, at all compatible with a revolutionary vision that thought of unity in terms of "peoples," not princes. At the same time, on the other hand, the restraints that had helped to limit war in the preceding century (even though the "perpetual peace" advocates had never thought much of them) were subjected to great stress, and some of these melted away under the new conditions of ideological fervor and the enmity it inspired. A new sort of war, more nearly total in both ends and means, resulted. The major traditions of the quest for peace nonetheless survived these fundamental changes, and now our task is to examine how they did so.

B. The Renewed Quest for Peace

1. *The Context and the Problem*

Wartime confronts the quest for peace with a paradoxical and uncomfortable situation. The fact of war itself presents the need for peace in its utmost urgency; yet, wartime tends to divide the ranks of the proponents of peace. Some will attach themselves to the nation's cause out of feelings that this is what loyalty requires. Others may go further and argue for unsparing prosecution of the war as a way of bringing about "real" peace as soon as possible. Those who remain in opposition to the war thus not only lose the companionship and support of erstwhile fellow travelers, but they may find their opposition reduced in the minds of the majority to nothing more than a dissenting minority political position; if they push hard against the war, they may even be accused of disloyalty to the nation. The more popular the war or the more it is perceived as just and necessary, the more difficult the stance of opposition becomes. We may view this problem briefly through a consideration of religion-based dissent in England during the period from 1789, the beginning of the French Revolution, to 1815, the year of Napoleon's final defeat at Waterloo. I will follow the analysis of the British historian Deryck Lovegrove, who focuses on a group of conscientious objectors little studied elsewhere: the "evangelical" religious dissenters.

Before turning to this analysis, though, it will be useful to prepare the context. We shall look briefly at a far better known example of English religious pacifism of a sectarian sort—the Quaker movement—and examine some results of its interaction with the governmental authorities on the question of war and military service over a period of more than a century prior to the evangelicals' opposition to military service during the Napoleonic Wars.[10]

By focusing on the evangelical dissenters, I mean in part to suggest that the phenomenon of radical Christian opposition to war is likely to break out unexpectedly. In any case, this example shows that in England during this period the Quakers were not the only representatives of the sectarian form of pacifism, despite their numbers and their relative prosperity as compared to the evangelicals. The Quakers' numbers, their social status, and their history gave them certain advantages in dealing with the state that the evangelicals did not share; thus, the case of the evangelicals is closer to that of the Schleitheim radicals than is that of the Quaker movement by the end of the eighteenth century.

Quaker pacifism had been formally institutionalized in 1660.[11] The evangelical dissenters of the late eighteenth century were in fact much like the Quakers of the 1650s and 1660s in their fresh representation of the radical dictates of the Christian message, as they understood it. Within the Quaker movement, on the other hand, the debate over war and military service had moved to a different level. In 1746 Richard

[10] I omit here any sustained discussion of the pacifism of the Quaker movement in England. An exhaustive study of English Quaker attitudes toward war and military service is provided by Peter Brock, who devotes three chapters in *Pacifism in Europe* (chapters 7-9) to this subject; see, also, the treatment of Quakerism in America during this period in his *Pacifism in the United States* (Princeton: Princeton University Press, 1968), part one, passim.

[11] See Brock, *Pacifism in Europe*, pp. 260-71, 305.

Finch, a Quaker merchant of London, published a small book called *The Nature and Duty of Self-Defence*, taking issue with the established Quaker position on war and arguing for a natural right of self-defense. Other Quakers immediately published works of their own upholding the established pacifist doctrine.[12] Finch later recanted, but he was not the only Quaker of this era to question the official pacifism of the movement. Brock writes:

> Not all Quaker peace dissidents returned to the ancestral pattern as Finch had done. . . . [T]hose Friends who could not accept the peace testimony usually remained silent on the issue and so escaped censure by their meetings—unless they were also tempted to accept service in the militia, if called for duty, or to place armaments on vessels they owned or captained.[13]

We glimpse here a phenomenon familiar to sociologists of religion who monitor the development of sectarian religious groups through their early generations. The Quaker lifestyle itself made for worldly success, prosperity, and respect; this in turn tended to produce conflicts of values among Quakers who, by the mid-eighteenth century, were well distant from the religious perceptions and motivations of the founders of the movement. A change, mirroring that found among the second-century Christians, appeared as some Quakers, appreciating the values the broader society represented, sought to justify bearing arms to protect that society and those values, with which these individuals were now very much at home. To oppose this, a special effort was needed to keep the questioned teachings alive and in force. The eighteenth-century intra-Quaker debate over pacifism was thus importantly an institutional debate over what Quakerism as a formal religious movement within society should be like. By looking at sectarian pacifism in this historical context through the evangelical

[12] Ibid., pp. 306-307.
[13] Ibid., pp. 307-308.

dissenters we avoid becoming enmeshed in this internal argument over the shape of institutional Quakerism.

Still, it is necessary to recognize that the social and historical milieu into which the evangelical dissenters' pacifism entered at the end of the eighteenth century had been formed, and was being formed, by the existence of the Quakers and their century-old pacifist stance—by the social prominence of many individual Quakers and by the number of persons who belonged to the movement as a whole. By the era of the Napoleonic Wars principles, laws, and practices had become established that constituted a working compromise between the military requirements of the state and religious pacifism. These defined the context into which the conscientious objection of the evangelical dissenters entered.

One aspect of the compromise was the legal provision that a man called for military service could, if he wished, hire a proxy to serve for him. This provision was not aimed specifically at pacifists, but evidence shows that in the Seven Years' War a number of Quakers had avoided military service in this manner, and the 1760 Yearly Meeting moved to halt the practice.[14] Yet the law remained in effect, providing at least a theoretical option for pacifists who would not themselves perform military service; this same allowance was, at the end of the century, still available to evangelical pacifists.

Fines were of course imposed for failure to muster or to provide a proxy, but Quakers also refused to pay such fines. Parliament responded by allowing "distraints," seizure of goods of individuals who did not comply with the law in one of the above ways. From the value of the goods, the authorities were enabled both to draw the fine and to provide funds to hire a substitute. This law discriminated in favor of the well-off; a 1786 law did hardly better by permitting Quaker pacifists without goods to pay £10, hardly an inconsiderable sum, in lieu of serving.

The final sanction against a conscientious objector without goods who refused or was unable to pay his fine or hire a proxy

[14] Ibid., p. 311.

was the threat of imprisonment, and some Quakers actually were jailed. Yet, the pressure of powerful Quakers mitigated this sanction as well, and in 1776 the attorney general of England declared that Quakers could not be put in prison for such cause.[15]

Whether these compromises were, as the Quaker historian Rufus Jones has characterized them, expressions of "great lenity" on the part of the authorities, or whether it is better to follow Peter Brock in noting that such legislation "could in no way satisfy Quaker scruples,"[16] or whether the truth lies somewhere in between, it is clear that the state had by the end of the eighteenth century adopted a quasi-recognition of the right of conscientious objection for religious reasons. Yet the provisions in question had been adopted in response to the pacifism of Quakers, and the evangelical dissenters were by no means automatically covered by them, as we shall see below. Lacking the Quakers' pacifist tradition, which extended back more than a hundred years, the evangelical conscientious objectors had to prove to the satisfaction of the authorities that their refusal to perform military service was genuinely religious and not otherwise motivated.

We turn now to examine the evangelical dissenters. Lovegrove notes that, at the beginning of this period, support for the French Revolution and opposition to English involvement in the fight against it were rooted in rationalist politics that favored "the democratic and levelling spirit already operating with such devastating results across the Channel."[17] Eight years later, though, in 1797, the weight of dissent had shifted to persons and groups—Lovegrove terms them "evangelicals" because of their emphasis on evangelism—also in religious dissent against the established Church. This opposition to the established powers on the subject of religion made it necessary for these persons and groups to tread warily in their opposi-

[15] On all these points see ibid., pp. 312-14; cf. pp. 314-27.

[16] Ibid., pp. 312-13; Brock cites Jones on p. 312.

[17] Deryck Lovegrove, "English Evangelical Dissent and the European Conflict, 1780-1815," in W. J. Sheils, ed., *The Church and War* (Oxford: Basil Blackwell, for the Ecclesiastical History Society, 1983), p. 263.

tion to the war, for this position also brought them into conflict with the establishment. As a result, the evangelicals found themselves having to stress their nonpolitical intent, and their opposition to the particular war across the Channel was phrased in terms of a general indictment of "the horror of war" and the good of peace.[18] The Christian's duty, in this view, was religious and moral, not political, as expessed in the following words from an address to the Hampshire association of Independent ministers in 1797:

> On the stable foundation of Christianity endeavour to the utmost of your power to promote the peace of the world, and to aid in giving the deadly blow to destruction and misery which have extended their triumphs so widely over the face of the earth. But to display the spirit of peace is not enough for a Christian. . . . To a pacific temper you must unite benevolence; and like Jesus of Nazareth go about doing good.[19]

At the same time, this withdrawal from the war had a practical political consequence: dissenters taking this position of conscience placed themselves in conflict with local militia regulations requiring service if chosen by ballot. While recognized ministers were given exemption, others were not. Dissenting congregations thus found themselves in the position of having to pay the fines imposed on men who out of conscience refused to serve—an expedient later used in the United States during the Civil War, when Quakers, rather than serving when drafted, sometimes paid for replacements who had no pacifist qualms.[20]

A few years further along, in 1803, the evangelicals' opposition to the continuing war had focused itself more closely on the effect the conflict was having on English morals at home. The nation was suffering from sexual immorality, profaneness, the evils brought by the slave trade, and (perhaps above

[18] Ibid., p. 267.
[19] Quoted ibid., p. 268, n. 18.
[20] See further ibid., pp. 269-70.

all) irreligion. The dissenters built on popular fear that the French might invade by saying such an invasion would be a proper punishment for England's decayed moral state. Summarizing the attitudes expressed in dissenters' sermons from this year, Lovegrove notes first that they all "regard war as a scourge and as a lamentable calamity." Many persons "are launched precipitately into an unexpected eternity, and civilian populations suffer the terrible experience of pillage, rape, and murder at the hands of marauding armies." Warfare, furthermore, has "an insidious moral influence" in general, "creating injustice, undermining the spirit of common humanity, inuring people to brutality and enervating vital religion." Finally, the sermons excoriate "the undue reliance placed upon material defences in preference to spiritual resources as being at least as harmful as the direct impact of violence."[21]

These dissenters were pure pacifists in the sectarian religious tradition. In England they were tolerated as *religious* groups, but such dissenters had to tread warily in drawing out the *political* implications of their moral stance against war. They had to be against war in general, not the particular war that was being fought; if they refused military service out of conscience, they had to pay fines and then see other persons induced to serve by cash bounties. Introverting their opposition to the war, they turned their fervor against personal immorality and irreligiousness at home.

Mutatis mutandis, the pattern was the same wherever there were pacifist sectarian groups on the Continent and in the United States, especially during the War of 1812. Paradoxically, war makes the rejection of war by such religious groups stand out in stark contrast, so that they become less able to make their pacifist voice heard in the context of the world outside the bounds of their religious beliefs.

On the other hand, a similar if opposite problem is faced by churches that uphold just war tradition: if they accept the possibility of a just war in general terms, then they may not oppose a particular war as unjust without seeming disloyal or involved

[21] Ibid., p. 272.

in partisan politics. Thus they find themselves beset by exactly the same pressures as the sectarians, though they typically resolve them differently.

The significance of this English example of dissent against war, then, is not only in the example it provides of how difficult it was for Englishmen to oppose the war against Napoleon out of religious conscience. It is also that this case reveals a pattern typical of how later sectarian pacifism has expressed itself in the modern world of secular nation-states, where conscientious opposition to war may be tolerated as a *spiritual* conviction but not as a *political* statement.

So far we have examined the quest for peace peculiar to religious sectarianism in the era of the French Revolution and the Napoleonic Wars. In the previous section, I have already treated the problems faced by the internationalist utopian tradition in the form of the "perpetual peace" ideal, arguing that the French Revolution made necessary a new conceptualization of this tradition of the quest for peace if it was to continue. There, too, we saw how the mainline just war idea, manifested in the practices of restraint from the "sovereigns' wars" of the *ancien régime* and in the developing theory of international law, also lost ground to the new realities of war shaped by revolutionary ideology, the creation of large national armies, and the effort to involve all of society in the war effort.

The remarkable thing is that, in the immediate aftermath of this era of warfare, things seemed to return to where they had been before 1789. Internationalism rose again, inspiring peace "congresses" in Paris, Brussels, Boston, and other places. Peace societies were formed in various countries (including one in the United States in 1815 and one in Britain in 1816), achieving in peacetime the union between internationalist idealism and sectarian pacifism that has been so difficult to maintain during a war. In 1839 another contribution to the "perpetual peace" literature appeared: Jeremy Bentham's *Plan for a Universal and Perpetual Peace*, which had, however, been written a half-century earlier.[22] With the restoration of the

[22] Jeremy Bentham, *Jeremy Bentham's Plan for an Universal and Perpetual*

monarchy in France, a sense of European unity was restored, and the balance of power was reestablished, albeit with a different list of major and minor players in the game.

It is easy to make much of this immediate continuity, as does Roland Bainton in the introduction to his chapter on the era "from Waterloo to Armageddon" (that is, from the end of the Napoleonic Wars until the beginning of World War I).[23] Yet much of what happened immediately was not to last, at least not in the same form. The changes set under way by the French Revolution and its aftermath, as these were identified in the previous section, had established a momentum of their own, and the energy of transformation continued to grow even amid the superficial appearance of a static return to the *status quo ante bellum*. I argued above that the "perpetual peace" movement would have to be rethought to make sense of the new conception of the nation-state; symbolic of the beginning of this reconception is the publication in 1840, the year following the appearance of Bentham's work, of a book by an American, William Ladd, titled *Essay on a Congress of Nations*. While reflecting the "perpetual peace" themes and their antecedents, Ladd sought to model his congress of nations on American governmental institutions and democratic principles.[24]

The post-1815 balance of power in Europe was quite different from the earlier one, and there were fewer players that really mattered. English dominance at sea was established beyond question; on land, the Russians, the Austrians, and the Germans dominated, while France was, for a time at least, relatively weak. Earlier substantial powers such as Spain, Holland, and Sweden had been reduced to supporting players. The prerevolutionary ideal of unity through a brotherhood of monarchs was hardly restored with the reestablishment of the monarchy in France; this remained weak, and France was to remain divided into monarchists, Bonapartists, and republi-

---

Peace, The Grotius Society Publications, no. 6 (London: Sweet & Maxwell, 1927).

[23] Bainton, *Christian Attitudes*, pp. 190-91.

[24] William Ladd, *Essay on a Congress of Nations*, ed. James Brown Scott (Washington, D.C.: Carnegie Institution, 1916).

cans right into the twentieth century. The erosion of restraint in war described earlier had taken place, and it was not easily to be revoked. A tradition developed, based on Karl von Clausewitz's concept of "absolute war," that redirected military thought away from restraint and limitation toward strategies and tactics geared to absolute victory.[25] Moreover, as noted earlier, the technological restraints on war still operating through the Napoleonic period increasingly fell before advances in industrialization, weaponry, and transportation. Finally, despite the popular success of the national peace societies and the international peace "congresses," any unity on the cause of peace that they achieved was more superficial than it may have seemed. Geoffrey Best identifies two quite disparate nineteenth-century themes, those of the "peace movement" and an opposing "war movement"—the former triumphant in the first part of the century, the latter dominant in the last part.[26] Even without the war movement, the peacetime success of the peace societies and congresses in bringing together sectarian pacifists and internationalist utopians could not be expected to last forever. This kind of unstable union did not, in fact, survive any major war.

The new currents did not unequivocally begin to emerge until toward the end of the nineteenth century; thus, the best course for our purposes is to scroll forward quickly to this period and examine the three major traditions in the quest for peace as they constituted themselves then and afterward. This brings us into the age of the codification of the law of war and, in the twentieth century, the definition of an international-law *jus ad bellum*. It brings us to the era of conscious, united political action by the "peace churches," as some of the sectarian pacifist groups now began to call themselves; and it brings us

[25] It is important to distinguish between the "Clausewitzian" tradition to which I refer here and the more dialectical position of Clausewitz himself, in which "absolute war" is countered by reflections on the need for less-than-absolute measures in actual wars. See further Karl von Clausewitz, *On War*, ed. and trans. Peter Paret and Michael Howard (Princeton: Princeton University Press, 1980).

[26] Best, *Humanity in Warfare*, pp. 130-38.

into an age of internationalism triumphant in the League of Nations, the United Nations, and the world order movement. We will be able to look at these only briefly, but in the following pages I will examine them as the vehicles by which the principal traditions in the quest for peace have developed into the present age.

2. *The Effort to Formalize Restraint in War*

An important feature in Western cultural attempts to limit the ravages of war has always been the reflection that peace at the end of a war is easier to establish if the war itself has not been so bitter as to induce persistent hatred. For this reason I have treated the broad tradition of restraint in war—the just war tradition, as I have defined it in other works—as one of the three main channels through which the quest for peace has flowed in Western history. In the medieval period this approach was manifested in the canon lawyers and theologians of the Church, on the one hand, and by knightly self-perceptions and concerns for self-interest, on the other. In the sixteenth and seventeenth centuries the burden of carrying this tradition began to shift to the theorists of international law. During the Enlightenment this trend continued, while statecraft and military concerns combined to produce a century-long phenomenon of limited warfare. Finally, in the last half of the nineteenth century and continuing into the twentieth, international law has sought to formalize and regularize restraints that in earlier times were but customary and consensual; military manuals on the law of war have followed in turn. This is the age of the military manuals on the conduct of war, of the Geneva conventions defining a "humanitarian" law of war, of the Hague conferences with their restraints on the use of certain weapons and means of war, and of twentieth-century efforts at arms control and disarmament. There is a voluminous literature on these topics, and I have myself added to it in other connections;[27] here I will touch only the high points in these developments.

[27] A diverse sample includes Best, *Humanity in Warfare*; the Classics of In-

What has been common to all these developments is the attempt to spell out the meaning of certain customary ideas of restraint in war, to extend that meaning in certain cases, to regularize it as a framework within which war should be fought, and to make it obligatory upon all concerned. The military manuals, including the original *General Orders No. 100* of the United States Army in the Civil War and all its successors right down to the present time,[28] have sought to ensure compliance by imposing rules of conduct upon military personnel from the top down. The international law approach has been to construct treaties in which the effort to impose restraint is carefully balanced against the willingness of the largest possible number of nations to sign the agreement in question.[29] The former approach is in principle more rigorous, for even though military necessity and the concept of reciprocity allow for departures from the code of conduct laid down by superior authority, there remains an irreducible possibility of court-martial for actions defined as illegitimate by the standards imposed. The My Lai massacre court-martials of the Vietnam War era in the United States are a recent example of this.[30] The international-consensus approach used in international law is inherently weaker in principle. Whatever a nation may have declared itself willing to do in peacetime, it may back away from it in wartime. Considerations of military necessity and

---

ternational Law series published by the Carnegie Institution; James Brown Scott, *The Spanish Origin of International Law* (Oxford: The Clarendon Press; London: Humphrey Milford, 1934); Dietrich Schindler and Jiri Toman, eds., *The Laws of Armed Conflicts* (Leiden: A. W. Sijthoff; Geneva: Henry Dunant Institute, 1973); Johnson, *Just War Tradition* and *Can Modern War Be Just?* (New Haven and London: Yale University Press, 1984).

[28] Contemporary examples include the U.S. Army's *Field Manual 27-10: The Law of Land Warfare* (Washington, D.C.: Government Printing Office, 1956). On the place of military professionalism in the ethics of war, see further Malham Wakin, ed., *War, Morality, and the Military Profession* (Boulder, Colo.: Westview Press, 1979).

[29] This tension can be glimpsed later in this chapter in the discussion of twentieth-century international law on war and peace; see Section C: "Internationalism and Universal Peace," below.

[30] Yet, at the same time, it appears difficult to secure convictions in such cases, as the My Lai example also suggests.

reciprocity are as alive here as in the application of the military manuals. Moreover, the limits established by treaty have already been filtered through such concerns by the time they are put on paper in final form. The international lawyer Georg Schwarzenberger speaks of a spectrum of obligations within existing international law on war: some provisions are self-evidently obvious and are almost always observed, such as prohibitions against torture and cruelty; others are attempts to extend the envelope of restraint and are quite unlikely to be observed in a condition of armed conflict, such as certain provisions attempting to restrain air warfare. Between these extremes lie the majority of international legal provisions on war, and these are more or less likely to be honored depending on which end of the spectrum they more closely resemble.[31]

It is not accidental that the first efforts of both sorts, *General Orders No. 100* (1863) and the First Geneva Convention (1864), appeared just when technological innovations had begun to make concrete the implicit changes in the face of war introduced in the revolutionary and Napoleonic Wars. The American Civil War was fought by citizen-soldiers on both sides; both North and South employed conscription when volunteers were insufficient; both had very large armies relative to the total population; for both, the aims of the war were of an ultimate character; on both sides, the distinction between combatants and noncombatants tended to dissolve under certain conditions. In addition to these factors, which were also present in the Napoleonic Wars, the logistic effects of the railroad first appeared in this war; and both sides also made extensive use of new types of weapons having greater destructive capability. The small-caliber exploding shell, or Minié ball, and the Gatling gun exemplify the latter, but this was also a war in which the use of rifles, rather than smooth-bore muskets, made for much greater loss of life on the battlefield.

In Europe, similar changes had also taken place. Large standing armies fed by conscription were becoming the

[31] Georg Schwarzenberger, *A Manual of International Law*, 5th ed. (London: Stevens & Sons, 1967), pp. 197-99.

norm—so much so that in 1870 they were denounced in a *Postulata* presented by a number of bishops to the First Vatican Council.[32] Large continental powers such as France and especially Germany were developing an awesome power to use their networks of railroads not only for logistical supply (which was the main use in the American Civil War) but also to mobilize reserve forces quickly and to move masses of armed soldiers speedily from one place to another. In addition, heavy industries like those of the Krupp family developed the ability to manufacture heavy-caliber, long-range rifled artillery, introducing a trend which, in World War I, produced the railway artillery used for countercity bombardment.[33]

The warfare of the eighteenth century had been restrained by a mix of moral, political, and technological factors. The French Revolution and the Napoleonic Wars removed the political restraints (however they may have been patched together again right after 1815); the industrial developments of mid-century removed the technological restraints. What remained were the moral ones, and an ambiguous and unstated consensus in this regard was not sufficient to hold the line of restraint against the pressures introduced by changes in the other factors. The military manuals and the new efforts to codify international law concerning the conduct of war were efforts to strengthen this last approach to restraint in war.

The manuals focused principally on the regularization of war and the imposition and maintenance of discipline among the new armies of civilians in uniform; secondarily, they sought to build upon the principle of humane treatment of civilians and of enemy soldiers taken out of combat by wounds or made prisoners of war. These emphases go all the way back to the first appearance of armies of common men in the early-modern period.[34] Traditionally the military manuals have had nothing to say about the weapons of war, leaving decisions on such matters to political authorities. The approach of the Ge-

[32] John Eppstein, *The Catholic Tradition of the Law of Nations* (Washington, D.C.: Catholic Association for International Peace, 1935), p. 132.

[33] See further Nef, *War and Human Progress*, chapter 18.

[34] See further Johnson, *Just War Tradition*, pp. 179-87.

neva conventions has been first of all to establish the principle of humanity as a guide to the treatment of various classes of noncombatants: first and foremost, sick and wounded military personnel; later, prisoners of war; eventually, civilians in the way of war.[35] The Hague conferences of 1899 and 1907 introduced the term "Hague law" as a parallel to the growing "Geneva law"; what was unique about Hague law was its effort to outlaw certain weapons (notably the dumdum bullet) while limiting others (notably the use of the airplane in warfare).[36] Also associated with the Hague conferences were largely unsuccessful efforts at disarmament, and subsequent attempts in this direction thus have the Hague conventions as their common ancestor.

The glory days of attempts to limit weapons and weapon systems, however, come in the post–World War I era. By contrast with the rather feeble efforts in this direction at the Hague conferences, the post–Great War period saw the banning of gas warfare by international convention and the limitation of naval power by types and number of ships, agreed to at the London Naval Conference.[37] The German pocket battleships aside (which did not so much break the rules as find loopholes in them), both conventions were observed in the second "great war" of 1939-1945. Since the end of that war, arms limitation efforts have focused most strongly on nuclear weapons, though such success as has been achieved has more to do with managing the growth of such weapons and weapon systems than in actually achieving limitation.[38] At the same time, though with no formal international agreement, there has been a *de facto* policy of nonuse of nuclear weapons by the powers that possess them, as well as some movement in the direction of preventing the spread of these weapons to other countries or

[35] See further Schindler and Toman, *The Laws of Armed Conflicts*, passim, for the Geneva conventions.

[36] Ibid., pp. 76-77.

[37] Ibid., pp. 99ff., 107f., and 109ff.

[38] See Michael Mandelbaum, *The Nuclear Question* (Cambridge: Cambridge University Press, 1979).

to revolutionary or terrorist groups (which, it is feared, would not prove so circumspect).

Of the main efforts to improve the chances of peace through restraint of war, as these have developed in Western history, weapons limitation as a principle has not been so successful as the idea of noncombatant immunity and a broad consensus on the principle of proportion. All these have suffered in the last hundred years as society has struggled to assimilate the combined effects of the democratization of war, the definition of the ends of war in terms of high-flown ideological ultimates, and a rapid expansion in the weapons of war and their capabilities. A body of recent peace research argues that arms limitation is a way to avoid war, noting the statistical correlation between past arms build-ups and the subsequent outbreak of war.[39] The trouble with this argument is twofold: first, it holds out of consideration the political or ideological background of tension against which both growth in armaments and the resort to war must be seen; second, it does not explain how arms control is to be achieved if, because of these background reasons, the nations in question have no desire for it. Another historical difficulty with arms control efforts is that they have tended to work only under three conditions: when the conflict is between nations of similar culture and value systems (as in the medieval ban on crossbows, which applied only in warfare among Christians); when the weapons banned are difficult to use discriminatingly and effectively (as in the case of poison gas, which can be blown back on its source or away to a civilian area); and when the weapons in question are obsolescent and not likely to be used anyway (as in the case of the dumdum bullets banned at The Hague).[40] Without these conditions, workable arms controls cannot simply be imposed from above; with them, *de facto* restraint in the use of certain types of weapons may follow even without a formal international

[39] See, for example, William Epstein, *The Last Chance: Nuclear Proliferation and Arms Control* (New York: The Free Press, 1976).

[40] See further Johnson, *Can Modern War Be Just?*, chapter 4.

agreement. (In my judgment, this is what has happened already with nuclear weapons.)

The goal of proportionality in warfare has been helped not by international agreements, but by another *de facto* development—the reemergence of armed conflicts limited by geography, targets, aims, or means employed.[41] It is likely that the threat of a general holocaust posed by strategic nuclear weapons has helped to further this trend by setting up implicit limits on escalation of hostilities between nations. At the same time, some of the limited wars since World War II have been grossly destructive in comparison with earlier wars: such conflicts as the Korean War, the Vietnam War (including its French period, its American period, and the present period of continuing conflict), the chronic Israeli-Arab War, and the Iran-Iraq War are *limited* wars; but there is no doubt that they have been *major* ones.

On the broad front of ensuring the protection of noncombatants, the humanitarian law of war defined by the Geneva conventions has had an easily recognizable and quantifiable effect on the conduct of war relative to prisoners of war and medical care for the sick and wounded during a war. The larger matter of noncombatant immunity in general is harder to assess. To use the phrase of Paul Ramsey,[42] "the memory of the distinction" between combatants and noncombatants was almost lost in the countercity artillery bombardment of World War I, the strategic bombing of cities in World War II, and the development of nuclear strategy around such concepts as "massive retaliation" and "mutual assured destruction." Moreover, the phenomenon of organized terrorism has produced direct, intentional attacks on noncombatants as a means of war against those authorities which the terrorists oppose. Yet the distinction remains nonetheless. The war crimes trials

[41] See further Johnson, *Just War Tradition*, chapter VII; for these categories of limitation, see John Baylis, Ken Booth, John Garnett, and Phil Williams, *Contemporary Strategy: Theories and Policies* (New York: Holmes & Meier, 1972), pp. 122-24.

[42] *The Just War: Force and Political Responsibility* (New York: Charles Scribner's Sons, 1968), p. 59.

at Nuremberg and Tokyo employed it; so did the court-martial action taken after the My Lai incident; and, paradoxically, the very fact of terrorist targeting of noncombatants has produced such revulsion that the memory of the moral duties owed to noncombatants may be stronger today than it was in 1944 and 1945.

Restraint in war as a means to peace remains an elusive goal. In part this is because of the nature of warfare in the contemporary age: democratized and likely to involve large numbers of persons, often highly ideological, able to be fought with weapons of horrific destructive power. But in part it is also because of the nature of the quest for such restraint itself. The effort to limit war can never be static; it must change continually as the nature of war is itself transformed. Thus the achievements of this aspect of the quest for peace must be measured in terms of relatives, not absolutes. While the principles remain as moral guides to what should be done, the practical application of these principles must be continually renewed.

3. *The Politics of Absolute Pacifism*

One of the most interesting developments in the quest for peace in the last century has been the transformation in the political presence of religious absolute pacifists. The central core of religious pacifism in Western culture is sectarianism, and the contemporary "peace churches" (including Quakers, Mennonites, Brethren, and others) come out of the tradition defined by such Radical Reformation groups as the Swiss Brethren and, before them, the medieval Waldensians. We have seen above how, during the Napoleonic Wars, it was impossible for English dissenting churches, themselves having a sectarian relationship to the established religion in English society, to transcend their religious apartness with a political program of opposition to the war in progress. The same was true later in the century. American religious groups in this same broad tradition—especially the groups later to go by the "peace church" name—did not take a general political role in opposition to the Civil War. Partly, to be sure, this was because they were mostly in the North and mostly opposed to slavery, but also because there was no way they could oppose the war on pacifist principles without seeming disloyal to the nation's cause. Thus they lay low, contenting their consciences with avoidance of *personal* participation in the war—the classic sectarian approach to the problem of violence in the actions of the state.

The twentieth century has seen a significant turnabout in the willingness and ability of religious pacifists to enter into the arena of general policymaking regarding war. While the first signs of this may be seen in the involvement of the "peace churches" in shaping the provision for conscientious objection in the draft law of the World War I era,[43] the whole subject of conscientious objection is actually quite close to the traditional sectarian pacifist aim of ensuring personal nonparticipation in violence. Making sure the draft law allowed them to avoid bearing arms was thus no real departure from past patterns.

We may, somewhat arbitrarily, mark the real change as beginning in 1935, with the adoption of eight "Principles of Christian Peace and Patriotism" by an assembly of Quakers, Mennonites, and Brethren meeting in Newton, Kansas. The principles themselves are a summation of the major points of traditional Christian sectarian opposition to war and violence. More interesting for our purpose is the accompanying paragraph, headed "Our Concept of Patriotism":

> As members of the Historic Peace Churches we love our country and sincerely work for its highest welfare. True love for our country does not mean a hatred of others. It is our conviction that only the application of the principles of peace, love, justice, liberty, and international goodwill will make for the highest welfare of our country; and the highest welfare of our country must harmonize with the highest welfare of humanity everywhere. . . . We feel that we are true patriots because we build upon the

[43] The term "peace church" itself did not come into existence until 1935; see Donald F. Durnbaugh, ed., *On Earth Peace* (Elgin, Ill.: The Brethren Press, 1978), p. 5.

> eternal principles of right which are the only foundation of stable government in our world community.[44]

This statement explicitly links the absolute pacifism of the sectarian tradition to internationalism—the theme that in the contemporary world carries the tradition of idealist utopianism earlier found in Dante's vision of *monarchia*, Erasmus's concept of political unity in Europe based on Christian principles, and the various plans for "perpetual peace" from Crucé to Bentham. The peace-church representatives who drew up this statement had found a way to be patriotic while holding true to their pacifist principles: they would frame their cause in terms of an internationalist vision of common human welfare. This has been a continuing theme ever since.[45] A 1951 statement from the Friends Peace Committee, London, exemplifies the juxtaposition of traditional Christian pacifism and the new internationalist thinking:

> Friends believe that Christians are required to reject war and to work out the ethics and politics of peace on the basis of forgiveness, generosity and active goodwill with sacrifice. They are required to build a world community based on friendship, understanding and co-operation, which are the fruits of Christian love, and to draw into fellowship even those who have hitherto relied on falsehood, self-aggrandisement and violence.[46]

There are two things to note about this development in the sectarian pacifist tradition of the quest for peace. First, the main emphasis of radical Christian movements has always been the reformation of Christianity as a whole and the evangelization of the world. Sectarian separation from society has

[44] Ibid., pp. 31-32.

[45] Such internationalism fits better the Protestant mainstream than it fits traditional sectarianism. For examples of the former see Robert Heyer, ed., *Nuclear Disarmament: Key Statements of Popes, Bishops, Councils, and Churches* (New York and Ramsey, N.J.: Paulist Press, 1982), pp. 246, 257, and 263, and Shannon, *War or Peace*, pp. 154, 156, 157; a striking case of the latter is Hershberger, *War, Peace, and Nonresistance*, chapter 9.

[46] Durnbaugh, *On Earth Peace*, p. 62.

been, when voluntary, a protective response to the frustration of that larger goal. Thus the tradition of the "ban," as enforced from the early Mennonite movement to the present-day Old Order Amish, has attempted to maintain the purity of the select group against the evil of the outside world, which in its hard-heartedness refuses to accept the full implications of the Christian message as the radicals understand it. Yet, this holding apart is the second-best course: best would be the conversion of the wider society to the "true Christianity" of the radicals' beliefs. Sometimes the separation has even been involuntary; then it is the larger society that draws the line of separation and places the sectarians beyond it. This was, for example, the case with the medieval Waldensians, whose apartness from society was the direct result of excommunication and persecution. Here too, though, the universalist ideal is not destroyed, and both sides espouse the goal of Christian unity and universality.

Secondly, the adoption of internationalist language and goals by the peace churches in the twentieth century is a manifestation of a larger development in Christian thinking about the Church in the world, one with its beginnings in the idealist progressivism of the nineteenth-century missionary movement and having a broad expression in the twentieth century through ecumenism both Protestant and Catholic. "The Christian Vision of World Community" is the title of the first article of the report of the 1972 World Council of Churches Consultation on Violence, Nonviolence, and the Struggle for Social Justice, held at Cardiff, Wales.[47] Similar language appears in other WCC documents and in statements from Protestant member denominations.[48] Likewise Catholic thought on war and peace has adopted the language of a world community in which there would be no war, as exemplified in the 1983 pastoral letter of the American Catholic bishops:

> The popes of the nuclear age, from Pius XII through John Paul II have affirmed pursuit of international order

[47] Ibid., p. 330.

[48] See further Muelder, "Pacifism," and Shannon, *War or Peace*, chapter 9; cf. Donald L. Davidson, *Nuclear Weapons and the American Churches* (Boulder, Colo.: Westview Press, 1983), chapters 5, 6.

as the way to banish the scourge of war from human affairs.

> The fundamental premise of world order in Catholic teaching is a theological truth: the unity of the human family—rooted in common creation, destined for the kingdom [of Christ], and united by moral bonds of rights and duties.[49]

In short, what we find in the peace-church adoption of internationalist language is not simple opportunism or an adulteration of the moral principles also motivating their absolute pacifist stance, though it is in stark contrast to the history of sectarian apartness from society—partly voluntary, partly imposed—that has characterized these religious groups in the past. At the same time, while it is not opportunism, the use of such language is certainly opportune, for it places this tradition of the quest for peace in close coalition with the idealist utopian internationalism of the Erasmian tradition.

Yet there are problems with such allegiances marked by fundamental conceptual differences with respect to the meaning behind the common language or the means to be employed in order to achieve the goal defined in that language. As remarked upon earlier, Martin Ceadel has studied in detail the break-up of the British peace movement, which was composed of diverse types of humanist and religious pacifists and internationalist utopians, under the stress of the beginnings of World War II.[50] More recently and, for Americans, closer to home is the attack on the idealist perspective, as represented by Jonathan Schell's *The Fate of the Earth*, by the theologian Stanley Hauerwas, who insists on the divergence of Schell's position from that of true Christianity. Schell would save the earth; but Christians, in Hauerwas's account, would instead be prepared to live out the consequences of their faith even though the earth—God's creation in the first place—might be destroyed after all.[51]

[49] National Conference of Catholic Bishops, *The Challenge of Peace*, paragraphs 235-36.

[50] See Ceadel, "Christian Pacifism."

[51] Hauerwas, "On Surviving Justly."

Alongside the espousal of internationalism there has been another prominent feature in the quest for peace as understood in twentieth-century radical Christian pacifism: the argument for nonviolence as an effective means of defense, so effective that it can be made to replace military means. This theme, too, had earlier roots and expressions. Bainton cites the case of the Universalist minister Adin Ballou, leader of the New England Non-Resistance Society, who in a book published in 1846 advocated a "prudential pacifism" based on the theory that "ordinarily one could assume that if one turned the other cheek, one would not be hit." Ballou holds up as an example the instance of an army unit "commanded to capture a town in the Tyrol. Finding there only women and children, the soldiers withdrew, not knowing what else to do because their instructions covered only fighting with soldiers."[52]

Recent advocates of this line of argument have presented a more complicated case. Nonviolence must be worked at, they argue; a pacifist nation must prepare its nonviolent defense with as much forethought and effort as it would spend on preparation for a violent means of defense.[53] In one scenario, before an invasion "[t]he entire populace has been continually educated by all the resources of school, church, and radio. . . . It has learned that while an individual may be restricted or punished, he can never be compelled to action against his will. . . ."[54] Defense services have been reorganized around "housing and teaching" and the relief of suffering. All this would aim at a national defense organized around four major principles:

1. no services or supplies to be furnished to invaders;
2. no orders to be obeyed except those of the constitutional civil authorities;

[52] Bainton, *Christian Attitudes*, p. 193. Bainton erroneously gives the publication date of Ballou's book as 1842. On Ballou see further Brock, *Pacifism in the United States*, pp. 441-45, 581-83, 590-604, et passim.

[53] Cf. Mulford Q. Sibley, ed., *The Quiet Battle* (Philadelphia: Pacifist Research Bureau, 1944), p. 322ff.; Yoder, *What Would You Do?*, pp. 25-32; Gordon Zahn, *An Alternative to War* (New York: Council on Religion and International Affairs, 1963).

[54] Sibley, *The Quiet Battle*, p. 322.

3. no insult or injury to be offered the invaders; and
4. all public officials to be pledged to die rather than surrender.[55]

The climax of this extended argument for nonviolent defense, in the form of a scenario of "what would happen if," is "a battle without arms": the invasion takes place, but the invaders find their conquest empty. No one obeys them; they cannot feed themselves, let alone make the country work to their advantage. The soldiers' morale falls, and discipline falters as they are reduced to "assaults upon unarmed citizens and ignominious robbing of shops and hen-roosts." Ultimately, the invading force simply packs up and leaves: "Before many weeks or months elapse, it is probable that the enemy government will hasten to cover up its blunder by recalling the inglorious and unprofitable expedition."[56]

The essay containing this scenario was written in 1942. Similar arguments—with similar scenarios—have appeared many times since. The case presented flies in the face of historical example, but the advocates of nonviolent defense retort that no nation has ever been properly prepared in nonviolent techniques. Thus, the experience of living in a country occupied by Nazi forces, which did not balk at assaulting unarmed civilians and robbing shops, and which certainly did not withdraw under their own volition, by definition does not count against the vision presented in the scenario. Nor do examples of contemporary totalitarian police states. The historical cases that do count—for it, not against—are the examples of the Gandhian resistance movement against the British in India and the American civil rights movement as led by Martin Luther King, Jr., in the 1950s and 1960s.[57]

Alongside the prudential arguments that nonviolent resistance would be successful in turning back an aggressor is another consideration: those who take this path must be willing to suffer martyrdom for their cause. This is stated explicitly in

[55] Ibid., p. 324.

[56] Ibid., p. 326.

[57] See Shannon, *War or Peace*, pp. 110, 114, 115, 140, 161-63, 170, 186, 205, 210, 219, 220, 221, 225, 227.

the above scenario for public officials, who must be "pledged to die rather than surrender"; yet it implies a broader obligation, as well. John Howard Yoder, a contemporary Mennonite theologian, puts martyrdom—either of the victim or of the victim's defender—among seven possible answers to the question of what one would do if faced with a violent attack on a defenseless loved one.[58] The principal thrust of the book in which this appears is in fact to argue for other alternatives in which *no one* would die, alternatives in which a nonviolent response to the situation would defuse the violence that is offered. Yoder is clearly one of those pacifists who believe in the practical and political efficacy of nonviolence. But the fact of possible martyrdom remains, and that the death of an innocent person is called "martyrdom," and not something else, shows why this stance is often today called "the pacifism of witness."[59]

It is this acceptance of the possibility of martyrdom that links those who argue for nonviolence-as-efficacious-defense to the broader, main line of the pacifist tradition of the quest for peace. For in this broader tradition the point is that one must not do evil (kill another person, even an aggressor) in order that good may come of it (an innocent person may live), *whatever the probable final outcome*. That outcome, for classic sectarianism, is in God's hands; and unfaith, not death, is the worst calamity that can befall a believer.[60] In strict terms, it is absolutely irrelevant whether the proffered violence occurs or does not, or whether nonviolence as a means of resistance does or does not work to prevent violent acts from happening.

The pacifism that argues for the efficacy of nonviolence as a means of resisting evil may thus be challenged on the grounds that it is not true pacifism. This was the approach taken by Reinhold Niebuhr in his 1932 book *Moral Man and Immoral Society*, which preceded and presaged his break with the Fellowship of Reconciliation two years later. For Niebuhr, "non-

[58] Yoder, *What Would You Do?*, pp. 13-32; see especially pp. 26-27, 30.

[59] Cf. the usage in Shannon, *War or Peace*, pp. 99-102.

[60] Cf. Hershberger, *War, Peace, and Nonresistance*, on nonviolent resistance, pp. 186-89.

violent means are not perfect proofs of a loving temper."[61] The real issue for Christians, he argued, is avoiding *coercion*, not avoiding violence as such: nonviolence may itself be coercive. Turning the matter around, once the decision has been made that coercion is morally permissible as a means of combating social injustice, Niebuhr reasoned that "the differences between violent and non-violent methods of coercion and resistance are not so absolute that it would be possible to regard violence as a morally impossible instrument of social change."[62]

Still, a distinction needs to be made between arguments from the case for nonviolence as efficacious to pacifism and arguments that begin with pacifism and merely argue for nonviolence as a preferred means of resisting evil within the pacifist framework. This does not completely avoid Niebuhr's criticism, that for Christians the real issue is coercion, but it does distinguish between prudential pacifism and the absolute pacifism of witness. This distinction is recognized by some analysts of contemporary pacifism, including Yoder in another book;[63] yet, in practice, it is often difficult to sort out the distinction in the beliefs of particular contemporary pacifists.

One way of attempting such a differentiation might be through the question of martyrdom. It is hard to believe that proponents of nonviolent-defense-as-efficacious take seriously the possibility that innocent people may in fact lose their lives. The belief seems instead to be that if nonviolence is the means of resistance chosen, the aggressor will not himself use violence. The examples chosen to bolster the case for the efficacy of such defense certainly all suggest this, from the case of the early-nineteenth-century pacifist Ballou (recall his case of the army withdrawal from the Tyrolean village) to the contemporary Mennonite Yoder (one- third of whose book *What Would You Do?* is given over to personal testimonies under the gen-

[61] Reinhold Niebuhr, *Moral Man and Immoral Society* (New York: Charles Scribner's Sons, 1932), p. 251.

[62] Ibid.

[63] Yoder, *Nevertheless*; cf. Edward LeRoy Long, Jr., *War and Conscience in America* (Philadelphia: The Westminster Press, 1968).

eral rubric "But Does It Really Work?").[64] Yoder, in fact, spends little space on the question of martyrdom: the possibilities that interest him more are those of "another way out,"[65] including conversion of the aggressor's violent intentions by acts showing natural love and the potential of providential acts for preventing the threatened violence from happening.

Still, the question of martyrdom remains—not only because it is central to the traditional sectarian position, but also because opponents of pacifism view the possibility of violence done to the innocent as such a great injustice. This view, of course, is at the heart of the "What would you do?" test when put to a conscientious objector in wartime. Its deep history can be found in the case classically stated by Ambrose and Augustine: that it is a Christian's duty to resist the evil of a violent attack on an innocent person, even at the cost of having to use violent means oneself.[66] This argument is often held to provide the theoretical base on which Christian just war thinking is based. Ironically, Christian just war thought and Christian absolute pacifism are quite close at precisely this point: both identify the evil in question not with the death of the innocent victim or of the defender, but with something else. For the pacifist, that evil is doing violence in response to violence; for the just war tradition, the issue is as classically phrased by Augustine:

> What is evil in war? It is not the deaths of some who would soon die anyway. The desire for harming, the cruelty of avenging, an unruly and implacable animosity, the rage of rebellion, the lust of domination and the like—these are the things which are to be blamed in war.[67]

For both these moral traditions, then, the fundamental moral question does not have to do with the evil of death: both accept

[64] See Yoder, *What Would You Do?*, pp. 81-111.

[65] Ibid., pp. 27-42.

[66] Ambrose, *Of the Duties of the Clergy* I.36; cf. Ramsey, *War and the Christian Conscience*, chapter 2.

[67] Augustine, *Against Faustus* XXII.lxxiv; cf. Aquinas, *Summa Theologica* II/II, q. XL, art. 1.

the possibility of death in the service of higher value. The soldier may risk death on the battlefield in the service of justice, yet the pacifist likewise may risk death by interposing himself between an attacker and his intended victim. The acts are morally similar; both are a world apart from the optimistic prudential nonviolence that finds in its methods a way to settle conflicts without resort to violence.

The sectarian pacifist tradition of the quest for peace, then, has in the contemporary era moved into alliance with two themes that are fundamentally utopian in character: internationalism and belief in the efficacy of nonviolent means of national defense. The classic sectarian position lives on; but it is to be found in separatist religious groups such as the Amish, not in such descendants of the Radical Reformation as the Quakers, the Mennonites, and the Brethren who, under the contemporary rubric of "peace churches," not only maintain for themselves a traditional pacifism of witness, oriented toward internal peace of the soul and peace within the religious community, but actively engage their energies in efforts to secure an end to war in the world at large.

C. Internationalism and Universal Peace

The search for peace through establishment of a superior order of government able to transcend petty rivalries has appeared in numerous forms in Western cultural history. It was the nature of the *pax Romana* of the late-classical world; it appeared again in the impetus toward restricting authority to make war in the tenth-century Peace of God movement; it appeared yet again, in quite different forms, in the thought of Dante and Marsilius of Padua in the fourteenth century, and of Christine de Pisan and others in the fifteenth. In these cases, practical politics and utopian idealism mixed together, with the former pointing in the direction of just war tradition and the latter pointing toward a pacifist utopian progressivism which envisioned the withering away of all war under the umbrella of a universal superstate. The Peace of God unambiguously fed into the consensus on the justification and limitation of war that coalesced between the twelfth and fourteenth centuries; Dante and Marsilius, while still able to think in broad just war terms, looked ahead to a world in which politics would be resolved by the establishment of a perfect order, which would then establish justice and thus create lasting peace by removing the causes of conflict. Erasmus, writing in the sixteenth century, is the key figure through which such a concept was brought forward into the modern era. His writings on war revolve around two foci: the horrors created by warfare and the ideal of universal and lasting peace to be established by virtue among rulers individually and cooperation among them collectively, both fruits to be gained through the common Christianity of European society. The theorists of "perpetual peace" in the seventeenth and eighteenth centuries built directly upon Erasmus's vision, and through them he continues to influence the shape of modern internationalism.

What unites the various expressions of this tradition in the quest for peace is the ideal that the structures of society can be recast so as to do away with war by removing the causes of conflict that lead to war. Thus we have Erasmus and the "perpetual peace" advocates describing in gory detail the horrors of war and tracing the causes of war to the venality and petty self-interest of rulers; in the contemporary age, this has translated into an almost loving depiction of the potential horrors of nuclear war,[68] a general opposition to "militarism,"[69] and in place of the denunciation of the vices of princes a denunciation of the vices of the nation-state and the international system of nation-states.[70]

Is this tradition of thought utopian, as I have numerous times called it? To its advocates, it seems more realistic than the approach of attempting to limit war in an age of weapons of world-destroying power, as just war tradition seeks to do; it also appears to them more realistic than an absolute pacifism of witness, which would seem to give the world up to the ag-

[68] See further the discussion of Schell at the end of this chapter.

[69] See, for example, Muelder, "Pacifism," passim.

[70] See above, note 38; cf. Falk, *A Study of Future Worlds*, pp. 7-10, 64-69, 140-41, and the discussion of Falk below in this chapter.

gressors. From such a perspective, internationalism is plain common sense; there is nothing utopian (in the sense of impractical idealism) about it. Yet there remain some good reasons to continue thinking of this tradition in the quest for peace as utopian, in exactly the same sense.

First of all, the Erasmian vision that animates modern internationalism was formed in an era when humanists were proposing ideal societies right and left;[71] to call internationalism "utopian" is simply to extend the term applied to an *imaginary* ideal society by Erasmus's contemporary Thomas More so as to make of Erasmus's vision a possibility that could be reached by *actual* European society. This is not an unreasonable extension of the term; More, after all, meant his *Utopia* as a critique of the England of his own time.

Secondly, as Rousseau noted caustically of Saint-Pierre in particular, the "perpetual peace" literature in general (Sully is the exception) did not really come to grips with the difficult politics that would be necessary to create such a world as its authors envisioned.[72] By this measure, the international law approach, which I shall discuss below as one contemporary example of this tradition in the quest for peace, is not utopian; but that is because it has sacrificed some part of the ideal in order to be able to work within the bounds set by the nation-state system. World order theory, the other contemporary example to be discussed below, holds close to the ideals; yet, when it seeks to deal with the need for a transition away from nation-states to world order, it falls into the fault of being merely programmatic.

Thirdly, contemporary internationalism is utopian in its vision of the moral base of world community—just as Dante had been in his ideal of the virtue of the *populus Romanus*; just as Erasmus had been in extolling the common Christianity of Europe in an age that was on the verge of the Protestant Reformation and a century of warfare rooted in religious difference; just as the "perpetual peace" advocates of the *ancien régime*

[71] Thomas More's *Utopia* is but the best-known example.

[72] See above, Chapter IV, notes 37-40.

had been in putting so much weight on the common ties that (they believed) united the peoples and monarchs of Europe. The problem before modern internationalists is far worse: how to conceive the basis for *world* community across myriads of linguistic and cultural boundaries, not to mention religious and ideological differences that even today are the root of major wars. One must either minimize the differences or find some means of transcending them. The contemporary world order movement has done both, as we shall see below.

Finally, though, to call a position utopian is not to dismiss it out of hand. There is a place for idealism in politics; otherwise, there is no language for expressing the common values that define a society or culture in terms of goals to be sought in the future. In this sense, utopianism may be a sign of confidence in a society or culture, a symbol of healthy, forward-looking dynamism. Even if the ideal of world government is not possible of achievement in practical political terms, the internationalist utopia remains as a critique of the shortcomings of the nation-state system and as a goad to achieving at least some proximate ends that might not otherwise have been conceived.

In the following pages I shall discuss two related but significantly different forms of this tradition in the quest for peace, as it has taken shape in the contemporary era. First I will examine the efforts to abolish resort to war by international agreement, the landmarks of which are the League of Nations Covenant, the Pact of Paris, and the United Nations Charter. Then I will treat of the contemporary world order movement as expressed in the thought of one of its principal exponents, Richard Falk.

1. *International Agreements and the Abolition of War*

Broadly speaking, international law has been one of the principal vehicles through which just war tradition has been carried in the modern period. In another context, therefore, I have treated the three international agreements that are the subject of the present discussion as twentieth-century attempts to recover the *jus ad bellum* that had largely been dissolved into *compétence de guerre* in the era beginning with Grotius in the time of the Thirty Years' War and ending with World War I.[73] Yet, seen as an effort to redefine the idea of justice in resort to war, these three agreements lack a great deal. Indeed, their cumulative effect, from a just war perspective, is to resolve the question of justice too simply into one of first use of force (deemed illegitimate) versus second use (deemed legitimate in response to the first), with "aggression" being defined as first use and "defense" defined as use of force in response.[74] From a just war perspective, this is hardly enough to encompass the myriad forms that aggression might take, and there might be occasions in which first use of force is genuinely defensive of values. In just war terms, then, the major international achievements represented by the League of Nations Covenant, the Pact of Paris, and the United Nations Charter have not gone far enough in recovering from three centuries of confusion between *jus ad bellum* and *compétence de guerre*.

Precisely what makes these agreements unsatisfactory from a just war perspective is what makes them attractive as expressions of the tradition of internationalist idealism in the quest for peace. For these agreements collectively embodied three major goals that had earlier proved elusive: the establishment of a "parliament" or "congress" of nations, the substitution of arbitration for war in the settlement of international disputes, and the renunciation of resort to war as an instrument by which one nation could seek to impose its will on another. The actual achievements reached by these agreements have not fulfilled all the promise attached to the goals by internationalist idealism; yet, as embodiments of the goals themselves, these three international compacts have gone far beyond what Rousseau and other critics of "perpetual peace" and its near relatives ever thought possible.

The first achievement of the League of Nations Covenant was the creation of a parliament of nations essentially similar

[73] James Turner Johnson, "Toward Reconstructing the *Jus ad Bellum*," *The Monist*, vol. 57, no. 4 (October 1973), pp. 461-68.

[74] See further ibid., pp. 464-65.

to what had been envisioned in the proposals for "perpetual peace" in the seventeenth and eighteenth centuries. What was different was, first, that now the principals who sent their representatives to this parliament were sovereign *nations*, some of them republican in governmental form, and not sovereign *individuals*; this just could not have been conceived of in the age of the French Revolution, when republicanism was new and mistrusted. In 1919, though, such was no longer the case; the international system had assimilated the difference in types of government. A second difference, in context more substantial, was that the national representatives to the League did not have the power that the "perpetual peace" proposals would have given them. Nations retained their sovereignty, and while in theory the League could reach agreements that would bind all members, in practice its influence was only moral or hortatory, not binding. A third departure from the earlier visions of such an organization's role was that the League itself possessed no military capability; thus, while it could call for arbitration instead of resort to force in disputes between its members, it did not have the superior force needed to oppose such actions by an individual nation, and which the Enlightenment theorists had thought necessary to ensure that such breaches of the peace would not occur in the first place. The idea had originally been Dante's in *De Monarchia*: the high sovereign must have such a clear superiority of force that no lesser body of persons could rationally think of opposing it; yet the League of Nations was not a *monarchia* but a confederation, and it lacked the power to enforce what it legislated. While Article 16 (3) supposed the existence of "forces of . . . Members of the League . . . cooperating to protect the covenants of the League,"[75] there could in practice be no such cooperation among the forces of member nations where their individual national interests seemed to recommend otherwise. This was a weakness that undermined the stringency of the covenant's

[75] International Intermediary Institute, The Hague, *The Permanent Court of International Justice* (Leiden: A. W. Sijthoff, 1922), Covenant of the League of Nations with Annex (pp. 2-28); see Article 16 (pp. 2, 4).

provisions for international arbitration and renunciation of war.

This said, we now need to examine these provisions, which are found in Articles 10-17 of the covenant.[76] Article 10 declares the League's concern to guarantee its members against aggression, charging the Council of the League with advising how to do this in particular cases. Article 11 extends the League's concern to "any war or threat of war," providing that there should be action to ward off such breaches of the peace; Articles 12 and 13, which will be treated more fully below, provide for international arbitration, and Article 14 defines in general terms the Permanent Court of International Justice, the principal international arbitration body. Article 15 has to do with disputes between League members not submitted to arbitration. Article 16 specifies sanctions that members of the League may take or, in some cases, are obliged to take against any member that resorts to war "in disregard of its covenants under Articles 12, 13, or 15," while Article 17 extends the same sanctions to nonmember nations that make war against member nations.

This was a grand design, going further than any international agreements had gone up to that time. The core of the "perpetual peace" movement had been the replacement of war by arbitration as a means of settling international disputes, and this aim was also the core of the provisions in the abovementioned articles of the League of Nations Covenant. Article 12 deals with disputes "likely to lead to a rupture" and provides for a three-month cooling-off period before war can be initiated. During this period, arbitration is to be tried, and Article 13 addresses disputes "suitable for submission to arbitration or judicial settlement." League members are to try arbitration first, before force; they are to accept arbitration awards in good faith; and in the case of disputes of the kind dealt with in Article 13, they are "not to resort to war with any Member of the League who complies therewith."

While there is a clear antiwar bias in these articles, they do

[76] Ibid., Articles 10-17 (pp. 10-20).

not completely outlaw war. The burden of the covenant is to push the possibility of war as far as possible down the list of options, so that most (if not all) disputes among nations can be settled before war seems the only solution. Peaceful means of resolving disputes are to come first, including arbitration, judicial settlement by the World Court, and/or investigation by the Council of the League. But much about this process is left unsaid. Which disputes are "suitable for . . . arbitration" and which not? Who decides? What if the dispute extends even to the question of whether it is arbitrable or not? What kind of sanctions may be imposed on nations refusing to accept arbitration or refusing to accept the results of arbitration in good faith, as provided in Article 13? The covenant speaks of situations in which the members of the League will have to take "necessary steps" to ward off a coming war, but it does not define clearly what those steps might include, or how to ensure that all members will cooperate in them. Indeed, the respect for national sovereignty in the covenant is so complete that even when economic sanctions are mentioned as a possible coercive measure against recalcitrant states, members faced with considerable "loss and inconvenience" do not have to abide by these sanctions.

The failures of the League to live up to its promise in keeping the peace are by now legendary, including the abortive attempt to use economic sanctions against Italy in order to force it to cease its empire-building war against Ethiopia. Yet, even if it did nothing else, the League provided a precedent for the kind of transnational parliament that had earlier been only an ideal, and it laid down a basis on which later efforts could be made.

One of these efforts was the General Treaty for the Renunciation of War, concluded in 1928 (also known as the Pact of Paris, after the city in which it was signed, and the Kellogg-Briand Pact, after the two principals who did most to bring it into being, U.S. Secretary of State Kellogg and French Foreign Minister Briand).[77] The three articles of this treaty bind its sig-

[77] U.S. Department of State, *The General Pact for the Renunciation of War.*

natories to "condemn recourse to war for the solution of international controversies, and renounce it as an instrument of national policy in their relations with one another" (Article 1), to seek solution of all disputes among themselves by peaceful means (Article 2), and to keep the treaty open for additional nations to sign for "as long as may be necessary for adherence by all the other powers of the world" (Article 3). This was an attempt to strengthen the antiwar bias already in the League of Nations Covenant; it has been popularly called "the agreement to outlaw war." Among those who regarded it as achieving this in law were the Roman Catholic theologians of the Conventus of Fribourg, who in 1931 issued a statement containing the following claims: because of the international agreements by then in force (notably the League of Nations and the Pact of Paris), "a war declared by a state on its own authority without previous recourse to the international agreements which exist cannot be a lawful social process. It would be repugnant to the dictates both of public law and of conscience. . . . *A fortiori*, modern war, that is war as understood and waged nowadays, could not be a legitimate social process."[78]

The existing agreements did not, in fact, outlaw *all* war; Secretary of State Kellogg made clear that in his interpretation of the 1928 treaty, "every nation is free at all times to defend its territory from attack or invasion and it alone is competent to decide whether circumstances require resort to war in self-defense."[79] Even the Fribourg theologians distinguished between aggressive and defensive use of force, arguing that "lawful defence" could be allowed "to repel force by force." But that was all they would allow: "[T]his legitimate defence does not imply *ipso facto* the right to take punitive measures against the ag-

---

Text of the Pact as Signed (Washington, D.C.: U.S. Government Printing Office, 1928).

[78] Eppstein, *The Catholic Tradition*, p. 140.

[79] Quoted by Morton A. Kaplan and Nicholas deB. Katzenbach, "Resort to Force: War and Neutrality," in Richard A. Falk and Saul H. Mendlovitz, eds., *The Strategy of World Order*, vol. II: *International Law* (New York: World Law Fund, 1966), p. 290.

gressor, or to set up the social process in such a way that the conflict between the aggressor and his victim is solved only by the arbitrament of the sword."[80] And even the need for such defense was expected to wither away in time as the results of "the co-ordinated protection of all States in common and the institution of arbitration."[81]

We thus have, implicit in the Pact of Paris and explicit in its interpretations, much more clearly than in the language of the covenant, a distinction between *aggressive* and *defensive* resort to military force; while the former may be said to be outlawed, the latter is permitted without restraint. Not only does this, as earlier suggested, confuse aggression with first use of force and defense with second use, it establishes a framework within which total war in response to an armed attack may seem to be not only legally permissible but morally righteous. The Kellogg-Briand Pact did not prevent World War II, but it justified the Allies in prosecuting total war against the Axis powers, using such means as countercity bombing and insisting on "unconditional surrender." It is against this backdrop, in turn, that nuclear strategy has developed, so that while a first use of nuclear weapons may be declared wrong, a second, responsive use (whether a limited tactical strike or a massively and indiscriminately destructive strategic one) appears unquestionably justified.[82]

Yet this is to move too far ahead of our story too fast. Not only could the signers of the pact have known nothing in advance about this subsequent history, but there was nothing inevitable about that history. While the pact did not outlaw *all* war, the truth remains that had all the nations of the world signed it, and had they then lived up to their treaty pledge to "condemn recourse to war for the solution of international controversies, and to renounce it as an instrument of national

[80] Eppstein, *The Catholic Tradition*, p. 141.

[81] Ibid.

[82] This is now a commonplace idea, the backbone of nuclear deterrence; for a discussion of the ideology behind it see Robert W. Tucker, *The Just War: A Study in Contemporary American Doctrine* (Baltimore: The Johns Hopkins University Press, 1960).

policy," then the age of war between nations would have ended. In such a case, Secretary Kellogg's reservation of the right of self-defense would have lost force: even those nations which, in their judgment, were being aggressed upon by non-military means could not have resorted to war to oppose such aggression, for they would have already renounced war as an instrument of national policy.

There is, then, a tension between the ideal aimed at in the treaty, well expressed in the popular phrase "the agreement to outlaw war," and the practical interpretation of the implications of the treaty in empirical relations among nations. Kellogg, despite the idealistic inspiration that led him to conceive of this sort of treaty, knew well the practical world of statecraft, where reservation of the right of self-defense was an intimate corollary of the principle that national sovereignty must be preserved. Again, this was not the vision of the "perpetual peace" idealists, for whom national sovereignty was reserved for domestic matters.

The United Nations Charter, drawn up in the aftermath of a world war that neither the League covenant nor the Pact of Paris had been able to prevent, incorporated major themes from both and went some distance toward remedying the weaknesses found there; at the same time, however, it did not remove them all, and it preserved other concepts that must, in terms of the quest for peace, be criticized. The articles in the charter most relevant to our purposes are Articles 2 and 51.[83] The former, building on the language of covenant and pact, prohibits members from "the threat or use of force against the territorial integrity or political independence of any state" and empowers the Security Council (though without clearly saying how) to preserve international peace. This article thus embodies the theme of renunciation of war as a means of settling international disputes and the provision for an international body to enforce the peace. Article 51, by contrast, grants the

[83] United Nations, *Charter of the United Nations and Statute of the International Court of Justice* (New York: United Nations Press, n.d.); see further Kaplan and Katzenbach, "Resort to Force."

power of self-defense against "armed attack" to all nations, whether acting individually or collectively. This right of self-defense remains in effect "until the Security Council takes the necessary measures to restore international peace and security." This article thus makes explicit what Secretary Kellogg had regarded as implicit in the Pact of Paris, the right of self-defense; it is also an interesting retreat from the optimism in Articles 12 and 13 of the Covenant of the League of Nations—as well as in Article 2 of the United Nations Charter itself—that international disputes could be settled by peaceful means.

Together, Articles 2 and 51 amount to being a prohibition of aggressive use of force by one nation against another along with allowance of defensive use. But it is not clear what "aggression" and "defense" mean, nonetheless. One possibility is that they resolve into the distinction between first and second use of force already mentioned above. This was the position of French President De Gaulle at the time of the 1956 Arab-Israeli Six-Day War; he criticized Israel's "opening of hostilities" by first use of force in the form of an air attack, but that same strike was regarded by Israel as a justified, if preemptive, self-defense against an attack the Arab states were about to launch. De Gaulle thus supported the concept of first use of force as illegitimate; another Frenchman, Henri Meyrowitz, in a book on the law of war, argues that this is what contemporary international law as stated in the United Nations Charter actually requires, though he himself disapproves of such reductionism.[84] On the contrary, American interpreters Morton Kaplan and Nicholas Katzenbach, while admitting that "most commentators would read the Article [51] to forbid self-defense except in case of armed attack," nonetheless argue that the actual wording of the article "does not clearly *forbid* self-defense prior to armed attack but only *sanctions* self-defense as permissible in case of armed attack."[85]

Is war, then, forbidden? The answer must be, as for the Cov-

[84] Henri Meyrowitz, *Le Principe de l'égalité des belligérants devant le droit de la guerre* (Paris: A. Pedone, 1970), pp. 144, 146-47.

[85] Kaplan and Katzenbach, "Resort to Force," p. 290, n. 3.

enant of the League of Nations and the Pact of Paris, that it is not. The reason is also the same: the persistence of national sovereignty, which the "perpetual peace" idealists would have severely abrogated but which, in the actual world of twentieth-century international politics, has proved impossible to move beyond. Indeed, the failures of world government have, in some quarters, produced a backflow of isolationist opposition, reminiscent of Marsilius's concept of the ideal state and, more recently, Rousseau's depiction of international peace as something to be achieved only when ties between societies are *minimized*, not when they are increased.[86] It is against these same failures and shortcomings, however, that the contemporary world-order movement must be viewed. For this movement, the steps taken by the covenant, the pact, and the charter (as well as numerous smaller efforts) represent limited but significant progress toward the ultimate goal of world government.

Before we turn to this theme, though, there remains one nagging problem concerning all the efforts mentioned above: they treat of *war*, a formal state of armed hostilities between nations, one of three possible states; the other two are peace and a *status mixtus* of these two extremes. Each status has its own character, and in each are certain rights and obligations that differ from those of the others. Yet the period since World War II has seen much armed conflict that is not, in the formal sense, war: revolutions, insurgencies, terrorist activity. Historically these had been regarded as domestic matters in which international agreements should not meddle. But the sheer prevalence of such phenomena has led international lawyers in the past two decades to attempt to extend what had earlier applied only to "war" (in the formal sense) so that it would cover all sorts of "armed conflict."[87] This is a positive move in the interests both of peace and the restraint of violence, for two rea-

[86] Cf. Laurence W. Beilenson, *Survival and Peace in the Nuclear Age* (Chicago: Regnery, 1981).

[87] Thus Schindler and Toman's compilation is entitled *The Laws of Armed Conflicts*; in an earlier era it would have been *The Laws of War* (cf. *The Law of Armed Conflicts* [New York: Carnegie Endowment for International Peace, 1971]).

sons. First, it establishes the principle that a state cannot avoid the prohibitions laid down against "war" by failing to make a *formal declaration* of war; this was a loophole that the League of Nations Covenant left wide open, and neither the Pact of Paris nor the United Nations Charter closed it. Second, it establishes the principle that even in a revolutionary or insurgency milieu the same sort of restraint should be observed that responsible nations ideally observe in their conduct toward one another. This holds both at the level of the law of war proper (the *jus in bello* of just war tradition) and at the level of the resort to force in the first place. If restraint in resort to force, cooling-off periods, and binding arbitration are worthwhile principles for the conduct of states toward one another, why should they not be worthwhile with respect to disputes of an intranational or domestic character?[88] Thus, the effort to redefine the restraints on "war" as restraints on "armed conflict" are an important step in the quest for peace, both between nations and within them.

2. *The World Order Movement and the Quest for Lasting Peace*

The contemporary world order movement may be regarded from two somewhat different angles: as a practical and pragmatic attempt to explore ways of extending the limited accomplishments of international law thus far in history, or as the vehicle for restating in contemporary terms the utopian ideals of a new international order earlier expressed by Dante, Erasmus, and the "perpetual peace" theorists. In fact it is both, lavishing considerable attention to practical details in analyzing the state of the existing international system (and suggesting how to improve it) and maintaining a high idealism regarding the values it seeks to achieve. There is now a formidable body of literature from this movement, including the studies from

[88] This is explicitly the argument of Richard John Neuhaus in his contribution to Peter Berger and Richard John Neuhaus, eds., *Movement and Revolution* (Garden City, N.Y.: Doubleday & Company, 1970).

the World Order Models Project (WOMP) of the Institute for World Order, a nongovernmental organization based in New York but drawing on the work of scholars from various countries, mainly in the United States and the Third World.

I will attempt a limited but representative look at the world order movement through one of its principal proponents and most tireless advocates, Richard A. Falk. Falk is one of the principals of WOMP, and his own works (books, edited books, and articles) on world order and related issues would fill a library shelf. He is at the center of this movement in the contemporary world, and an examination of his thought will provide the most appropriate and representative vista on the movement as a whole. Within Falk's still growing body of work, his 1975 volume, *A Study of Future Worlds*,[89] is the best general statement of the idealist and practical sides of the world order movement and their linkage.

The end to war was a principal goal of Erasmus and the "perpetual peace" movement; in the eighteenth century (specifically, with William Penn) and the early nineteenth, the peace movement added the goal of economic betterment, to be achieved through international cooperation and trade—a goal that was also held to be a means of reducing the likelihood of war, since general prosperity would mean less need to go to war over economic matters. Both these values—the end of war and economic prosperity through international cooperation—carry forward into the world order movement. In laying out a "relevant utopia" according to the values of WOMP/USA (the consensus of values reached by Americans working on the World Order Models Project), Falk lists these as the first two of four controlling values:

1. the minimization of large-scale collective violence;
2. the maximization of social and economic well-being;
3. the realization of fundamental human rights and conditions of political justice; and

[89] See above, note 70.

4. the maintenance and rehabilitation of ecological quality (pollution and resources).[90]

Noting that the chief aims embodied in these values are "the prevention of catastrophe and the alleviation of misery," not "the positive realization of human potentialities," Falk appends a list of eight "additional values" oriented toward "the quality of life." These are somewhat more specific and closer to statements of actual programmatic goals than the four major values. They include 1) "[s]ecuring the conditions of social life in each society that promote harmony, joy and creativity," 2) eliminating governmental coercion and manipulation, 5) "[e]xperimenting with different social and political [means] for organizing human activities," 6) affirming a diversity of lifestyles, 7) using female value perspectives along with male ones when approaching social issues, and 8) ensuring that science and technology are employed in ways that support, rather than negate, the four primary values.[91]

These are all, of course, explicitly affirmed by Falk to be rooted in American experience and perspectives: the list of primary and secondary values that might be generated from India or Latin America (two other areas producing their own "preferred models of world order" in the form of "relevant utopias") would be expected to be different. This frankness about cultural diversity, coupled with an approach designed to cope with it through a mix of erasing, transcending, and tolerating differences, distinguishes this movement from earlier related movements such as that of the "perpetual peace" idea. Neither Dante nor Erasmus nor the peace advocates of the eighteenth and nineteenth centuries could seriously think beyond their own cultural perspectives. Most of their anticipation of unity among nations flowed from convictions about the cultural unity of Western Europe. When an outsider—for instance, the Turkish Empire—was included in the speculation, it was with the proviso that the other should behave like a good European. This was a residue from medieval concepts of natural law that,

[90] Falk, *A Study of Future Worlds*, pp. vii, 11-30.
[91] Ibid., pp. 30-31.

in retrospect, were clearly culture-biased, yet were sincerely believed to represent what any "natural" individual, in whatever culture wherever in the world, could understand to be good and seek to achieve, purely out of the abilities present in him by his nature. The nineteenth century introduced, along with imperialism, the concept that the European nations needed to "civilize" the rest of the world; such a concept continues into international law, as for example in Georg Schwarzenberger's reference to the "dictates of civilization" in the law of war.[92] In this perspective, not too different after all from that of earlier eras, behavior according to the conventions of European society was something to be imposed on the rest of the world in whatever way appropriate. Diversity among cultures was recognized and admitted—but deplored. The existing power balance reinforced the implications of this view.

Not only recognizing the diversity of values rooted in cultural differences, the pluralistic, relativistic approach of the contemporary world order movement exemplified by Falk attempts to find ways to live with that diversity. Nonetheless, a central element of the motivation behind this movement is the perception that the problems confronting the world are universal, not conditioned by diverse value perspectives. Thus the list of major values may also be read as a list of problems to be resolved: violence and war; poverty and maldistribution of wealth; abuses of human rights under unjust political systems; loss of ecological quality under the stresses imposed by pollution and overutilization of natural resources. We can see this developing in Falk's analysis as he focuses on "population as a world order factor,"[93] "the war system,"[94] "ecological pressures,"[95] and various issues raised by technological innovation.[96] These same concerns run throughout the more extended analyses provided later as bases for the "preferred

[92] Schwarzenberger, *A Manual of International Law*, pp. 197-99.

[93] Falk, *A Study of Future Worlds*, pp. 86-96.

[94] Ibid., pp. 96-103.

[95] Ibid., pp. 103-112.

[96] Ibid., pp. 112-40.

world polity" that, it is argued, ought to replace the present system.[97]

Let us look a bit more closely at two of these concerns, one inherited from earlier stages in the internationalist utopian tradition (the abolition of war) and the other relatively new (the concern for the ecological health of the world). The other two issues can be seen in relation to these. The prioritization within the four major values that this suggests is in fact implicit in Falk's concern for the avoidance of catastrophe, whether a "nuclear catastrophe"[98] or an "ecological catastrophe."[99]

The first is familiar territory. Warfare is "*endemic* in international relations."[100] At fault is the state system, for it inherently encourages conflict and warfare. The current international system is a "war system,"[101] and it drives toward "global disintegration" through "the combination of modern technology with competitive patterns of international behavior."[102] The rise in domestic authoritarianism the world over is connected to the same phenomena: domestic authoritarianism leads to arms procurement and hence to war. At the same time, a reverse process is also at work: domestic militarization increases the violence used by governments against their own citizens and increases human rights abuses.[103] Yet in truth, as Falk argues another familiar theme from the "perpetual peace" tradition, military strength may "only marginally" be connected to national security. He cites the case of Japan and the relations that obtain between the United States and Canada, as well as those "among states in most parts of Latin America."[104] Real security, by contrast with that which is only military, is to be found in peaceful relations with other states

[97] Ibid., chapters 3-6.

[98] Ibid., pp. 43-46.

[99] Ibid., pp. 46-49; cf. p. 281.

[100] Ibid., p. 99; emphasis is his.

[101] Ibid., p. 96.

[102] Ibid., p. 97.

[103] This case is made extensively in another book by Falk, *Human Rights and State Sovereignty* (New York and London: Holmes & Meier, 1981).

[104] Falk, *A Study of Future Worlds*, p. 98.

and domestic well-being fostered by prudent—that is, nonexploitative—economic development. Thus Falk integrates Rousseau's concern for domestic well-being into his own internationalist "relevant utopia."

As for the ecological theme, here too "catastrophe" looms because of structural problems arising from the interstate competition inherent in the existing international system. Falk writes, "There is an approaching need to agree upon limits that apply to such fundamental matters as human numbers and per capita life-style," then asks, "How many people, at what level of consumption, *can* the world support for the indefinite future?"[105] The state system, by being organized in such a way as to foster competition in the consumption of limited resources, rather than cooperation in their use in order to maximize the benefit of the greatest number of people, makes it impossible to "transcend the immediacies of the present" and deal with the long-term problem of defining and setting appropriate limits.[106]

The solutions to such problems are to be found, as is the case generally for this tradition in the quest for peace, in a higher level of governmental order: "it hardly matters," comments Falk, "whether our preference model . . . is called 'the United Nations' or not."[107] Actually, the model he develops is somewhat different from the United Nations as it has existed since 1945. His highest level of transnational organization is called a World Assembly and it has three component parts: the Assembly of Governments, the Assembly of Peoples, and the Assembly of Organizations and Associations. Below this would come a Council of Principals, operating through its Central Coordinating Board and a Secretary General. The actual implementation of transnational planning and decisionmaking would be through four "systems," one for each of the problem areas of world security, economics, human development, and ecological balance.[108] In line with the above discussion of the

[105] Ibid., p. 151; emphasis is his.

[106] Ibid., pp. 151-52.

[107] Ibid., p. 234.

[108] Ibid.; see chart, p. 234, and discussion, pp. 237-74.

problems posed by the "war system" and by selfish competition for resources heedless of the results, we will look at two of these: the World Security System and the World System for Ecological Balance.

The World Security System, as developed here, has three main branches: the World Security Forces, a World Grievance System, and a World Disarmament Service. The first would "try to operate as a police force rather than an army";[109] its duties would include "Peace Observation along troublesome frontiers . . . and the coercive implementation of disarmament obligations."[110] Falk envisions efforts to develop weaponry suited to the "police" nature of these forces, "weaponry that could temporarily and harmlessly neutralize—rather than kill, maim, or injure."[111] Falk would, however, maintain a "minimal kind of nuclear deterrent" to cope with "pathological tendencies."[112] But in consideration of the general national disarmament he hopes will be achieved, Falk sets the size of the transnational security force at 200,000, "or even less," with regional and supplementary forces in reserve. Finally, in the tradition of expecting that a new transnational structure will lead to the end of armed conflict, he envisions that the peacekeeping forces might perform most of their functions without the use of weapons at all.[113]

The other two legs of the world security stool, as envisioned

[109] Ibid., p. 243.

[110] Ibid., p. 242.

[111] Ibid., p. 243. Falk does not explore this thought, though it would be interesting to do so. Might it imply the use of incapacitating gases, in possible violation of existing international agreement on gas warfare? Might it imply rubber bullets such as the British forces use in Northern Ireland, despite their ability to cause serious injury? Might it imply a generalized "Star Wars" defense capability against nuclear weapons such as proposed in the Reagan administration's Strategic Defense Initiative? I mention these items in particular because they have in the past been singled out as "inhumane" or "destabilizing" by critics who share many of the general value goals enunciated by Falk. By contrast, the value conception that points toward the need to develop such weaponry is that of just war tradition's *jus in bello*.

[112] Ibid., p. 245.

[113] Ibid., p. 246.

by Falk, are an international arbitration system and national disarmament—again, familiar themes from this broad tradition in the quest for peace. The latter is simply *assumed*, as Falk notes, and no space is spent on how to get from here to there. Keeping the world disarmed would be the function of a new transnational civil service, the World Disarmament Service, which would operate essentially through supervision of the disarmament agreement and public reporting of their findings.[114] As for the settlement of international disputes through arbitration, the proposed World Grievance System is rather a thought experiment than a detailed proposal; the discussion does not even show how existing international judicial institutions and agreements for arbitration of disputes would be incorporated into this new system.

The single most important aspect of the new World System for Ecological Balance appears to be the proposed World Environment Authority.[115] This body would be concerned with, among other things, balancing "immediate health and food requirements against deferred burdens on environmental quality and possibly even on human health."[116] It would be both a policymaking body and an agency able to settle disputes and enforce its decisions,[117] after the model of regulatory agencies in the United States. The difference is that this one would be concerned with transnational, global problems. Its work would be supplemented by the World Forum on Ecological Balance, which would "seek to elaborate an ideology for ecological policy that takes account of diverse perspectives,"[118] and by an agency concerned with resource supply and demand, conservation of resources, and policy on economic development.

In short, this proposal for a new model of world order builds on the existing internationalist utopian tradition and extends it via contemporary concerns for human rights, ecological balance, and pluralism of values rooted in cultural diversity.

[114] Ibid., pp. 246-48.
[115] Ibid., pp. 269-73.
[116] Ibid., p. 269.
[117] Ibid., p. 270.
[118] Ibid., p. 273.

While Falk happily and frequently calls this new system a utopia, he also presents it as a proposal for actual change in the system of world order, setting up a timetable for its achievement over a thirty-year period beginning in the 1970s and ending in the early 2000s. The latter date is crucial for him, since he posits that this is when the feared catastrophes caused by the existing system will occur. Thus, there is both a "domestic imperative" and a "global imperative" to seek such a transnational system of world order.[119] This, too, is a style of argument familiar in the tradition: right reason and common-sense concern for one's own self-interest point in the direction of the new higher level of governmental order.

Despite the moral concern that steps begin to be taken to adopt such a system as proposed, and despite some considerable use of quantitative data, charts, and the like in Falk's analysis, this model of a new world order nonetheless suffers from the same lack of specificity about how to achieve the utopian vision that marked earlier stages in this tradition of thought. The pattern that repeatedly recurs, and is found here as well, is this: a problem is discerned to exist (war, destruction of the ecological balance, or whatever); its causes are identified with some element in the existing interstate system (whether that be in the confrontation between pope and emperor, the rivalry between independent monarchs, or the competition between autonomous states); a solution is posited that would involve a *structural* change, which would in itself remove the causes of whatever problem is at issue; and the claim is made that prudent self-interest, rightly understood, will lead mankind to adopt this new superior order. Problems that might be created by the transition are ignored, as are (in all but the most general sense) steps necessary to bring the new order into being. Finally, there is no development of the possible implications the new order might have on the values that brought it into being: it is simply assumed to foster their further development. This last point applies differently in different utopian systems. In Falk's, for example, it needs to be asked whether the new

[119] Ibid., pp. 308-322; between these there is also a "regional imperative."

world system would not gradually impose change on the plurality of values and differences among cultural systems that now exist, and whether such change would be good. Rousseau, posing the same sort of question in response to Saint-Pierre's system, concluded that it would not. The question at least needs to be treated seriously in the design of utopian systems of world order and in their critical evaluation.

One final issue, not central but related, is the connection between the internationalist utopian tradition of the quest for peace and the contemporary antinuclear movement. Antinuclearism is a broad phenomenon, with versions implied by all three of the major traditions identified in this book; yet the connection with internationalism seems particularly close. Present in Falk's own work,[120] the asssociation is nowhere more visible than in a book to which I have earlier referred several times, Jonathan Schell's *The Fate of the Earth*, which soon after publication took an eminent position in the literature of the antinuclear movement.

A primary sign of Schell's connection with the internationalist utopian tradition is the likeness of structure between his argument and that typical of this tradition of thought. There is first the depiction of the evils of war, which in the case of Schell's description of the horrors of nuclear war takes up most of his first chapter and all of the second;[121] there is the identification of this peril with the existing "sovereignty system"[122]—though earlier in the book he writes, "It is fundamental to the shape and character of the nuclear predicament that its origins lie in scientific knowledge rather than in social circumstances";[123] there is the appeal to a commonalty greater than the particulars that divide nations from one another (put most strikingly not in the usual fashion of appeals to universal brotherhood, but in Schell's depiction of "the sec-

[120] The need to avoid "nuclear catastrophe" is one of the principal motivating themes in *A Study of Future Worlds*; see pp. 43-46 et passim.

[121] In fact, such description is the meat of the book, repeated again and again in subtle detail; but for a rather straightforward example see pp. 36-54.

[122] Schell, *The Fate of the Earth*, pp. 186-88.

[123] Ibid., p. 100.

ond death," the death of all life on earth);[124] and there is the solution offered, "the choice," or the mutual international renunciation of war. Indeed, argues Schell, the rationality of this last has already been forced into history: "There is . . . no need to 'abolish war' among the nuclear powers; it is already gone."[125] What is most notably lacking is the provision of some new political structure (like Falk's "relevant utopia") that will resolve the problem described. Yet, though Schell specifically refuses to undertake such a task himself, he clearly regards it as the only ultimate solution:

> In this book, I have not sought to define a political solution to the nuclear predicament—either to embark on the full-scale reexamination of the foundations of political thought which must be undertaken if the world's political institutions are to be made consonant with the global reality in which they operate or to work out the practical steps by which mankind, acting for the first time in history as a single entity, can reorganize its political life. I have left to others those awesome, urgent tasks, which, imposed on us by history, constitute the political work of our age.[126]

The popular fame of Schell's book, I suggest, lies in the power with which it evokes the myth of war that lies behind the humanistic utopian tradition of the quest for peace. We have seen in the previous chapter how, even in the eighteenth-century age of limited war, persons speaking out of this tradition took pains to describe the bloodiness of the battlefield as a way of strengthening their argument for systemic political change; Schell takes this approach to new heights, aided by the awesome destructive capability of the strategic nuclear weapons possessed by the United States and the Soviet Union. Yet this is a mythic appeal, a statement out of a particular perspective: among those most critical of Schell have been persons who agree almost entirely with his depiction of what would

[124] Ibid., chapter III.
[125] Ibid., p. 193.
[126] Ibid., p. 219.

happen if nuclear war were to break out, but who nevertheless insist that *precisely because* of the state system as it exists, *precisely because* of deterrence as it exists, the nuclear holocaust painted in such matter-of-fact detail could never happen. Their response is a statement of a contrary myth of war, and the existence of such a contrary interpretation of the same basic facts about nuclear weapons should remind us of the mythic roots of both perspectives. In short, nuclear weapons and the threat they pose are new, but the argument is old.

CONCLUSION

MORAL IDEALS AND THE QUEST FOR PEACE

This has been a book about the quest for peace in Western moral tradition, and secondarily it has been about moral tradition itself. In the foregoing pages, I have identified three broad ways of thinking about peace and how to achieve it, following these streams of thought as they have come together and developed through history. The process of making a culture is a long one; and, in a contemporary climate of concentration on the needs of the present, I have wanted to inject some little bit of reflection on our continuity with the past. I have not attempted to argue that the three traditions treated in this book are the *only* forms the quest for peace has taken in Western culture, and certainly not that every thread in the fabric of contemporary debate over issues of war and peace can be traced to one or more of these three streams of thought.[1] I

[1] Were this the place to debate the issue, I think that anyone observing the complexity and variety within contemporary Western culture would have to grant that influences from other cultures have in some cases made their way into Western thought on peace and war. A case in point is the impact of Gandhi on American use of nonviolent resistance for political ends—not a topic treated above. Yet this case also exemplifies an important truth about such influences: they have to be assimilated into the idiom of our own culture to have significant impact. Gandhi's thought began to be taken over by Americans as early as the 1920s; see Charles Chatfield, *The Americanization of Gandhi* (New York: Garland Publishing Co., 1976). A more recent and for many Americans the most powerful vehicle was, however, provided by Martin Luther King, Jr., and the civil rights movement. King, though, and his colleagues in the Southern Christian Leadership Conference were inheritors of far broader and deeper streams of cultural moral influence than this one, and the stamp they gave to nonviolent resistance was peculiarly American, peculiarly rooted in the black experience, and peculiarly couched in the language of biblical faith as mediated by the black-American church. Thus, the perspective on nonviolence found in the contemporary American "peace movement," which

do insist, though, that these are the *major* forms this quest has taken, that each of them has a presence in the contemporary world, and that we stand to learn something about how we to-day think about war and peace by reflecting on how others have done so in the past.

One of the reasons these three ways of approaching the subject of peace stand out over history is that they represent three quite distinct perspectives on history, morality, and politics. Just war tradition is, in the parlance of political thought, "realistic" about history—that is, it is pessimistic about the prospects of achieving peace in any final way and about the reconciliation of humankind in some form of political community (or communities) not yet conceived. In theological terms, human history is a time when sin holds sway, and perfection, whether moral or political or any other kind, is beyond human reach. For Augustine this was symbolized by the *civitas terrenae*, the "city of earth," which was capable of its own goodness and justice but (because divine grace had not yet finished its work of transformation) was not yet the *civitas Dei*, or "city of God," which lies at the end of history. The just war idea, as related to this view, represents an effort to maximize the justice of the "city of earth" and to hold evil in check there while also responding to the transforming effect of love on human moral concerns. In later medieval thought, as just war tradition coalesced, its purpose was couched in terms of the need to maintain natural law against evildoers; princely authority to punish evil became a way of ensuring peace by establishing a political order in which justice could be done. For Luther, more pessimistic than either Augustine or his medieval predecessors concerning the possibilities of history, all human existence after the Fall stands on the edge of collapsing into destruction because of the omnipresence of sin and evil. It is not enough, in his view, that Christians already belong to the kingdom of God; for one foot is always (in this life) planted in the earthly

has important links going back to the civil rights movement, is one that has been shaped by American experience and moral values, not one drawn directly from Gandhi and the Indian revolution. My argument, put generally, is that such indigenous streams of influence need to be attended to most.

realm, where it is their duty to combat evil and help to uphold the forms of order that preserve the world so long as God's work of salvation is not yet done. Here just war tradition functions also to bolster the state, which is ordained by God for the purpose of restraining evil and establishing an endurable—if not enduring—peace.

In all these positions (and others within just war tradition that might be added to the list) morality implies being involved with the world, even at the cost of having to act in terms dictated by the nature of that world. Thus the politics of all these positions mirrors the concepts that define just war tradition: violence is permitted in the service of good (including order, justice, and peace), but it is also restrained lest it add to the burden of evil. Life in history is thus a life in tension, a holding action that will continue so long as history continues. The goods to be achieved are real ones, but they can never be got fully, or by means entirely without cost in values forgone, or once and for all time. The achievement of peace is a feat of maintaining a precarious balance; in this tradition, peace is not so much a state of being as it is the action of maintaining the balance through perpetual adjustment. Making these adjustments thus becomes definitive of the art of statecraft; at the same time, the goal of morality is to hold high the values that define the ends of political community while maintaining the constraints that establish the bounds beyond which statecraft cannot go to achieve those values without endangering their very existence.[2]

A second, and quite different, conception of history, politics, and morality is found in the utopian tradition of the quest for peace. Here history is the medium in which the ideal can be achieved, and politics is the art of achieving that ideal and maintaining it once achieved. The roles assigned to morality vary somewhat and, in contemporary expressions of this perspective, are sometimes downplayed; yet, one theme that runs throughout this tradition, from Dante through Erasmus and the "perpetual peace" theorists and on to the present, is the

[2] See Johnson, *Can Modern War Be Just?*, chapter 8.

moral vision of the ideal human community in which all live at peace. This theme of universal human commonalty is fundamentally a moral vision, a value toward which all moral strivings ought tend. Thus, in this perspective, the end of history is an immanent expression of a transcendent moral ideal. Again, the terms of theology are particularly apt: since all humankind is one in God, we may all become one people in the history of this earth. The quest for peace thus means, for this tradition of thought, the quest to make a reality out of this ideal of human community; and politics is judged not by its ability to hold evil in check, but by its capacity to show progress in moving toward such community. Even though actual historical expressions of this tradition of thought about peace reveal some connectedness with the concept of just war (for example, the reservation of a place for a "peacekeeping" force even in a new and all-inclusive international political order), the underlying difference in perspective is far more fundamental (for no one in the utopian tradition really takes seriously that such a force would actually be necessary, as everyone would come to realize the good of the new order and participate in it). This tradition rejects violence as evil in itself; politics, then, must ultimately move beyond the threat or use of violent force. Just war tradition offers sharp contrast: violence is an instrument for good or evil, depending on how it is used, by whom, and for what ends; politics exists as a way of making sure violence is used for good.

The third perspective we have glimpsed in this study is that of sectarianism; it is a position that, while distinct from the other two, incorporates elements found in each. Like just war tradition, sectarianism is pessimistic about human history; yet it is more radically pessimistic, because for it the earthly realm is ultimately doomed. Whether its doom lies in final conversion or in damnation is all that remains in dispute, but the world of this age will surely not be the kernel of the new, ideal age that is yet to come. Alongside this radical pessimism about the secular lies a kind of utopian idealism about the communities of the sectarians themselves: they are living the life of the new age already, and they must keep the secular world from dragging them back into its concerns and necessities. Thus the sectarian community is, in theological terms, the kingdom of God already on earth; for its morality is the love that is found in the gospels, and its politics that of the *ecclesia*, the congregation of God, the True Church. Life in this community is peace; nothing outside this community qualifies to be called by that word. Violence is not evil in itself, but it has no place in this community: it is "ordained by God outside the perfection of Christ," in the formula of the Schleitheim Brethren, and has to do only with the world outside the sectarian community. Thus, violence is one of the aspects of the world that must be avoided; yet merely avoiding it is not peace, for peace is a much fuller idea that refers to all aspects of the life of the sectarian community. There is some irony in the fact that the sectarian tradition has typically expressed its version of the quest for worldly peace through an absolute pacifist rejection of violence and war, while from within the peace of the sectarian community both war and the absence of war, as these are found in the outside world, manifest that world's terminal sickness. Both war and the peace (or not-war) of this world are smells that rise from a polluted sea: one is more pleasant than the other to live with, but the sea itself is what must be dealt with.

Each of these perspectives generates its own myth of war, and each has its own concept of peace. Thus, not only do we find three traditions of the quest for peace flowing from these perspectives, we actually have three different goals that are all called by the same name: "peace." The peace of the sectarian community is the result of God's love, lived out in the common life by those who have received it. For those outside that love, there is no peace. The peace of just war tradition is the restraint of evil, which can never be completely stamped out but always threatens to break out anew. It is an interim state of life, hard won and precious to possess, but all too easy to see vanish again. The peace of the utopian tradition is the realization in human history of a moral ideal, the new political order of the community of humankind, in which justice will be done and violence and war will wither to nothingness. Absent the causes of war in disorder and injustice, there will be no war. Peace, then, is more than not having war: it is the final ideal that results from the prior achievement of two other ideals, right order and justice. Yet there is a dialectical relation here, as well; for, throughout this tradition of the quest for peace the conscious and deliberate effort to avoid war (by settling disputes through arbitration, for example) is treated as a means toward bringing in the new universal order.

What each concept of peace provides is a part of a larger whole. Conceived as an ideal life in perfect community, it is something to have and to hold forever; conceived as a state of temporary rest in the moral struggle to overcome evil in the world, it is never a state of affairs about which anyone can dare become complacent, for it can all too easily pass away. Conceived as a possible achievement to be won by human striving, it sets a goal for moral and political efforts to reach goodness; conceived as a gift of divine grace, it reminds us that the ideal, precisely because it is ideal, ever remains transcendent and not fully to be grasped by human initiative. Conceived as a goal for all of humankind, it expresses a fundamental optimism about overcoming the walls of cultural and political separation that bedevil the world we know; conceived as a state achievable only in the relatively small, separate community united in common belief and mutual concern, it reflects the best of what experience teaches about life in the family, among friends, in voluntary associations—in all the particular communities in which persons live out their lives. Each of these three concepts of peace is only partial; each of the perspectives behind these concepts has its own limits; each of the traditions expressing these perspectives has its peculiar faults as well as its peculiar virtues. A synthesis among them may not be possible—or desirable, to the adherents of each, since they simply see matters differently from the others. Yet, each one stands to learn something from the others, even if what is learned is only that one's own way of thinking is not the only *possible* one.

So much for the view across the three perspectives and their respective moral traditions. From what I have said, it should be clear that I think of a moral tradition as an expression of a particular way of viewing the world. These three traditions of the quest for peace are thus the products of three unique visions of reality, and the unique vision of each is the "given" in its particular moral tradition.

Yet a moral tradition is also something that develops through human reflection and action, and it is the continuity that links such reflection and action which defines the tradition. That the medieval canonist Gratian preserved what Augustine had said about just war and gave it canonical authority is more than just a common expression of a similar point of view; it is a forging of historical links between past and present and an affirmation that the links thus made are morally significant. The same holds for the theorists of the Enlightenment—or of today—who read Erasmus on peace and make his insights part of their own moral reflection. Given enough such actions, we have a moral tradition, a stream of connections that makes past experience and wisdom part of what is significant for moral reflection in the present. I have elsewhere called this conscious act of forging connections with the past and utilizing connections already forged the memory of "significant history," arguing that the memory of such history is what constitutes moral identity.[3] This book as a whole, then, is by this definition an exercise in attempting to understand the moral identity of Western culture as it has taken shape over history and as it has been constituted by that history.

I have thus meant this book to be more than a simple account of the past, for *this particular* past is one out of which our perceptions about peace and war have largely come. We use that past rightly when we find our own continuities and discontinuities with it; this is, to my mind, what it means to learn—at least in the sense of moral knowledge—from history. This study of the major Western traditions of the quest for peace as these have developed in the past is intended, then, as a contribution toward the quest for peace in our present day.

[3] See James Turner Johnson, "On Keeping Faith: The Uses of History for Religious Ethics," *The Journal of Religious Ethics*, vol. 7, no. 1 (Spring 1979), pp. 98-116, and "Historical Tradition and Moral Judgment," *The Journal of Religion*, vol. 64, no. 3 (July 1984), pp. 299-317.

SELECT BIBLIOGRAPHY

Alighieri, Dante. *De Monarchia.* Oxford: The Clarendon Press, 1916.

———. *Monarchy and Three Political Letters.* New York: The Noonday Press, 1954.

Althaus, Paul. *The Ethics of Martin Luther.* Philadelphia: Fortress Press, 1972.

Ambrose of Milan. *Of the Duties of the Clergy.* Pp. 1-89 in Schaff, Philip, and Wace, Henry, eds., *A Select Library of Nicene and Post-Nicene Fathers*, second series, vol. X. New York: The Christian Literature Co.; Oxford and London: Parker & Co., 1896.

———. *On the Christian Faith.* Pp. 199-314 in Schaff, Philip, and Wace, Henry, eds., *A Select Library of Nicene and Post-Nicene Fathers*, second series, vol. X. New York: The Christian Literature Co.; Oxford and London: Parker & Co., 1896.

Aquinas, Thomas. *Summa Theologica.* 3 vols. London: R. & T. Washbourne; New York: Benziger Brothers, 1912-1922.

Augustine. *The Basic Writings of St. Augustine.* 2 vols. Ed. with introduction and notes by Whitney J. Oates. New York: Random House, 1948.

———. *The Political Writings of St. Augustine.* Ed. with an introduction by Henry Paolucci. Chicago: Regnery, 1962.

Bainton, Roland H. *Christian Attitudes toward War and Peace.* New York and Nashville: Abingdon Press, 1960.

Barber, Richard. *The Knight and Chivalry.* New York: Charles Scribner's Sons, 1970.

Barnes, Timothy David. *Tertullian: A Historical and Literary Survey.* Oxford: The Clarendon Press, 1971.

Baylis, John; Booth, Ken; Garnett, John; and Williams, Phil. *Contemporary Strategy: Theories and Policies.* New York: Holmes & Meier, 1972.

Beales, A.C.F. *The History of Peace*. New York: L. MacVeagh, The Dial Press, 1931.

Beilenson, Laurence W. *Survival and Peace in the Nuclear Age*. Chicago: Regnery, 1981.

Bense, Walter F. "Paris Theologians on War and Peace, 1521-1529." *Church History*, vol. 41, no. 2 (June 1972), pp. 168-85.

Bentham, Jeremy. *Jeremy Bentham's Plan for an Universal and Perpetual Peace*. The Grotius Society Publications, no. 6. London: Sweet & Maxwell, 1927.

Berger, Peter, and Neuhaus, Richard John, eds. *Movement and Revolution*. Garden City, N.Y.: Doubleday & Company, 1970.

Best, Geoffrey. *Humanity in Warfare*. New York: Columbia University Press, 1980.

Bonet, Honoré. *The Tree of Battles of Honoré Bonet*. Cambridge: Harvard University Press, 1949.

Born, Lester K. *The Education of a Christian Prince by Desiderius Erasmus*. New York: Octagon Books, 1965.

Bowder, Diana. *The Age of Constantine and Julian*. New York: Harper & Row, 1978.

Brock, Peter. *Pacifism in Europe to 1914*. Princeton: Princeton University Press, 1972.

———. *Pacifism in the United States*. Princeton: Princeton University Press, 1968.

Brown, Peter. *Religion and Society in the Age of St. Augustine*. London: Faber & Faber, 1972.

———. *The World of Late Antiquity*. Cambridge: Harvard University Press, 1978.

Cadoux, C. John. *The Early Christian Attitude to War*. New York: The Seabury Press, 1982.

Caputo, Philip. *A Rumor of War*. New York: Holt, Rinehart & Winston, 1977.

Ceadel, Martin. *Pacifism in Britain, 1914-45*. Oxford: The Clarendon Press; New York: Oxford University Press, 1980.

Chastellain, Georges. *Le Livre de paix*. Pp. 341-422 in Chastellain, Georges, *Oeuvres*, vol. 7. Brussels: F. Heussner, 1865.

Chatfield, Charles. *The Americanization of Gandhi*. New York: Garland Publishing Co., 1976.

Clausewitz, Karl von. *On War*. Ed. and trans. by Peter Paret and Michael Howard. Princeton: Princeton University Press, 1980.

Clement of Alexandria. *Paedagogus*. Pp. 207-298 in Roberts, Alexander, and Donaldson, James, eds., *The Ante-Nicene Fathers*, vol. II. Buffalo, N.Y.: The Christian Literature Publishing Co., 1885.

———. *Stromata*. Pp. 199-568 in Roberts, Alexander, and Donaldson, James, eds., *The Ante-Nicene Fathers*, vol. II. Buffalo, N.Y.: The Christian Literature Publishing Co., 1885.

Contamine, Philippe. *War in the Middle Ages*. Oxford: Basil Blackwell, 1984.

Cookson, J. E. *The Friends of Peace: Antiwar Liberalism in England, 1793-1815*. Cambridge and New York: Cambridge University Press, 1982.

Crucé, Emeric. *The New Cyneas of Emeric Crucé*. Ed. and trans. by Thomas Willing Balch. Philadelphia: Allen, Lane & Scott, 1909.

Daniélou, Jean. *Origen*. New York: Sheed & Ward, 1955.

de Vaux, Roland. *Ancient Israel, Its Life and Institutions*. New York: McGraw-Hill, 1961.

Delbrück, Hans. *History of the Art of War within the Framework of Political History*. 4 vols. Westport, Conn.: Greenwood Press, 1975-1985.

Derocque, Gilberte. *Le Projet de paix perpétuelle de l'Abbé de Saint-Pierre*. Paris: Librairie Arthur Rousseau, 1929.

Devisse, J. *Hincmar et la loi*. Dakar: Publications de la Section d'Histoire, Université de Dakar, 1962.

Durnbaugh, Donald F., ed. *On Earth Peace*. Elgin, Ill.: The Brethren Press, 1978.

Eisenbeis, Walter. *Die Würzel Sh-L-M im Alten Testament*. Berlin: Walter deGruyter & Co., 1969.

Eppstein, John. *The Catholic Tradition of the Law of Nations*.

Washington, D.C.: Catholic Association for International Peace, 1935.

Epstein, William. *The Last Chance: Nuclear Proliferation and Arms Control*. New York: The Free Press, 1976.

Erasmus, Desiderius. *Adages*. See Phillips, Margaret Mann, *The "Adages" of Erasmus*.

———. *Bellum Erasmi*. London: Thomas Berthelet, 1533.

———. *The Correspondence of Erasmus, Letters 142 to 297*. Toronto and Buffalo, N.Y.: University of Toronto Press, 1975.

———. *Desiderius Erasmus: Christian Humanism and the Reformation, Selected Writings*. Ed. by John C. Olin. New York, Evanston, and London: Harper & Row, 1965.

———. *The Education of a Christian Prince*. See Born, Lester K., *The Education of a Christian Prince by Desiderius Erasmus*.

Falk, Richard A. *Human Rights and State Sovereignty*. New York and London: Holmes & Meier, 1981.

———. *A Study of Future Worlds*. New York: The Free Press, 1975.

——— and Mendlovitz, Saul H., eds. *The Strategy of World Order*, vol. II: *International Law*. New York: World Law Fund, 1966.

Fuller, J.F.C. *The Conduct of War, 1789-1961*. New Brunswick, N.J.: Rutgers University Press, 1961.

Fussell, Paul. *The Great War and Modern Memory*. New York and London: Oxford University Press, 1975.

Gager, John G. *Kingdom and Community: The Social World of Early Christianity*. Englewood Cliffs, N.J.: Prentice-Hall, 1975.

Gallie, W. B. *Philosophers of Peace and War*. Cambridge: Cambridge University Press, 1978.

Gewirth, Alan. *Marsilius of Padua: The Defender of Peace*. 2 vols. Vol. I: *Marsilius of Padua and Medieval Political Philosophy*; vol. II: *The Defensor Pacis*. New York: Columbia University Press, 1951-1956.

Gonnet, Jean, and Molnar, Amadeo. *Les Vaudois au moyen âge*. Turin: Editrice Claudiana, 1974.

Grotius, Hugo. *Of the Rights of War and Peace*. London: n.p., 1682.

Harnack, Adolf von. *Militia Christi: The Christian Religion and the Military in the First Three Centuries*. Trans. with introduction by David McInnes Gracie. Philadelphia: Fortress Press, 1981.

Hauerwas, Stanley. "On Surviving Justly: An Ethical Analysis of Nuclear Disarmament." Pp. 1-20 in Jill Raitt, ed., *Religious Conscience and Nuclear Warfare*. Columbia: University of Missouri Press, 1982.

Heath, Ian. *Armies of the Dark Ages, 600-1066*. Worthing, Sussex: Wargames Research Group, 1980.

Helgeland, John. "Christians and the Roman Army, A.D. 173-337." *Church History*, vol. 43, no. 2 (June 1974), pp. 149-163, 200.

———; Daly, Robert J.; and Burns, J. Patout. *Christians and the Military: The Early Experience*. Philadelphia: Fortress Press, 1985.

Herr, Michael. *Dispatches*. New York: Alfred A. Knopf, 1977.

Hershberger, Guy Franklin. *War, Peace, and Nonresistance*. Scottdale, Pa., and Kitchener, Ont.: Herald Press, 1944, 1953, 1969.

Heyer, Robert, ed. *Nuclear Disarmament: Key Statements of Popes, Bishops, Councils, and Churches*. New York and Ramsey, N.J.: Paulist Press, 1982.

Hoffmann, Stanley. *The State of War*. New York, Washington, D.C., and London: Praeger, 1965.

Hornus, Jean-Michel. *It Is Not Lawful for Me to Fight*. Revised ed. Scottdale, Pa., and Kitchener, Ont.: Herald Press, 1980.

International Intermediary Institute, The Hague. *The Permanent Court of International Justice*. Leiden: A. W. Sijthoff, 1922.

Johnson, James Turner. *Can Modern War Be Just?* New Haven and London: Yale University Press, 1984.

———. "Historical Tradition and Moral Judgment: The Case

of Just War Tradition." *The Journal of Religion*, vol. 64, no. 3 (July 1984), pp. 299-317.

———. *Ideology, Reason, and the Limitation of War*. Princeton: Princeton University Press, 1975.

———. *Just War Tradition and the Restraint of War*. Princeton: Princeton University Press, 1981.

———. "On Keeping Faith: The Uses of History for Religious Ethics." *The Journal of Religious Ethics*, vol. 7, no. 1 (Spring 1979), pp. 98-111.

———. "Toward Reconstructing the *Jus ad Bellum*." *The Monist*, vol. 57, no. 4 (October 1973), pp. 461-88.

Kant, Immanuel. *The Philosophy of Kant: Immanuel Kant's Moral and Political Writings*. New York: Modern Library, 1949.

Kaufmann, Gordon D. *Theology for a Nuclear Age*. Philadelphia: The Westminster Press, 1985.

Keegan, John. *The Face of Battle*. Harmondsworth, Middlesex: Penguin Books, 1983.

Kittel, Gerhard, ed. *Theologisches Wörterbuch zum Neuen Testament*. 10 vols. Stuttgart: W. Kohlhammer, 1932-1979.

Kot, Stanislaw. *Socinianism in Poland*. Boston: Starr King Press, 1957.

la Noue, François, Sieur de. *The Politicke and Militarie Discourses of the Lord de la Noue*. London: T. C. and E. A. by Thomas Orwin, 1587.

Ladd, William. *Essay on a Congress of Nations*. Ed. by James Brown Scott. Washington: Carnegie Institution, 1916.

Ladurie, Emmanuel L. *Montaillou: The Promised Land of Error*. New York: Random House, 1979.

Lange, Christian Louis. *Histoire de l'internationalisme*. 3 vols. Kristiana, Norway: Aschehoug, 1919-1963.

Lasserre, Jean. *War and the Gospel*. Scottdale, Pa., and Kitchener, Ont.: Herald Press, 1962.

The Law of Armed Conflicts. New York: Carnegie Endowment for International Peace, 1971.

Lieber, Francis. "Addenda and Notes for Inclusion in Lieber's

Code." Ms. and other materials in the Lieber Collection of the Huntington Library, San Marino, Calif.

———. *Lieber's Miscellaneous Writings*, vol. I: *Reminiscences, Addresses, and Essays*. Philadelphia: J. B. Lippincott & Co., 1881.

Lienhard, Marc. *The Origins and Characteristics of Anabaptism/Les Débuts et les caractéristiques de l'Anabaptisme*. The Hague: Martinus Nijhoff, 1977.

Long, Edward LeRoy, Jr. *War and Conscience in America*. Philadelphia: The Westminster Press, 1968.

Luther, Martin. *Luther's Works*. 54 vols. Ed. by Jaroslav Pelikan and Helmut T. Lehmann. St. Louis: Concordia Publishing House; Philadelphia: Muhlenberg Press and Fortress Press, 1955-1976.

Luvass, Jay, ed. and trans. *Frederick the Great on the Art of War*. New York: The Free Press; London: Collier-Macmillan, 1966.

Mandelbaum, Michael. *The Nuclear Question*. Cambridge: Cambridge University Press, 1979.

Marsilius of Padua. See Gewirth, Alan, *Marsilius of Padua: The Defender of Peace*.

McEvedy, Colin. *The Penguin Atlas of Medieval History*. Harmondsworth, Middlesex: Penguin Books, 1961.

McNeill, John T. "Asceticism versus Militarism in the Middle Ages." *Church History*, vol. 5, no. 1 (March 1936), pp. 3-28.

Meeks, Wayne A. *The First Urban Christians: The Social World of the Apostle Paul*. New Haven and London: Yale University Press, 1983.

Meyrowitz, Henri. *Le Principe de l'égalité des belligérants devant le droit de la guerre*. Paris: A. Pedone, 1970.

Molnar, Amadeo. *A Challenge to Constantinianism: The Waldensian Theology in the Middle Ages*. Geneva: WSCF, 1976.

National Conference of Catholic Bishops. *The Challenge of Peace: God's Promise and Our Response*. Washington, D.C.: United States Catholic Conference, 1983. Second draft, in *Origins*, vol. 12, no. 20 (October 28, 1982), pp. 305-328.

Nef, John Ulrich. *War and Human Progress*. New York: Russell & Russell, 1950.

Niebuhr, H. Richard. *Christ and Culture*. New York: Harper & Brothers, 1951.

Niebuhr, Reinhold. *Moral Man and Immoral Society*. New York: Charles Scribner's Sons, 1932.

O'Brien, William V. *The Conduct of Just and Limited War*. New York: Praeger, 1981.

Oman, Charles W. *A History of the Art of War in the Middle Ages*. Revised ed. Ithaca, N.Y.: Cornell University Press, 1960.

Origen. *Against Celsus*. Pp. 395-669 in Roberts, Alexander, and Donaldson, James, eds., *The Ante-Nicene Fathers*, vol. IV. Buffalo, N.Y.: The Christian Literature Publishing Co., 1885.

Pedersen, Johannes. *Israel, Its Life and Culture*. 2 vols. London: Oxford University Press, 1959.

Penn, William. *An Essay toward the Present and Future Peace of Europe*. Philadelphia: Peace & Service Committee, Friends General Conference, 1944.

Phillips, Margaret Mann. *The "Adages" of Erasmus: A Study with Translations*. Cambridge: Cambridge University Press, 1964.

Pisan, Christine de. *The Book of Fayttes of Armes and of Chyvalrie*. Trans. of *Les Faits d'armes et de chivalrie* by William Caxton; ed. by A.T.P. Byles. London: Oxford University Press, 1932.

———. *The "Livre de la paix" of Christine de Pisan*. The Hague: Mouton & Co., 1958.

Previte-Orton, C. W. *The Shorter Cambridge Medieval History*. 2 vols. Harmondsworth, Middlesex: Penguin Books, 1961.

Ramsey, Paul. *The Just War: Force and Political Responsibility*. New York: Charles Scribner's Sons, 1968.

———. *Nine Modern Moralists*. Englewood Cliffs, N.J.: Prentice-Hall, 1962.

———. *War and the Christian Conscience*. Durham, N.C.: Duke University Press, 1961.

Rousseau, Jean-Jacques. *L'État de guerre and Projet de paix perpétuelle*. Introduction and notes by Shirley G. Patterson. New York and London: G. P. Putnam's Sons, 1920.

Russell, Frederick H. *The Just War in the Middle Ages*. Cambridge, London, New York, and Melbourne: Cambridge University Press, 1975.

Saint-Pierre, C. I. Castel de. *Selections from the Second Edition of the Abrégé du Projet de paix perpétuelle*. The Grotius Society Publications, no. 5. London: Sweet & Maxwell, 1927.

Schell, Jonathan. *The Fate of the Earth*. New York: Avon Books, 1982.

Schindler, Dietrich, and Toman, Jiri, eds. *The Laws of Armed Conflicts*. Leiden: A. W. Sijthoff; Geneva: Henry Dunant Institute, 1973.

Schwarzenberger, Georg. *A Manual of International Law*. 5th ed. London: Stevens & Sons, 1967.

Schweitzer, Albert. *The Kingdom of God and Primitive Christianity*. New York: The Seabury Press, 1968.

Scott, James Brown. *The Spanish Origin of International Law*. Oxford: The Clarendon Press; London: Humphrey Milford, 1934.

Selge, Jurt-Victor. *Die Ersten Waldenser*. 2 vols. Berlin: Walter deGruyter & Co., 1967.

Shannon, Thomas A., ed. *War or Peace: The Search for New Answers*. Maryknoll, N.Y.: Orbis Books, 1980.

Sheils, W. J., ed. *The Church and War*. Oxford: Basil Blackwell, for The Ecclesiastical History Society, 1983.

Sibley, Mulford Q., ed. *The Quiet Battle*. Philadelphia: Pacifist Research Bureau, 1944.

Smith, W. Robertson. *The Religion of the Semites*. New York: Meridian Books, 1956.

Stayer, James M. *Anabaptists and the Sword*. Lawrence, Kans.: Coronado Press, 1972.

Sully, Maximilien de Béthune duc de. *Sully's Grand Design of*

Henry IV. The Grotius Society Publications, no. 2. London: Sweet & Maxwell, 1921.

Swift, Louis J. "Augustine on War and Killing: Another View." *Harvard Theological Review*, vol. 66 (1973), pp. 369-83.

———. *The Early Fathers on War and Military Service*. Wilmington, Del.: Michael Glazier, 1983.

———. "St. Ambrose on Violence and War." *Transactions and Proceedings of the American Philological Association*, vol. 101 (1970), pp. 533-43.

Tertullian. *On Idolatry*. Pp. 61-78 in Roberts, Alexander, and Donaldson, James, eds., *The Ante-Nicene Fathers*, vol. II. Buffalo, N.Y.: The Christian Literature Publishing Co., 1885.

———. *On the Soldier's Crown*. Pp. 93-104 in Roberts, Alexander, and Donaldson, James, eds., *The Ante-Nicene Fathers*, vol. II. Buffalo, N.Y.: The Christian Literature Publishing Co., 1885.

Theissen, Gerd. *The Social Setting of Early Christianity: Essays on Corinth*. Philadelphia: Fortress Press, 1982.

———. *Sociology of Early Palestinian Christianity*. Philadelphia: Fortress Press, 1978.

Thouzellier, Christine. *Catharisme et Valdéisme en Languedoc à la fin du XIIe et au début du XIIIe siècle*. Louvain: Editions Nauwelaerts; Paris: Beatrice-Nauwelaerts, 1969.

Tucker, Robert W. *The Just War: A Study in Contemporary American Doctrine*. Baltimore: The Johns Hopkins University Press, 1960.

United Nations. *Charter of the United Nations and Statute of the International Court of Justice*. New York: United Nations Press, n.d.

United States Army. *Field Manual 27-10: The Law of Land Warfare*. Washington, D.C.: Government Printing Office, 1956.

United States Department of State. *The General Pact for the Renunciation of War. Text of the Pact as Signed*. Washington, D.C.: U.S. Government Printing Office, 1928.

Vattel, Emmerich de. *The Law of Nations; or, The Principles of Natural Law*. Translation of the edition of 1758 by Charles G. Fenwick. Washington, D.C.: Carnegie Institution, 1916.

Victoria, Franciscus de. *De Indis et De Jure Belli Relectiones*. Washington, D.C.: Carnegie Institution, 1917.

Wakin, Malham, ed. *War, Morality, and the Military Profession*. Boulder, Colo.: Westview Press, 1979.

Walker, Williston. *A History of the Christian Church*. Revised ed. New York: Charles Scribner's Sons, 1959.

Walters, LeRoy. "The Just War and the Crusade: Antitheses or Analogies?" *The Monist*, vol. 57, no. 4 (October 1973), pp. 584-94.

Weigley, Russell F. *The American Way of War*. New York: Macmillan; London: Collier-Macmillan, 1973.

Williams, George Huntston. *The Radical Reformation*. Philadelphia: The Westminster Press, 1972.

Yoder, John Howard. *Nevertheless: Varieties of Religious Pacifism*. Scottdale, Pa.: Herald Press, 1971.

———. *What Would You Do?* Scottdale, Pa., and Kitchener, Ont.: Herald Press, 1983.

———. *When War Is Unjust*. Minneapolis: Augsburg Publishing House, 1984.

———, ed. and trans. *The Legacy of Michael Sattler*. Scottdale, Pa.: Herald Press, 1973.

Zahn, Gordon. *An Alternative to War*. New York: Council on Religion and International Affairs, 1963.

Zampaglione, Gerardo. *The Idea of Peace in Antiquity*. Notre Dame and London: University of Notre Dame Press, 1973.

Zwingli, Ulrich. *Huldreich Zwinglis Sämtliche Werke*. 13 vols. Ed. by E. Egli and G. Finsler. Berlin: C. A. Schwetschke und Sohn, 1904-1968.

INDEX

Library of Congress
Cataloging-in-Publication Data

Johnson, James Turner, 1938-
The quest for peace.

Bibliography: p. Includes index.
1. Peace—Moral and ethical aspects—History.
2. Peace—Religious aspects—History. I. Title.
B105.P4J64 1987 172'.42'09 86-30568
ISBN 0-691-07742-8